Contents

The Necessity of Witness

The Necessity of Witness

Stanley Hauerwas's Contribution to Systematic Theology

Ariaan W. Baan

PICKWICK *Publications* · Eugene, Oregon

THE NECESSITY OF WITNESS
Stanley Hauerwas's Contribution to Systematic Theology

Pickwick Publications
An Imprint of Wipf and Stock Publishers
199 W. 8th Ave., Suite 3
Eugene, OR 97401

www.wipfandstock.com

ISBN 13: 978-1-4982-0162-9

Cataloguing-in-Publication Data

Baan, Ariaan W.

The necessity of witness : Stanley Hauerwas's contribution to systematic theology / Ariaan W. Baan.

xii + 234 p. ; 23 cm. Includes bibliographical references and index.

ISBN 13: 978-1-4982-0162-9

1. Hauerwas, Stanley, 1940–. 2. Theology, doctrinal. I. Title.

BJ1278.5.H38 B23 2015

Manufactured in the U.S.A.   08/13/2015

Preface

AT THE BEGINNING OF his second book, Luke the evangelist tells how Jesus instructs his disciples:

> But you will receive power when the Holy Spirit comes on you; and you will be my witnesses in Jerusalem, and in all Judea and Samaria, and to the ends of the earth. (Acts 1:8)

These words, spoken by Jesus just before his ascension, have prompted Christians to understand themselves as witnesses, as people being called by their Lord to bear testimony of him through their words and lives. Particularly since the second half of the last century—an era in which Christianity lost its dominant role in Western culture—witness terminology has helped Christian theologians formulate how Christians can relate to the societies they live in. By speaking of the vocation to be witnesses, these theologians express how Christians have been grasped by the good news of the gospel and how they can speak about what they find to be true without imposing their view on others through apologetics.

Over the last three decades, the American ethicist and theologian Stanley Hauerwas has made a comprehensive case for witness. Hauerwas argues that witness is necessary for the church. To be faithful and truthful, Christian communities must commit themselves to the practice of witnessing. But he also argues that witness is necessary for the academy—for theologians, philosophers and others involved in intellectual reflection about the world we live in. Hauerwas's claim is that we cannot understand the true character of all that is without the practice of Christian witnessing.

From the first time I read Hauerwas, I was fascinated by his ideas about witness. I became more and more convinced that these ideas are significant for anyone thinking about the meaning of Christian faith in our late modern societies. This book is born out of this fascination. And so I will carry out a systematic theological exploration of Hauerwas's account of Christian witness to examine if his claims about the necessity of witness make sense.

Nicholas Healy's *Hauerwas: A (Very) Critical Introduction* was published shortly after I'd finished the manuscript for my book. According to Healy, Hauerwas's theology is too thin. Due to his reliance on Alasdair MacIntyre's social theory and his "ecclesiocentrism," Healy argues Hauerwas pays too little attention to traditional theological questions about who the God Christians worship is and how this God works in our world. Though Healy's approach differs from mine—his is, as the title suggests, much more critical—in our actual analyses of Hauerwas's work there are a quite a few similarities. I'll refer to these points of agreement in several footnotes in chapter 5.

For Hauerwas, theology is a craft, a skill that can only be learned by training from a master. And from my experience, Gerrit Neven and Rinse Reeling Brouwer are the most skillful and dedicated masters a PhD student could wish for. I was Rinse's assistant as an undergraduate and when I specialized in systematic theology Gerrit supervised my master's thesis (on George Lindbeck). It was Gerrit who encouraged me to write a research proposal in 2005, and without the help of Rinse I never could have written it. But these two are very different supervisors. Rinse was closely involved with the project, there was no paragraph, no footnote over which he did not cast his eagle eye and give advice on. Gerrit's great quality, however, was to remain at arm's length. This allowed him the benefit of a broad overview and to recognize, and to be strict with me, when he knew I could do better. I'm truly indebted to these profound professors.

This project began back in 2006 when I was hired by the Theological University of Kampen. By the time I'd finished in 2013, I was working in Groningen for the Protestant Theological University of the Netherlands. And although my university merged with another institution and then moved to Groningen it continued to support my research. For this and more, I owe them a lot. I'm also extremely grateful for the support of my colleagues from the theological university PThU. I want to thank in particular Hanna Ploeg, Titia Struik, Mechtild Alferink, Jeanet Landsman, Carlien Geelkerken, Theo Witkamp, Ciska Stark, and Lieke Werkman for their constructive cooperation.

At the beginning of my research, I discussed the outline of my book with Hans Reinders, professor of ethics at VU University, Amsterdam. He helped me to get in touch with Stanley Hauerwas. In 2008, at a conference in Rome I discussed my project with Stanley. And during that conversation a throwaway remark that "in fact, my work is all about witness" was to become a great inspiration for me. In 2012, I met Hauerwas again at the meeting of the Society for Christian Ethics in Washington, DC. We discussed the project and he looked over a draft of chapter 5. This conversation helped me see that "Stanley Hauerwas" is not just a research subject but an approachable and friendly man, who is prepared to help others think critically about his own work.

In 2009 Herman Paul and Bart Wallet began a project to publish some of Hauerwas's work in Dutch. I'd like to thank them both for this initiative and for inviting me to join their team of translators. In 2010 *Een robuuste kerk* was published. Thanks to this book much more attention is being given to Hauerwas's ethics and theology in the Netherlands compared to when I started my research.

I'm also grateful to those experts I consulted about the parts of chapter 2 where I discuss the various fields in which the terms "witness" and "testimony" are used. Carlien Geelkerken advised me on witnessing in law, Dineke Houtman on the Jewish interpretations and Gé Speelman on the Islamic interpretations of witness and testimony. Onno Zijlstra commented on what I'd written on Wittgenstein, and Pieter Vos on my paragraph about Kierkegaard. I'm very grateful to Marjo Korpel for her careful reading of the complete manuscript. Further, I must thank Ed Noort, professor emeritus of Old Testament at the University of Groningen and Bert Jan Lietaert Peerbolte, professor of New Testament at vu University, Amsterdam for their careful comments on the biblical sections in chapter 2 and chapter 4. I owe many thanks to Akke van der Kooi and John de Boer for their beautiful translation of the poem by Fedde Schurer from Frisian to English in chapter 5. Moreover, I'm grateful for Akke's friendship and guidance: like Rinse and Gerrit, she's been a theological mentor to me. During my years in Kampen I also enjoyed my friendship with Volker Kuester. As theologians we disagreed on almost everything but we agreed that it's also fun to disagree.

Harm Goris, assistant professor of systematic theology at Tilburg University, commented on a draft of chapter 3 during the PhD Conference of the Netherlands School for the Advanced Study of Theology and Religion in 2009. The Christian Articles Conference organizers offered me the opportunity to present my research in 2011. The Annual Barth Conference in the Netherlands also invited me to present a draft of my final chapter. At this conference, Hans G. Ulrich, professor emeritus of ethics from the University of Erlangen–Nürnberg, responded generously to my research for which I thank him.

This book could not exist without the help of Gerard van Zanden. It is a great pleasure to work together with such a skilful and critical editor who is also such a promising theologian. Nick Harvey did a great job of transforming my broken sentences into fluent English. Overall, it has been refreshing for me to be in touch with other *doctorandi* working on very different projects from mine but struggling with very similar problems, people such as Pieter Dronkers, Daniel Drost, Wietske de Jong and Gerben van Manen, and in Groningen Wijnand Boezelman, Isaiah Munali, Rianne Voogd and Jacobine Gelderloos.

I thank my church, my friends and my family for giving me a life outside the academy. It is a blessing to work for the protestant church in Baflo, and to be a member of the local church in Winsum. It is a blessing to have old friends like Jan, Rob, Bindert, Jelbert, Pieter and new friends like Oege Wietse, Imkeline, Ilja, and Jos. It is a blessing to have such a dedicated father, a caring mother, two loyal brothers, and a supportive family in law. It is a blessing to have children, Fedde, Ella and Yne who disturbed me at precisely those moments when I—muttering to myself as I clicked away at my keyboard—risked getting lost in my work.

This book is dedicated to the women in my life, women who showed me what it means "to live truthfully in a world without certainty": Maaike van Die, my grandmother, Jantje Hulshof, my grandmother-in-law, Heleen Coumou, my mother, Lammy Hulzebos, my mother-in-law, and Christy Pijning, my wonderful, wonderful wife.

Hauerwas's Contribution to Systematic Theology

HAUERWAS'S MOST EXTENSIVE WRITING on witness can be found in *With the Grain of the Universe*, the book that comprises the Gifford Lectures which he gave in 2000–2001 at the University of St Andrews in Scotland. In these lectures he comes to speak about what he calls "the necessity of witness" (207–41). On the back cover of *With the Grain of the Universe*, Hauerwas is described as "contemporary theology's foremost intellectual provocateur."[1] Such praise may improve sales figures, but it's doubtful whether it enhances academic reputation. As academics, we tend to listen to the provocateur, laugh about his artful teasing, before getting back to serious business. It's easy to read Hauerwas like this and refute his argument for the necessity of witness as if it's just another "typically Hauerwasian" provocation. Hauerwas himself, however, wants his readers to take him seriously. Thus he writes, "Mine is a thesis clearly aimed to get attention, but more important, it is one that I think true" (10). In this book, I will indeed take his argument seriously and I'll indicate that Hauerwas has good reasons to argue that witness is necessary for living faithfully as God's creature, and for thinking truthfully about God and his creation.

During the last decades, a lot has been published about Hauerwas. Whether he likes it or not, Stanley Hauerwas has become an authority in Christian ethics and theology.[2] Numerous monographs have appeared in which different aspects of his thinking are discussed—his account on virtue, his vision on narrative, his approach to political ethics—and most of

1. This statement was originally made by Jean Bethke Elshtain in *Time Magazine*: Elshtain, "Theologian."

2. In the online databases on ebscohost.com there are almost 400 articles with the subject "Hauerwas," including about 150 academic articles and reviews.

them are dedicated to the relation between ethics and the community of the church. But while Hauerwas's contribution to debates in Christian ethics have been widely discussed in secondary literature, this is not true of his contribution to systematic theological issues. Some significant review articles on *With the Grain of the Universe* have been published,[3] but there are no extensive works, no monographs, dedicated to Hauerwas's contribution to systematic theology.[4] Moreover, while many of Hauerwas's interpreters agree that witness is a central idea in his work, none of them undertakes a thorough discussion of Hauerwas's understanding of Christian witness, let alone a systematic theological examination.[5]

The reason for this omission is obvious: though in many of his publications Hauerwas refers to systematic theological issues, in most of his texts the main focus is on theological ethics. Indeed, Stanley Hauerwas has become famous for his characteristic views on pressing ethical themes such as abortion, the nation state and war.[6] However, especially since the publication of *With the Grain of the Universe*, no one can deny that Hauerwas's contribution to systematic theology requires attention and needs to be evaluated.

In this study, I will suggest that Hauerwas's major contribution to systematic theology is his thought on the necessity of Christian witness. This book offers a thorough examination of Hauerwas's account of witness and an explanation of how these ideas contribute to systematic theological reflection on the character of the church, the work of the Holy Spirit and on the truth of Christian beliefs. Moreover, for a genuine systematic theological examination we must know whether this account is persuasive, we must test if there are valid reasons to accept it. The five chapters of this book can be conceived as five successive phases of such a test.

- Chapter 1 gives a description of the "material" which is being tested. It begins with an introduction of Hauerwas's account of witness in *With the Grain of the Universe* and it ends with an overview of how the theme of witness relates to other themes in Hauerwas's work.

3. These articles will be discussed in chapter 1.

4. In *Ethics as Grammar*, Brad Kallenberg reads Hauerwas's work as a Christian answer to some crucial philosophical insights by Ludwig Wittgenstein. While Kallenberg's monograph has many significant implications for systematic theology, it is not so much a *systematic* theological study as it is a *philosophical* theological study on the character Christian ethics.

5. Already in 1993, Hütter spoke of Hauerwas's ethics as an ethics of witness in his dissertation *Evangelische Ethik als kirchliches Zeugnis*. But Hütter does not give a thorough analysis of Hauerwas's understanding of witness. Strikingly, although Hütter and others entitled their Festschrift for Hauerwas *God Truth and Witness*, none of them discusses the meaning of witness in the work of Hauerwas.

6. See for instance, *Resident Aliens*, Hauerwas's bestseller written with William H. Willimon.

- Chapter 2 is a comparative test. I map out what the terms witness and testimony mean in different fields—such as law, modern and ancient philosophy, the Old and New Testament, and the Christian tradition—and I determine how Hauerwas's account relates to these different meanings. The outcome of this test will be ambiguous. In one way it will turn out that, though Hauerwas himself does not reflect on how his account relates to all these conceptions of witness, he has quite a good intuition for the "logic" of witnessing. Yet, due to this lack of reflection, some aspects of his account remain somewhat vague and abstract. Moreover, he pays little attention to the Old and New Testament texts which refer to God calling men as his witnesses.

- Chapter 3 tests whether it's possible to clarify the vagueness of Hauerwas's account. For this test I use philosophical analyses on everyday, legal, and other conceptions of witnessing. The conclusions of this chapter will be twofold. In many respects Hauerwas's account withstands the test. By the end of this chapter it is possible to explain how Christian life must be conceived as a testimonial life and in what ways the Christian community can be understood as a community of witnesses. But, as we will see, through this test new problems arise.

- Chapter 4 examines how Hauerwas's account of witness relates to Scripture. I will discuss some crucial Bible texts on witnessing: the prophecies in Isaiah of God's vocation of Israel, the story in Acts of Jesus's vocation of the disciples, the visions in Revelation of faithful witnesses and the speeches in John in which Jesus is witnessing of himself. In this chapter I will test whether (and if so, to what extent) these texts offer support for Hauerwas's account of witness. Again, the outcomes of this test will be twofold. On the one hand, it appears that there is indeed Scriptural support for the basic aspects of Hauerwas's understanding of witness, however some of the discussed Bible books also refer to characteristics of the witness and his testimony which do not fit so easily with Hauerwas's account.

- Chapter 5 is a systematic theological test. With the help of my interpretations of the different Bible books in chapter 4, I develop a criterion in the form of three rules of discourse for an adequate systematic theological reflection of witness. The first rule is about the witness's vocation, the second is about the assistance of the Holy Spirit and the third rule is about the relationship between witnessing and truth. These rules are formulated in such a way that they are acceptable, not only for Hauerwas and those who sympathize with his theology, but also for the majority of his critics. In this chapter I test whether and to what extent Hauerwas's reflections on the character of Christian witness conform to these rules. Through this test I will try to give a well-balanced systematic theological evaluation of how Hauerwas understands witness.

The analyses in these five chapters strictly concentrate on the theme of witness. Instead of giving a complete overview of Hauerwas's work in chapter 1, I will concentrate on what he has written on witness and how this relates to other important themes in his work. In the chapters that follow, I will not compare "Hauerwas's ideas" to "philosophical" and "biblical" ideas but will strictly focus on how his account of witness relates to those practices, philosophical texts and Bible pericopes which explicitly speak of witness and testimony. And we'll see that through this focus it's possible to give a thorough evaluation of how Hauerwas speaks of witness.

In this book I have to deal with a tension between the word "witness" and that to what the word refers. We need words to understand what's going on in the Christian life—and "witness" is a very useful term. And this word and the way it's used can be examined. But what the word refers to—the "testimonial life,"—cannot be subjected to examination. In some ways this tension is already present in Acts 1:8. Luke the evangelist uses "witness" when he tells about the vocation of the apostles but at the same time this term cannot fully express what it means for the apostles to have met the risen Lord and to be called by him. In Hauerwas's work, a similar tension can be discerned. Hauerwas speaks of "witness" because it helps to describe the Christian life. Yet, he also seems to realize that his reflections cannot fully grasp what Christian life is about. This tension is also present in this study. I'll indeed examine whether Hauerwas's claims regarding the necessity of witness are correct. But that to which this claim ultimately refers—people witnessing through their lives to the one true God—cannot be subjected to my tests and evaluations.

Though this book gives a systematic theological examination of Hauerwas, I must admit that I use the term "systematic theology" with some reserve. I realize that many contemporary theologians, including Hauerwas himself, dislike the noun "system."[7] Therefore it's good to say in advance that

---

7. In the introduction of his books, Hauerwas often makes remarks about the unsystematic character of his work. See for instance *Christian Existence Today*: "That does not mean I have any ambition to develop a grandiose system. I simply do not think so systematically, as is clear from the unsystematic and occasional nature of my work" (8). See also *Sanctify them in the Truth*: "Therefore, I do not assume that my task as a theologian is to make what the church believes somehow more truthful than the truth inherent in the fact that this is what the church believes. One of the reasons, moreover, why I resist those who urge me to "pull it all together" is that attempts to do so impose false unity on the wonderful anarchy of the life called church" (2–3).

it's not my intention to impose a system on Hauerwas's thoughts on witness. I simply speak of systematic theology because it is the most common term for the discipline I practice and I use the term "systematic theological approach" because I know of no better way to describe what I'm doing in this book.[8] Moreover, I must add that for Hauerwas the distinction between the disciplines of theological ethics and systematic theology is relative. For him, systematic theology and theological ethics are not so much different fields of research but rather different perspectives on the same reality of Christian faith. Hauerwas believes that theological ethics and systematic theology can only be meaningful discourses in relation to each other. On one side he argues that ethical "ought-issues" cannot be divorced from theological "is-issues." We can only know what people ought to do, if we know what kind of creatures they are, in what kind of world they live, and how God is involved is this world. But, on the other hand, for Hauerwas systematic theology cannot be done in abstraction from theological ethics.[9] He argues, for instance, that a proper understanding of the true character of God, man and the world requires not just intellectual but also moral transformation. Therefore, while this book offers a systematic theological analysis of Hauerwas's account of witness, it will also show how in this account witness is considered as an *ethos*, a moral practice which is crucial for our understanding of all that is.

Roughly speaking there are three ways of reading a theological (or ethical, or philosophical) author. Firstly, an author could be *portrayed* from a distanced position. In such a reading "the phenomenon" of Stanley Hauerwas could be described as, for instance, a typical representative of late modern American theology.[10] Secondly, the author's work could be *criticized* from a suspicious point of view. In such a reading, a hidden agenda in Hauerwas's work could be revealed, and his ideas could be rejected as fideistic, sectarian or tribalistic.[11] And, lastly, an author can also be *explained* in a

8. Schwöbel gives an accurate description of the discipline of systematic theology: "The task of systematic theology is organized exposition of how the Christian faith interprets reality, with reference to its inherent certainty of its truth, and the closely associated guidance for action" ("Systematic Theology," 45).

9. See for instance Hauerwas's remarks in *The Peaceable Kingdom*: "Indeed, I think in many ways the separation of ethics from theology has had unfortunate consequences. Ethics is but one aspect of the theological task and little hangs on whether it has integrity as a specifiable discipline" (54). See also *Against the Nations*: "Our task as theologians remains what is has always been: namely, to exploit the considerable recourses embodied in particular Christian convictions which sustain our ability to be a community faithful to our belief that we are creatures of a graceful God" (44).

10. See for instance the portrait by Elshtain, "Theologian." See also Webb, "The Very American."

11. See for instance the critique by Miscamble, "Sectarian Passivism."

way which is both affirmative and corrective. As this introduction indicates, in this book I offer such a reading of Hauerwas's work. I am an affirmative reader. I'm convinced that Hauerwas's understanding of witness makes sense, and I've written this book to show this. Yet, I'm not naive and am also very aware of the strong rhetoric in Hauerwas's texts and I've tried not to let myself be confused by it. I will continue to ask if his arguments are clear and lucid and if his ideas are biblically and theologically tenable. Indeed, I'll not hesitate to criticize Hauerwas for being unclear or incomplete or mistaken. But I'll also try to improve his account of witness by proposing clarifications, completions and corrections, as I see them.

Nevertheless, I must also admit that some of Hauerwas's basic convictions will not be questioned in this book: namely those about how we must practice theology. Along with "postliberal" theologians in the English-speaking world, Hauerwas can be characterized as a theologian belonging to "the school of Anselm and Karl Barth," a theologian who considers himself to be in the service of the movement of *fides quaerens intellectum* (faith seeking understanding).[12] Like Anselm and Barth, Hauerwas conceives faith as a particular gift by God to the Christian community.[13] For him, the theologian's task is to use the intellect to reflect on God as the giver of faith, and on how this God enters into a relationship with man. However, he believes we are mistaken when we think that the intellect is the foundation of faith or an instrument which can prove its truth. Thus, in the school of Barth, Anselm *and* Hauerwas, theology makes sense only as the explication of God's gift of faith to the church.

In his book *Types of Christian Theology*, Hans Frei argues that there are very good reasons to theologize in this way.[14] For the what he calls "type 4" theologians, the language of faith—the retelling and reflecting on of stories of God and Israel and God in Jesus Christ by the church in all ages and

12. Fodor, "Postliberal Theology." For a further discussion of how Hauerwas relates to postliberal theologians like Hans Frei and George Lindbeck, see Wells, *Transforming Fate*, 52–61. See also chapter 1.5.1.

13. Barth, *Anselm*. Hauerwas discusses Barth's book in *With the Grain of the Universe*: "Barth understood one of the tasks of theology to be the silencing of certain questions. That is one of the reasons he admired Anselm's work, just to the extent that Anselm helped the fool see that to ask more questions of the revealed Word of God is to fail to see how that Word calls into question the form of our question" (190). See also 154–55, 165–66, 187.

14. In his Gifford Lectures (146n) Hauerwas refers to Frei's discussion of Karl Barth in *Types* but he does not discuss Frei's typology. In "The Church as God's New Language," Hauerwas does explain how he relates to Frei's theology but he does not refer to Frei's typology. This essay was published in *Christian Existence* but originally written for a Festschrift for Frei: Green, *Scriptural Authority*. An insightful discussion of Frei and his typology can be found in DeHart, *Trial of the Witnesses*, 128–42.

places—has priority over "external languages" such as philosophy, science and the dominant stories in our society. Frei describes Barth as the typical representative of this theology (38–46). According to Barth, there's no use trying to explain *why* God has chosen to reveal himself through Christ. Theologians can and must explicate what it means to believe and confess *that* God revealed himself in Jesus Christ. According to Frei, the great strength of this type of theology is that it is not reductive. Christian theology is not reduced to an external description of Christianity and theological reflection does not become a secret language, but is capable of persuading even "cultured despisers."[15] It's clear that Hauerwas also belongs to this type. For him, Christian theology reflects on the particular narrative about God and Israel, about God in Jesus Christ and about Jesus Christ calling his disciples. In *With the Grain of the Universe* he argues that theology cannot *prove* that this narrative makes sense but only show *how* it makes sense.[16]

Frei further describes how in this type of theology Scripture and philosophy each has a different role (78–91). Scripture has a normative role—as the collection of books given to the church. The church constantly retells the stories of Israel and Jesus, and in this retelling it interprets the changing intellectual, cultural, social and political contexts in which Christians find themselves. The task of Christian theology is to serve the church in this process of retelling and reinterpretation. It helps the church by expounding how in the light of the Bible, Christians can understand themselves, God, and the world they live in. As we have seen above, for this task theologians need the intellect. But the theologians of this type do not restrict themselves by only using their own intellect, or the intellect of some specific ecclesial authorities. They creatively use all available "tools" which are helpful for performing their task of explicating Christian faith. Here philosophy comes in, because theologians know from age-long experience that philosophical analyses, ideas and arguments are extremely helpful for them. Thus for this type of theology, philosophy has a heuristic role. It does not prescribe what theologians must think, but helps them "to think better."

Regarding his approach to Scripture and philosophy, Hauerwas can be conceived as a typical representative of this type of theology. Scripture is normative in his theology. For him, the Bible can only be read correctly

---

15. Though Frei (*Types,* 34–38) has a preference for type 4, he also shows that there is another non-reductive type of theology. In type 3, the language of faith has no priority over external description but they are considered as autonomous yet reciprocally related discourses. This type is exemplified by Friedrich Schleiermacher who uses external description to explain to the "cultured despisers" the true meaning of the language of faith. See also DeHart, *Trial of the Witnesses,* 139–42.

16. This will be further explained in chapter 1.

as a book for the church—and not, say, as a classic in American culture.[17] Philosophy, however, has a more modest role in his work. Though he often refers to philosophers such as Aristotle, Wittgenstein and Macintyre, he uses their insights in a rather specific way, namely to articulate the particular characteristics of Christian faith.[18] Nevertheless, in the chapters in *With the Grain of the Universe* which reflect on the character of Christian witness, there are few references to Scripture or philosophy. Hauerwas does not clarify his account of witness with the help of contemporary philosophical reflections, nor does he justify it by referring to the various biblical texts about God calling man as witnesses. In fact he's simply having a dialogue with other theologians, and in this dialogue he expounds his understanding of witness. Still, the crucial implication of his Gifford Lectures is that there are philosophical arguments *and* biblical grounds for his exposition on Christian witness. What I'll try to do in the chapters in which I discuss philosophical reflections and Scriptural texts is test whether this implicit suggestion is correct. In other words, I'll consider whether there's philosophical and Scriptural support for his understanding of witness. Moreover, in chapter 5, I refer again to the same places in Scripture, this time to formulate an "intersubjective criterion" which I use to make a systematic theological evaluation of Hauerwas's account of Christian witness.[19]

In all these chapters I will *not* question the basic views on the role of philosophy and Scripture in Christian theology which are typical for the school of theology to which Hauerwas belongs. On the contrary, I adopt these views and test whether Hauerwas actually conforms to the criteria of a "type 4 theologian." Thus, the presupposition of my study is that Frei is right, i.e. that there are good reasons for practicing this type of theology. Although this presupposition will not be questioned, I hope this book will indicate that theology in the school of Anselm, Barth *and* Hauerwas makes sense.

But Hauerwas is not the only theologian who speaks about Christian witness without explicitly referring to philosophical arguments and biblical justifications. The same is true for two theologians who are very close to him: John Howard Yoder and James McClendon. In *The Christian Witness to the State*, published in 1964, Yoder gives an analysis of how Christians relate to the nation state and how they could witness to peacefulness. In *Witness*, the third volume of his systematic theology, James McClendon discusses how the life of the Christian community relates to society. But

17. Hauerwas makes this argument in *Unleashing the Scripture*.

18. See for instance the "use" of Aristotle in the essay "Character."

19. Hauerwas himself searches for biblical grounds in an article written with Charles Pinches: "Witness." This article will be further discussed in chapters 1 and 4.

neither Yoder nor McClendon wonders how their view on witness relates to philosophical analyses on the witness and his testimony and to the biblical texts about God calling men to be his witness. In his book *Church, World and the Christian Life*, Nicholas Healy described the responsibility of the church as to "witness to its Lord, to make known throughout the world the Good News of salvation in and through the person and work of Jesus Christ."[20] But in his book, Healy refers neither to Scripture nor to philosophical reflection to explain what witnessing is and why it is a typical practice of the church. Most recently, Craig Hovey in his book *Bearing True Witness* uses philosophical analyses of witness to develop a thorough examination on the character of Christian witness (which seems close to Hauerwas's understanding of witness). However, Hovey gives but a short discussion on the significant biblical pericopes on witness.[21]

In this respect this book fills a gap. By describing a quest for philosophical arguments and Scriptural support for Hauerwas's account, it contributes to the ongoing debate on the character of Christian witness. It offers an overview of how everyday, legal, and other conceptions are related to the way Christians understand themselves as witnesses. It offers an interpretation of various philosophical analyses (using other sources than Hovey does), and an exposition of how these analyses help to clarify theological reflections on the character of Christian witness. It offers a reading of the different voices in Scripture which speak about God calling men as his witnesses, and an examination in which the texts are related to systematic theological ideas.

It may be appropriate to make two final remarks about this study and its author. Firstly, though I don't doubt that this book will betray how I'm shaped by my Calvinist upbringing and by my Barthian teachers, this a not a "denominational evaluation" in which the writer examines if the "Methodist theology" of Stanley Hauerwas fits the criteria of a "Reformed" theology in the tradition of Calvin and Barth. Along with Hauerwas, I believe that denominational differences are of minor interest in theology these days, and that Christian theologians must write for all denominations.[22] Thus when I speak of the church, I refer to the one, holy, catholic, and apostolic Church represented by all denominations accepting the Nicene-Constantinopolitan Creed and when I speak of Christians' vocation to be witness, I think of all people who consider themselves Christians.

20. Healy, *Church, World,* 6.

21. Most of Hovey's references to Scripture can be found in *Bearing True Witness,* 117–37.

22. Hauerwas's understanding of the church is discussed in chapter 1.

Secondly, I am a Christian theologian living in one of the most secularized countries of the world: the Netherlands. The reformed churches of the Netherlands used to have a huge influence on Dutch culture, society, and politics. But these days are long gone. Nowadays, the mainstream churches in the Netherlands are learning to exist in the margins and they need a theology that can help to interpret this new situation and to recover the church's identity. I admit that one of the reasons I love to study Hauerwas is I believe his theology could help us Dutch Protestants recover our vocation and form a community of witnesses. I believe that, if interpreted correctly, Hauerwas's work shows a way for us to live truthfully and faithfully in a world without certainties. But that is not what this book is about. It is not written to argue that Stanley Hauerwas is the best guide for Dutch Protestants. It is written to indicate how the theology of this Texan Methodist helps all Christian theologians to understand the true meaning of the words of Jesus Christ: "you will be my witnesses."

——————————————————————

Stanley Hauerwas and the Necessity of Witness

THIS CHAPTER INTRODUCES HAUERWAS and his account of Christian witness. I will show what, in my view, is the leading notion of his Gifford Lectures, and a crucial theme in his other works: *for a full understanding of Christian faith, we need the practice of witnessing.* Most of this chapter is dedicated to *With the Grain of the Universe.* The first section is a brief analysis of the book, the second and third sections discuss the understanding of witness Hauerwas develops in the last part of his book. The fourth section is about two significant articles on witness written after the publication of his Gifford Lectures. The chapter concludes with a short biography and a discussion of witness in Hauerwas's other works.

1. BY THEIR FRUITS YE SHALL KNOW THEM—NOT BY THEIR ROOTS

Stanley Hauerwas never expected to be asked to give the Gifford Lectures. As he writes in the preface of *With the Grain of the Universe,* "it was with the delight that comes only from an unimagined gift that I received the invitation to be the Gifford lecturer at the University of St. Andrews in 2000–2001" (9). Hauerwas was surprised to be invited, not just because of the status of the lectures—"one of the most prestigious lecture series in the world"[1]—but also because the prescribed subject of these lectures was natural theology: something Hauerwas did not feel completely comfortable lecturing on. Over the years, he had written inspiring articles about the courage to relinquish violence, about the amorality of medical ethics

———
1. Limpitlaw, "Gifford Lectures," 6.

and the weakness of the values of liberal democracy—but he never wrote about the relation between God and natural reasoning. Indeed, in his work he has always stressed the particularity of the Christian narrative and has been skeptical about attempts to make universal claims about God and the world. Nevertheless, Hauerwas accepted the invitation. After four years of preparation he went to Scotland's oldest university to lecture on "the natural" based on the thoughts of three renowned Gifford lecturers: William James, Reinhold Niebuhr and Karl Barth.

With the Grain of the Universe is like a well-balanced symphony: six same-sized chapters, two on each Gifford lecturer, introduced by a substantial overture, concluded with a magnificent finale, and with the extensive footnotes playing a sophisticated countermelody. The eight chapters in the book correspond with the eight lectures given at Saint Andrews. The first lecture introduces the subject of "natural theology" and problems related to this subject: how can we best speak theologically about the natural? In the next two lectures, William James is presented as an illustration of the problem: his account makes it impossible to speak theologically about the natural. Then Reinhold Niebuhr's theological approach is discussed as the apparent solution to the problem. However, the sixth and seventh lectures argue that the actual solution comes from an unexpected source: Karl Barth's *Church Dogmatics*. In the last lecture, Hauerwas gives his final answer: in order to speak theologically about the natural we should learn to listen to the witness of the church.

In the first lecture, Hauerwas discusses the last will and testament of Lord Gifford, the founder of the Gifford Lectures. This lecture can be read as Hauerwas's attempt to respect Gifford's will. Gifford dedicated his lectures to "Promoting, Advancing and Diffusing the Study of Natural Theology." For him, natural theology was not just "the Knowledge of God, the Infinite, the All, the First and Only Cause, the One and Sole Substance, the Sole Being" but also "the Knowledge of the Relations which man and the whole universe bear to Him" and "the Knowledge of the Nature and Foundations of Ethics or Morals."[2] According to Adam Gifford's will, his lectures should treat their subject without "reference to or reliance upon any supposed special exceptional or so-called miraculous revelation."[3]

Hauerwas explains that he can only respect Gifford's will by expounding why he has a radically different view of the nature of natural theology. Though he agrees with Gifford that natural theology is about everything,

2. Hauerwas, *With the Grain*, 19, quotes "Lord Gifford's Will," in Jaki, *Lord Gifford*, 72–73.

3. Hauerwas, *With the Grain*, 26, quotes "Lord Gifford's Will," 74.

about God, man and the world, he thinks it cannot be practiced by relying on reason alone. Hauerwas argues that the way Gifford speaks about natural theology isn't "natural" at all: it is a typical outcome of the historical process of modernity. In modernity, the features of theology change dramatically. While in Aquinas's *Summa Theologica* natural knowledge of God is integrated in a trinitarian theology, Enlightenment theologians came to think about natural theology as "a given that can clearly be distinguished from theology proper" (31). Hauerwas calls this change "the epistemological overcoming of theology" (36). After this overcoming, Christian convictions are not self-evident anymore. Their content is supposed to be secondary to natural thinking and therefore theologians such as Adam Gifford claimed that the truth of Christian convictions can only be secured by a natural theology. Influenced by Immanuel Kant, others chose another strategy to theologize under the conditions of modernity. They left the natural world to science and turned to "the only place left in which language about God might make sense, that is, to the human—and not just to the human, but to what makes the human 'moral'" (37–38). For these theologians, God-talk made sense only in the sphere of the ethical and as a result they were "devoid of the recourses needed to demonstrate that theological claims are necessary for our knowledge of the way things are and for the kind of life we must live to acquire such knowledge" (38).

In the second and third lectures, Hauerwas presents the work of William James as representative of this second strategy. James turned natural theology into religious psychology. For him, genuine religion was not about the way things are, but about man's innermost feelings: through individual experiences, religion teaches us about the true nature of ourselves:

> James gave voice to the character of Christianity in modernity: Christianity makes sense only as disguised humanism. That Christianity might make sense as something else is a possibility that James rejected. (64)

For Hauerwas James is the perfect example of how Christian convictions about God and the world were reduced to irrelevant "over-beliefs" (71). Yet, there is an interesting "nevertheless" in Hauerwas's account of James. Hauerwas is captivated by James's pragmatic account of religion. James suggests that religious faith can be verified by testing it in practice. In James's own words: "By their fruits ye shall know them, not by their roots."[4] Hauerwas endorses this pragmatic account. With James he holds that "theological

---

4. Hauerwas (*With the Grain,* 66) quotes James, *Varieties of Religious Experience,* 37. James, in turn, quotes the Gospel of Matthew, "by their fruits ye shall know them" (Matt 7:20 KJV) and discusses Jonathan Edwards's *Treatise on Religious Affections.*

ideas will be true if they have a value for concrete life" (68). Moreover, he learns from James that "some ideas are true only in relation to other ideas" (68). Hauerwas thinks that James's pragmatic account might be helpful for his own project: if James's claims are true, then Christian beliefs about "the way things are" cannot be treated separately as a theory about nature, but must be understood in their relation to "the kind of lives Christians live." In the third lecture, this argument is used to turn James's account on its head. Hauerwas argues that in a pragmatic approach there are no valid reasons either to put aside orthodox doctrine as over-belief or to reduce communal Christian practices to individual religious experience. As we will see, this argument is further elaborated on in the last lecture.

The lectures on Niebuhr are perhaps the most controversial.[5] In the fourth and fifth lectures, Hauerwas argues that Reinhold Niebuhr's account of Christianity is not an alternative to James's understanding of religion but a continuation of it. According to Hauerwas's analyses, Niebuhr's theology is nothing but anthropology: it's not about the nature of God, but the nature of man.

> Niebuhr's project was not natural theology, if by that you mean the attempt to "prove" God; rather, he sought to naturalize theological claims in a manner that would make them acceptable to the scientific and political presumptions of his day. (114–15)

Niebuhr is described as an apologist who tries to prove that "the truth of Christianity consisted in the confirmation of universal and timeless myths about the human condition that made Christianity available for anyone without witness" (39). For Hauerwas, the costs of this apology are high, indeed, too high: in Niebuhr's theology God is domesticated, "capable of doing no more than providing comfort to the anxious conscience of the bourgeois" (138). For Niebuhr, just like James, Christian convictions do not provide any genuine knowledge about the way things are or about the way man should live. Christian faith is not about God and being, but about being human. Consequently, the form of Christianity promoted by James and Niebuhr is nothing but an endorsement of the convictions and social orders of liberal society.

Then Karl Barth is summoned. The theologian, who is famous for not wanting to be a natural theologian at all, is called upon to save natural theology. What makes Barth attractive to Hauerwas's project is that he does *not* attempt to demonstrate how theology makes sense. Barth speaks about God and creation from the presupposition that they make sense: that it is God

---

5. See for instance Novak, "Defending Niebuhr."

who makes sense. Hauerwas's discussion of Barth begins with Barth's *Nein* to Emil Brunner and the sharp dialectic of the second edition of *The Epistle to the Romans*. Hauerwas argues that this "No!" to the world (and to theologies that do not begin with such a "no") is not Barth's last word but the necessary beginning of any form of proper theology. For Barth, speaking about "our existence" or "the existence of the world" without any further specifications does not make sense but is an illusion of sin. The "peculiar, indeed unique and in the end only true existence" (187) only applies to God who in revelation destroys our illusions. But human speech *can* make sense. God offers faith, and this faith creates an analogy between human words and divine being. By this *analogia fidei* it is possible to speak meaningfully, not just about God but about ourselves and the world we live in. By following this analogy we find that neither the world nor our lives are subject to necessity or fate. Instead, we find that we are creatures and that the world is God's creation.

Hauerwas describes Barth's concept of *analogia fidei* as "an attempt to display the metaphysical claims intrinsic to theological speech" (189). Barth does not want to build a metaphysical system, because he conceives such a system as the mere illusion of the subject. Nevertheless in his theology something "metaphysical" happens: "we speak, and in speaking we discover that we are caught up, together with that about which we speak, in an endeavor that must be described as 'metaphysical'" (189). Since Barth's theology is not based on prior metaphysical claims but displays the metaphysical claims intrinsic to theological speech, it is able to overcome the problems of classical metaphysics. And this overcoming of metaphysics is also the overcoming of any Gifford-like epistemology. Barth did not get stuck in the question "How do we know God?" for he saw that this question is relative to the question "Who is God?" In his *Church Dogmatics* Barth showed how "our speech is at once a witness to God and a revelation of our nature as God's creatures" (191).

Since Barth did overcome Gifford-like epistemology, Hauerwas presents him as "the 'great natural theologian' of the Gifford lecturers" (9–10).

> Barth, in spite of his disavowal of natural theology, provides the recourses necessary for developing an adequate theological metaphysics, or, in other words, a natural theology. Of course, I assume that "natural theology" simply names how Christian convictions work to describe all that is as God's good creation. (142)

This section has made clear that Hauerwas's description of Karl Barth as the "great natural theologian" of the twentieth century cannot be pushed aside as just another Hauerwasian provocation. Hauerwas has serious reasons for making this claim. Barth is a great natural theologian because he did not let himself be misled by the adjective "natural." He's under no illusions that he cannot speak about things as they are without "presuppositions," but supposes "the natural" as creation.[6] Barth does not leave the natural to science as Niebuhr and James did. Not unlike Aquinas's *Summa Theologica*, his *Church Dogmatics* speaks frankly "about all that is" as God's creation.[7]

But Hauerwas's argument does not finish with his lectures on Barth. In the final lecture, Hauerwas explains that this special knowledge about God's creation can only be communicated by witnesses, people showing in their speech and in their action that "all that is" is the creation of the triune God. And since the church is presented as a community which trains men in the skills of witnessing, Hauerwas even claims that the existence of the church is necessary for any knowledge of nature, and for practicing natural theology. If Christian convictions are separated from the ecclesial practices of producing truthful and faithful witnesses, they are not only useless or meaningless but false: because such a separation violates Christian convictions. This is what happens in any Gifford-like natural theology: true convictions about the triune God are twisted into false ideas about God as watchmaker. And these ideas cannot shape witnesses, because: who wants to dedicate his life to a watchmaker?[8]

Now the outline of the book has been sketched, its title can be explained. As Hauerwas tells us in the first lecture, the title originates from a phrase by the theologian he is most indebted to: John Howard Yoder. Hauerwas quotes Yoder at length:

> The point that apocalyptic makes is not only that people who wear crowns and who claim to foster justice by the sword are not as strong as they think—true as that is: we still sing, "O where are Kings and Empires now of old that went and came?" It is that people who bear crosses are working with the grain of the universe. One does not come to that belief by reducing social processes to mechanical and statistical models, nor by winning some of one's battles for the control of one's own corner of the fallen world. One comes to it by sharing the life of those who sing about the Resurrection of the slain Lamb. (17)[9]

6. On the idea of supposing the natural as creation, see the review article by Ochs, "On Hauerwas."

7. See for Hauerwas's discussion of Barth's relation to Aquinas 184–85n.

8. Hauerwas finishes his last lecture with an exposition on the church and the university. He makes a plea for a Christian university "as a site where Christians might rediscover the difference that being Christian makes for claims about the world" (232).

9. Yoder, "Armaments," 58. This phrase is also the motto of *With the Grain of the Universe*.

To grasp the statement "that people who bear crosses work with the grain of the universe" we must realize that implicitly Yoder refers to Scripture, to two sayings by Jesus. One can be found in the Gospel of John:

> Very truly, I tell you, unless a grain of wheat falls into the earth and dies, it remains just a single grain; but if it dies, it bears much fruit. (John 12:24)

And the other found in the Gospel of Matthew:

> whoever does not take up the cross and follow me is not worthy of me. (Matt 10:38)[10]

Yoder's statement suggests that Christians are cross-bearers, a people whose existence is dependent on the ultimate cross-bearer, Jesus Christ. In other words: Jesus is the grain that dies in the earth and bears fruit in the community of his disciples. Just as seed constantly multiplies, these cross-bearers work with the grain and sow it again and again. Yoder suggests that working with this specific piece of grain has universal implications. By bearing crosses, these people reveal that this single kernel is "the grain of the universe." In his Gifford Lectures, Hauerwas takes up this insight of Yoder and argues that the followers of Jesus Christ should be conceived as a testimonial people, a people bearing witness through their words and their lives.

2. THE LECTURES ON KARL BARTH

Now we can examine Hauerwas's account of witness more closely. In the third section of this chapter, I will consider how Hauerwas appeals for the necessity of witnessing in his last Gifford lecture. He maintains that we can only speak properly about the natural if we are prepared to listen to the witness of the church. In this section I will discuss the lectures on Karl Barth. In these lectures Hauerwas begins to elaborate on this idea that we need witnesses to understand the character of the natural. In fact, witness is a key term in Hauerwas's interpretation of Barth. He uses it both to explain the impact of Barth's work and to characterize Barth's life. The present section gives an analysis of these lectures in three steps. First, I will give an introduction to how Hauerwas reads Barth's life and work. Then I will consider his reception of Barth's account of witness before thirdly discussing his critique on Barth.

---

10. Unless otherwise indicated, all Scripture quotations are from the New Revised Standard Version.

Before examining his Gifford Lectures in detail, a brief remark on Hauerwas's use of language is required. Stanley Hauerwas is not the sort of scholar who gives precise definitions of all the terms he uses in his texts. Mostly he just uses words that help him make his point, hoping that his writings will reveal—to the readers *and* to the author—the exact meaning of the applied word. This also concerns Hauerwas's use of the word "witness." Hauerwas does not give a definition in advance but in his lectures he gradually discloses what "witness" means. Therefore, the best way to explain Hauerwas's understanding of the term is by following his writing. If we try to do this, however, it turns out that his use of the term is slightly confusing. Hauerwas has a strong preference for the term "witness" and scarcely uses the noun "testimony" and the verb "to testify."[11] As we know, the English term "witness" has many meanings. As a noun, "witness" refers either to a person who is a "witness," or to a report, a testimony. As a verb, "to witness" refers either to the act of observing or to the act of reporting. To understand Hauerwas's account of witness we must realize that he uses the verb "to witness" almost exclusively in the second sense. In *With the Grain of the Universe* "witnessing" is "witnessing to," it means reporting, testifying or even showing. For Hauerwas, the noun "witness" applies either to a witnessing person or to what is given by this person; his testimony. But in some instances it remains unclear whether "witness" refers to a person or to testimony (for instance, in the title of the first section of the last lecture: "No Witness, No Argument"). Although this indistinctness may seem somewhat confusing, it will turn out below that it does not cause serious problems for our analysis. What shall be shown in this section is that Hauerwas presupposes a close relation between the person who is a "witness," his or her act of "witnessing," and the "witness" which is given through this act. Thus, what is given cannot be separated, either, from the act of giving or from the subject of the giver. For Hauerwas, a witness always belongs to someone, to a particular witnessing subject.

2.1 The Witness of Karl Barth

As we have seen above, the main argument in the lectures on Barth is that the *Church Dogmatics* provides the recourses necessary for developing an

---

11. Hauerwas uses the noun "testimony" and the verb "to testify" only in paraphrases of Barth. See for instance: "According to Barth . . . God's creation is never absent testimony to its creator. . . . For Barth all creation . . . testifies in gratitude to the grace of the creator" (167). In this chapter I will follow the language of the Gifford Lectures and not use the terms "testimony" or "testify." See chapter 2.1 for a discussion of the meaning of "witness" and "testimony" and their derivatives in relation to Hauerwas.

adequate natural theology. Barth explains to his readers that the natural should be understood as God's good creation. But, according to Hauerwas, Barth realizes that he can only show the natural as creation by training the vision of his readers. Hauerwas, therefore, reads the *Church Dogmatics* as a "training manual" (179).

> Earlier I said that the *Church Dogmatics* is a manual designed to train Christians that the habits of our speech must be disciplined by the God found in Jesus Christ. I can now add that this training, which requires both intellectual and moral transformation, enables Christians to see the world as it is, and not as it appears. (182–83)

According to Hauerwas, the *Church Dogmatics* transforms the intellectual and moral vision of its readers so that they can see the world as it is: God's creation. This training is not offered to all humanity, but to the specific group of women and men who are ready to be trained. These people are those living in the church and calling themselves Christians.[12] Moreover, the *Church Dogmatics* not only trains the *vision* but also the *skills* of its readers. And on this very point Hauerwas speaks about witness:

> The *Church Dogmatics*, with its unending and confident display of Christian speech, is Barth's attempt to train us to be a people capable of truthful witness to the God who alone is the truth. (176)

For Hauerwas, Barth's dogmatics reminds Christians that Jesus Christ has called them as his witnesses *and* instructs them how they could faithfully answer this call. In other words, it trains Christians in the *skills of witnessing*. This community of skilled witnesses teaches mankind that the natural is God's good creation.

By the end of his seventh lecture, Hauerwas comes to speak about Barth's ethics of sanctification. He emphasizes that in the *Church Dogmatics* ethics and dogmatics are intertwined:

> All the volumes of the *Dogmatics* are Barth's "ethics," because Barth rightly saw that the truthfulness of Christian speech about God is a matter of truthful witness. (194)

---

12. In fact the *Church Dogmatics* is more than a training manual offered to the church. In his lectures, Hauerwas emphasizes how Barth has been trained by the church of all ages to read the bible, to understand doctrine, to live the Christian life. From this perspective, Barth's dogmatics could also be understood as the "product" this ecclesial training.

In Hauerwas's reading, Barth's ethics of sanctification speaks more explicitly and coherently of what is already indicated in the other parts of his work: Christians have been called to bear witness through their lives and the Holy Spirit makes this life of truthfulness and faithfulness possible. Thus, for Barth witness is not the exclusive identity of an elite of faithful believers. The very fact that a Christian has been baptized already witnesses to the God who made the existence of Christians possible. The vocation for a Christian to be a witness is the vocation to become in an active and truthful way what they already are in a passive and often unfaithful way. And witnessing truthfully is an act of sanctification. Through the Holy Spirit it is possible that man gives a faithful answer to God's call and lives a life of sanctity.

Hauerwas indicates that for Barth, witnessing involves truthful speech *and* faithful action. Christians bear witness not just by retelling the story of creation, reconciliation and redemption, but also by enacting this story in their lives. This witnessing which takes place in the church is primarily addressed to God, but it also addresses man. In one way, the church is a community in which witnesses bear witness to each other by speaking about God's covenant with man and by living this narrative. In another, the church bears witness to the world through its utterances and its practices. And Barth stresses that witnesses will not always find a receptive audience. Truthful witnesses are rejected—both by unfaithful ecclesial communities and by incredulous societies. In Hauerwas's words:

> The Christian ministry of witness, therefore, will disturb some people, and they will react to the pressure of the witness with counterpressure. (198)

But those who learn to listen to the witness of the church will find that even creation itself is not without witness to its Creator:

> For Barth, all of creation, and not humans alone, testifies in gratitude to the grace of the creator. (167)

Finally, Hauerwas indicates that for Barth, theology itself is no more than a practice of witnessing. The theologian's task is not to explain Christian faith in general terms but to bear witness of the church's witness. In his lectures, Hauerwas presents Karl Barth as the paradigmatic example of a witnessing theologian:

> In his life and in his work, Barth sought nothing other than to be a witness to God's reconciling and redeeming work in Jesus Christ. (146)

The title of the sixth lecture is "The Witness of Karl Barth." For Hauerwas this witness contrasts sharply with "The Liberalism of Reinhold Niebuhr" (the title of lecture 4) and "The Faith of William James" (the title of lecture 2).[13]

2.2 Barth and the Witness of the Church

In his seventh lecture, Hauerwas extensively discusses the role of the church in Barth's theology. For Barth, the church is not a conceptual idea but a visible people witnessing to God's revelation through audible speech and perceptible action. In the extensive footnotes, Hauerwas argues that the *Church Dogmatics* should be understood in relation to these ecclesial practices of witnessing. Implicitly, Barth's dogmatics suggests that one cannot understand the truth of Christian convictions in abstraction from the audible speech and perceptible action of a witnessing church.[14] In this discussion of Barth's ecclesiology, Hauerwas makes some observations about the character of witness that are significant for our understanding of Hauerwas's own account of Christian witness.

Hauerwas observes that for Barth, witnessing is vital for understanding Christian faith:

> The church's struggle to produce truthful witnesses is an ongoing task; to the extent that such witnesses exist, by their fruits you shall know them. For Barth, therefore, the question of the distinctive character of the Christian life as a witness to God is inseparable from, in fact is the necessary condition for, any account of the truth of Christian convictions. (200)

13. Hauerwas does not discuss how Barth in chapter xvi of his dogmatics speaks of Jesus Christ as the first and ultimate witness, cf. *Church Dogmatics* iv/3. But in fact, Barth's idea that the unique witness of Jesus Christ is the *conditio sine qua non* for the witness of the church, is the basic presupposition of Hauerwas's reflections on the character of Christian witness.

14. In the footnotes of the lectures on Barth, Hauerwas carefully explains how his reading of Barth relates to other interpretations. He puts it positively: "My point is simply that Barth's position on theological truth at least requires that Christians must be who they say they are—and that is not without significance for questions of truth" (200n). He also puts it negatively: "I do think, however, that Barth is committed to some account of the self-involving character of claims that would make any attempt to separate what is asserted from the speaker problematic" (200n). On the one hand, this interpretation differs somewhat from Hunsinger, *How to Read Karl Barth*, 65–75. According to Hauerwas, Barth is closer to an understanding of truth which acknowledges "the self-involving character of speech about God" (176n). But on the other hand Hauerwas disagrees with Johnson who suggests that for Barth "God is what God achieves in Human Beings" (*Mystery of God*, 50). Hauerwas remarks: "I suspect that Barth would think Johnson's paraphrases cross a boundary, making the witness of Christians equivalent to that to which they witness" (195n).

Hauerwas's suggestion is obvious. In some way Barth's account of truth resembles James's. While for James "theological ideas will be true if they have a value for concrete life" (68), for Barth "Christian orthodoxy cannot be Christian truth without living Christians" (200). However, unlike James, Barth neither rejects orthodox doctrine as "over-belief" nor reduces communal Christian practices to individual religious experience. Thus, according to the seventh Gifford lecture, it is Barth and not James who understands the true meaning of the phrase "by their fruits ye shall know them, not by their roots."

The idea that we cannot understand Christian faith unless it is through witnesses consists of two claims. Firstly, Hauerwas suggests that in the *Church Dogmatics*, witness is the ultimate form of theological *communication*. Knowledge about the triune God and his works of creation, reconciliation and redemption can only be communicated by a people devoted to this God, a people daring to live with him. Secondly, Hauerwas claims that in the *Church Dogmatics*, Christian witness is an indication of the truth of what's being communicated. The "fruit" of the church's witness can also be conceived as an *argument* for the truth of Christian convictions.[15] To put it formally: witnessing through speech and acts must be conceived as a report which supplies information, and this report itself is an argument for the truth of the supplied information.

2.3 Hauerwas's Critique on Barth

Hauerwas realizes that in some respects his reading of Barth's life and work is un-Barthian. In the seventh lecture he remarks:

> Of course, Barth always maintained that we can never be sure that God will make our speech God's speech. The *Church Dogmatics,* however, is good evidence that God has done just that. And if our God is the God who has made himself known through the promise in Israel and the life, death, and resurrection of Jesus, we should not be surprised that when our speech becomes God's speech, that is, when we participate in God's revelation, we find ourselves involved in a story. (191)

---

15. Hauerwas does not explicitly speak about this distinction between communication and argument. Yet, he does use the term "argument" cf. "as Barth uses it, the language of the church is itself already an argument just to the extent that his descriptions and redescriptions cannot help but challenge our normal way of seeing the world" (182).

More than Barth, Hauerwas stresses that Christians are able to give truthful and faithful answers to God's call to be his witnesses—and he presents Barth's life and theology as evidence for this claim. In other words, Hauerwas argues that if witnessing is vital for knowing the truth of faith, and if God is indeed a God of grace, then God will not withdraw but send his Holy Spirit to his people to make the church into a community of truthful and faithful witnesses.

According to Hauerwas, Barth's theology ultimately lacks concreteness. In his ecclesiology, he oscillates between claims which are essential yet abstracted from concrete ecclesial practices and claims which are empirical yet accidental and without theological significance. For Hauerwas, Barth's failure is that he does not explain how human agents become witnesses, how they are involved in the Spirit's work. The reason for this is that Barth's is an "overly cautious account of the role of the church in the economy of God's salvation" (202). According to Barth, the church cannot be trusted in its calling to be God's witness. Hauerwas quotes Joseph Mangina, who argues that what fails in Barth's account of the church is the glad acceptance "of the church itself as the binding medium in which faith takes place" (145).[16] In Hauerwas's own words:

> Barth is not sufficiently catholic just to the extent that his critique and rejection of Protestant liberalism make it difficult for him to acknowledge that, through the work of the Holy Spirit, we are made part of God's care of the world through the church.[17] Barth, of course, does not deny that the church is constituted by the proclamation of the gospel. What he cannot acknowledge is that the community called the church is constitutive of the gospel proclamation. (145)

16. Mangina, "Bearing," 294–95.

17. In the footnotes, Hauerwas mentions that for this analysis he is indebted to Hütter, "Barth's Catholicity." Earlier Hütter criticized Barth in a similar way, saying that what is lacking in Barth's theology is the acknowledgement of the Holy Spirit binding himself first to Word and Sacrament and then to the life in the church in general (see Hütter, *Evangelische Ethik*, 55). In the second part of this book, Hütter presents Hauerwas as a theologian who theologizes from this presupposition that the church is the binding medium in which faith takes place. Further, Hauerwas mentions that it was Healy who started this critique in "Logic." Strikingly, Healy did withdraw his critique recently: "Karl Barth" Now he appeals *in favor* of Barth's ecclesiology and criticizes Hauerwas (and also Hütter). See for instance: "Barth might ask of Hauerwas and of those who follow his lead whether in their laudable—and quite reasonable—effort to recover an ecclesial politics, they have not veered a bit too far towards presenting—and, in some cases, maybe even thinking of?—the church, the Christian life and its forms and institutions, as an 'end in itself'?" (296). See also Healy, "Practices," and more recently *Hauerwas*.

In a footnote Hauerwas further explains his critique by another quote from Mangina:

> In brief, is the church merely a human echo or analogy of Christ's completed work, as in Barth? Or is it also somehow the herald of new activity in which God is engaged between now and the eschaton? (195n)[18]

In fact, Hauerwas's critique on Barth is not just pneumatological but also soteriological and epistemological. More than Barth, Hauerwas stresses the necessity of the existence of the church as a concrete people both for man's salvation and for his knowledge of the true character of God, himself and the world. Therefore, Hauerwas also disagrees with Barth's famous claim that while the church would be lost if it had no counterpart in the world, the world would not necessarily be lost without the witness of the church. If the witness of the church actually matters, if it is vital for knowing about God's redemption, then we should not be restrained, but must articulate what difference the church actually makes in the world. Stanley Hauerwas thus needed the theological rigor of Karl Barth to demonstrate why we cannot practice theology without the witness of witnesses, indeed without becoming witnesses ourselves. Yet, in the end, the radicalness of this claim also distances him from Barth.

3. THE FINAL LECTURE

The title of the last lecture of *With the Grain of the Universe* is "The Necessity of Witness." Hauerwas starts by looking backwards, concluding that what he has tried to show in his Gifford Lectures is that Christian discourse (including theology) and ecclesial action is not self-referential: Christians are witnesses, their truthful words and faithful deeds refer to the triune God. He then elaborates on this, especially in the first section: "No Witness, No Argument." The lecture has a significant soteriological impact—it suggests that the church's witness is necessary for human salvation—but its central claim is epistemological: Hauerwas argues why the church's witness is necessary for genuine theological knowledge.

In this section, I will examine the final Gifford lecture in detail, since in this text Hauerwas unfolds his own account of witness. The section consists of four parts. The first discusses the pneumatological and the second the pragmatic argument for witness. The third part is about witness and martyrdom and the fourth is about Hauerwas's other examples of truthful witnessing. I

18. Mangina, "Bearing," 282.

will invoke the help of Hauerwas's reviewers throughout, referring to articles by the philosophers Paul J. Griffiths and Peter Ochs in *Modern Theology*, to Hauerwas's response to Griffiths and Ochs, also in *Modern Theology*, and to a piece by Brad J. Kallenberg in *The Journal of Religious Ethics*.

3.1 Why Witness? A Pneumatological Answer

The last lecture does not introduce a new understanding of witness, but repeats and elaborates on the conclusions of the lecturers on Barth: witnessing is not "applied Christianity," it is a vital part of Christian faith. Christians are called to bear witness, and by speaking the truth about God's work, by acting in accordance with these convictions, Christians answer God's call. Their witness is primarily addressed to God, but they also witness for each other and for the world. Moreover, for Hauerwas witnessing is not restricted to particular words or deeds, Christians bear witness with their entire life, through all their words and practices.

Again, Hauerwas stresses the epistemological importance of Christian witnessing. For Hauerwas, the witness of the church is more than an echo of Christ's witness, it is the fruit of a new activity by the Holy Spirit. He argues that without the concrete witness of people showing "the grain of the universe" there is no Christian faith, only a void ideology or metaphysical system that refers neither to God nor to human practice. In his own words: witnesses "must exist if Christians are to be intelligible to themselves and hopefully to those who are not Christians" (212). Only through witnessing do Christians become what they are, do they learn to know their role in the story of creation, reconciliation and redemption. Only by studying these practices of witnessing can non-Christians understand Christianity. Thus, only through witnessing words, acts and lives, does Christianity become intelligible as the practice of faith in God.

This stress on the theological importance of concrete ecclesial practices is quite un-Barthian. While Barth emphasizes the continuing influence of sin in the concrete life of Christians and the church, Hauerwas has more confidence, not in human beings but in the constancy and persistence of the work of the Holy Spirit. But why exactly is this practice of witnessing crucial for understanding Christian faith? In the first section of the last lecture, two different but interrelated answers to this question can be discerned: a pneumatological and a pragmatic answer. Hauerwas's pragmatic answer is the most extensive, but it presupposes his pneumatological answer.

In the first section of the last lecture, Hauerwas frequently refers to Bruce Marshall's *Trinity and Truth*. Marshall describes the Holy Spirit as a teacher, who persuades not by giving additional reasons or evidence "but by eliciting our assent to a way of structuring the whole" (214).[19] Hauerwas agrees with Marshall and speaks about Christians as a people who are instructed by the Spirit to look at the world in a particular way. The Holy Spirit shows Christians that their claims about the way things are is "not without persuasive power and/or support of argument" (208). The power of the Holy Spirit overturns epistemic priorities and changes both the human heart and mind, so that man is capable of loving and knowing the truth of the gospel.

> Christian practices and beliefs cannot be self-justifying because Christians, as Barth insists, must be witnesses to the God who is the Father, Son, and Holy Spirit. Just as the Son witnesses to the Father so the Spirit makes us witnesses to the Son so that the world may know the Father. (207)

Thus, for Hauerwas witnesses are people who have been persuaded by the Holy Spirit. By helping these witnesses and inspiring them to give a truthful and faithful answer to God's gift of grace, the Spirit involves human beings in the interplay or—though Hauerwas does not use this word—*perichoresis*[20] between Father, Son, and Holy Spirit. And therefore Hauerwas finally makes a bold claim:

> The truth of Christian convictions can be known only through witnesses because the God Christians worship is triune. If the truth of Christian convictions could be known without witness, then that truth would no longer be the work of the Trinity, and those who espoused it would no longer be Christians. (211–12)

Of course, Hauerwas does not deny that it's possible to convey Christian convictions through accurate observers of the Christian religion, but he does deny that the *truth* of those convictions can be communicated in other ways than through witnessing. This is why the fundamentalist's attempt to give "coercive evidence" for the truth of Christian convictions is self-destructive. Coercive evidence and "knockdown arguments"[21] are not

19. Marshall, *Trinity*, 182.

20. Hauerwas does, however, speak of *perichoresis* in his discussion of Barth in the sixth lecture (181n). Kallenberg uses the term in his discussion of Hauerwas: "Consequently, because Christians worship a God whose peaceable *perichoresis* displays tri-unity, Christian witness is strongest when the mode of their truth claims about God is isomorphic with the content spoken. Christians must speak peacefully about the Prince of peace. In Hauerwas's view, Christians witness to a triune God by means of their shared form of life" ("Strange New World," 205).

21. See also "To put is as forcefully as I can, if there were a 'knock-down' argument

the work of the Holy Spirit but a product of human pride and sin. If such evidence is constructed, it is evidence for something that is not Christian faith. Though Hauerwas does not use many words to clarify this claim, his suggestion is clear, at least for those who know his work.[22] Coercive evidence is the kind of evidence that is imposed by force, and such evidence can only betray the true character of the triune God.

Thus, the ultimate reason why the truth of Christian convictions can only be known through witness is not that those who are involved have the best understanding of their own faith. The ultimate reason is that the true God, the God who alone is the truth, is not a monopolizing tyrant, but a triune God who communicates, intrinsically (with himself) and extrinsically (with the world). The life of the Trinity is constituted by love, and this very love is communicated through witnessing: the Son witnesses to the Father and the Spirit witnesses to the Father and the Son by making a truthful and faithful ecclesial community out of proud and sinful people. Consequently, that experienced witnesses have a better understanding of their own faith than outsiders is a result of the work of the Holy Spirit. Put formally, Hauerwas suggests that witness is necessary for the intelligibility of Christian faith because of the specific features of the subject of this faith, the triune God. This subject can only be known in a way that fits the subject, or better: this subject can only be known by the way the subject makes himself known. And since this subject makes himself known by making truthful and faithful witnesses, the very existence of these witnesses is an argument for the truth of this faith.[23] As he does in the lectures on Barth, Hauerwas actually makes two epistemological claims. Since the Holy Spirit communicates and argues by bearing witness and by making witnesses, witness is both the only true form of theological communication *and* the only true argument for the truth of Christian convictions.[24]

---

capable of demonstrating the truth of what Christians believe about God and the world that made witness irrelevant, then we would have evidence that what Christians believe in is not true" (212n).

22. See further Kallenberg, "Strange New World," 203–5.

23. In the last lecture, Hauerwas does not restate his own argument in this formal way. In the fifth lecture (142), however, he refers to a similar argument in favor of Barth's theology made by the Scottish theologian T. F. Torrance.

24. In Hauerwas's own words: "The witness of Christians may or may not take the form of argument at different times and places, but if the Holy Spirit does not witness to the Father and Son through the witness of Christians, then Christians have no arguments to make" (210). Though Hauerwas does not suggest that the work of the Holy Spirit is restricted to what he does for to the church, in his Gifford Lectures he does not refer to works by the Spirit outside the church.

3.2 Why Witness? A Pragmatic Answer

Hauerwas not only uses pneumatological language to argue for the necessity of witness but holds that it is possible to give a "pragmatic display" of his argument:

> That the truth of Christian convictions requires witnesses is but the "pragmatic" display of the fact that the God who has created and redeemed the world has done so from the love that constitutes the life of the Trinity. (211)

Hauerwas does not present his pneumatological argument independently of his pragmatic analysis of concrete ecclesiastic practices. Indeed, in the last lecture he is constantly changing his tune: sketches about the character of Christian practices are restated in trinitarian phrases, and vice versa. Yet the justification of the pragmatic display can only be pneumatological: if it is the work of the Spirit to make witnesses, then traces of this work can be discerned in the lives of faithful Christians through non-reductive description. And if the Spirit actually works in the church, then it is possible to give a pragmatic analysis of these lives which does not deny but rather confirms that the Spirit is the primary subject of Christian witness.

Why exactly is witness vital for the understanding of Christian convictions? The pragmatic answer is that ideas and practices cannot be separated from each other, but should be understood in their interrelatedness. As Hauerwas puts it,

> The work that "witness" does differently from "conviction" is to remind us that the grammar of faith, the Christian faith, cannot be known (or, more forcefully, "does not exist") unless it is embodied in faithful lives.[25]

Thus, in his last Gifford lecture Hauerwas reveals what he has learned from James: theological ideas are true only if they have a concrete value for life. Put negatively, if scholars only focus on Christian convictions or Christian practices and neglect that conviction and practice come together in the "speech act" of witnessing, their accounts will be inaccurate. And if Christians cease to witness, Christian faith changes to become an unintelligible and irrelevant religion of the past. Put positively, if Christians relearn to live truthfully and faithfully, Christianity becomes what it should be: the enactment of the story of creation, reconciliation and redemption in the

---

25. "Hooks," 92.

community of the church. And if scholars take these practices seriously, they will understand what Christianity is about: "By their fruits ye shall know them, not by their roots."

For Hauerwas, witnesses communicate in a particular way and to describe this communication he often uses the verb "to show." Witnesses communicate through showing. By speaking and acting, witnesses show others the meaning of a belief. For instance, a Christian who tells the story of the Prodigal Son speaks of God as a forgiving father, and forgives her neighbors since she knows she herself is forgiven: she is a witness showing others what forgiveness is. Moreover, Hauerwas has learned from James that "some ideas are true only in relation to other ideas" (60). This insight helps him to see that truthful references to a specific belief do not only presuppose other convictions but refer implicitly or explicitly to a totality of beliefs. Thus, while at first sight words, deeds and lives show the meaning of some specific beliefs—for instance, beliefs regarding forgiveness—these in fact cannot be abstracted from other beliefs, they presuppose a larger whole. Therefore, Hauerwas says that in some ways a Christian witness shows the meaning of Christian faith, and that together faithful Christians show what the world is like, what it means to be human, and who God is.

> Christianity is unintelligible without witnesses, that is, without people whose practices exhibit their committed assent to a particular way of structuring the whole. (214)

In *Modern Theology* Hauerwas adds,

> Such a showing ... cannot be coercive because the story that shapes the witness is a story of a God who would have us love freely. (90)[26]

But as we have seen above, for Hauerwas witnessing is not just a form of communication but also an argument for the truth of Christian convictions. And he attempts to phrase this claim not only in pneumatological but also in pragmatic terms. We must, however, not misunderstand this attempt. Hauerwas is not suggesting that through witnessing Christians seek to justify their own faith. Witnesses are not "evidence" which can be separated from the totally of Christian beliefs, "they are a people whose lives embody a totally of beliefs" (214). Moreover:

---

26. In a more recent article ("Witness," 135) Hauerwas explains that his understanding of showing originates from Wittgenstein. See further chapter 2.10.

> To be a witness does not mean that Christians are in the busi-
> ness of calling attention to ourselves but that we witness to the
> One who has made our lives possible. (207)

But if witness is not evidence, how can witness be an argument for the truth
of Christian convictions?

In his review article in *Modern Theology*, Peter Ochs explains that
Hauerwas has a pragmatic view on truth. For Hauerwas, truth

> is not a predicate of our immediate intuitions of the world, but
> only of the temporally extended relationship that we have with
> the world. This means that truth is a predicate of our behavior
> in the world, which means the way that life in the world shapes
> us, over time. (78)

Since truth is a predicate of human behavior, there is no use in examining
whether Christian faith "corresponds with reality." Hauerwas argues in his
Gifford Lectures that faith itself is a possible source for how we understand
reality. What can be tested, in Ochs's reading of Hauerwas, are the relationships Christians have with the world, i.e. the behavior of those being
shaped by Christian faith.[27] By this test, it is possible to determine whether
Christianity does what it should do: produce truthful and faithful witnesses
of Christ, a people whose speech and action is not self-centered but refers
to their Lord.

In his reaction in *Modern Theology*, Hauerwas concurs with Ochs's
reading: "Christian convictions can be tested (a testing that the convictions
themselves require) via the challenges which cannot help but come through
the practices that make the Christian faith what it is" (91). Thus a practice
of faithful witness is an argument for the truth of Christian convictions,

---

27. In "On Hauerwas" Ochs considers how the "scriptural theology" propagated by
Hauerwas could be related to philosophy and science. Science, philosophy, and theology each have their own separate sphere: "Science claims its own superiority as a discipline for observing what goes on in the finite world of creation; philosophy claims its
superiority as a discipline for articulating the grammar of social discourse and the logic
of inquiry; scriptural theology claims its own superiority as a discipline for articulating
the ultimate presuppositions that inform a way of practicing philosophy, and thereby of
practicing science. Viewed in this way, theology is no longer subjugated to the methods
and judgements of philosophy and science, as it has been in the modern academy. But
it also refrains from subjecting them to any misuse of its own sphere of knowledge"
(84). In this fruitful relationship, theological claims can and must be tested with the
help of scientific research and philosophical investigations: "This means that the job
of philosophy is also, on the basis of scriptural assumptions, to frame the theologian's
logic of inquiry and grammar of social discourse. According to the pragmatic logic of
inquiry, the pronouncements of theology must be testable within the world of everyday
experience that is also observed (in different ways) by scientists" (84).

because it is a positive and concrete outcome of the continuing test of these convictions in the lives of believers. Moreover, for Hauerwas "showing" is not only communication, but successful showing is itself an argument for the truth of what is being shown. Thus he speaks of successful witnessing not just as a practice of *faithfulness* but also of *truthfulness*. In other words: what can be described in a pragmatic approach is the existence of a people showing that self-centeredness is not human fate, that it is possible to be grateful to God, and to have mercy on our neighbors. From this pragmatic perspective we can conclude that, though witnessing is a human practice, this practice cannot exclusively be ascribed to human agents but must also be ascribed to the Holy Spirit.

3.3 The Witness of the Martyrs

Hauerwas explains his argumentation in the first section of the last lecture by referring to martyrdom. Martyrdom is a form of truthful witnessing, in fact "the most determinative display of what being a witness entails" (212).[28] First, Hauerwas remarks that in some way the life and death of martyrs can be conceived as "evidence": the fact that some Christians are willing to die for their faith proves that Christian faith is something worth dying for. But then he adds that the martyr does not need the evidence of martyrdom. Indeed, the more Christians learn to follow Christ, the less they are in need of proof from others to confirm their faith. And when a Christian dies for his faith it is not in order to believe it, but because he believes the gospel.[29] Thus, though martyrdom proves that Christian faith has certain characteristics, it cannot prove that Christian faith is true.

> In other words, that martyrs die for their faith does not *prove* that Jesus is risen; on the other hand, that some people have assented to a totality of beliefs that includes the belief that Jesus is risen surely means that martyrs will die for their faith. (214)

And, exactly because faithful Christians are not in the business of justifying their own beliefs, but believe that they have been justified by Jesus Christ, they can live as witnesses to Christ and are prepared to suffer and die for

28. With Marshall, Hauerwas suggests that "the Christian martyr's willingness to die for his or her faith in Christ is similar to the scientist's commitment to experimental results, though any pragmatic similarity that can be drawn between science and theology is inexact" (212). In *With the Grain of the Universe* this suggestion remains somewhat unclear but it is clarified by Ochs's suggestion that Christian faith is *tested* by the practice of witnessing.

29. See further 210n.

the one they bear witness to. A full pragmatic account of martyrdom must recognize this. It must refer to the witness of the witness, to the testimony of the martyrs. In his discussion of Bruce Marshall's example of the martyrdom of Maximilian Kolbe, a Roman Catholic priest who voluntarily took the place of a condemned prisoner at Auschwitz, Hauerwas remarks,

> to say that St. Maximilian's death is rightly described as martyrdom, that is, as an act by which one shares in the self-sacrificial love the triune God shows to the world through the cross, is a description not only of that act but also of a complex set of beliefs about God and how God acts in the world. Therefore, whether the description of St. Maximilian's death is rightly described as martyrdom involves questions of how that description fits in the larger web of beliefs. (213)

As faithful witnesses, martyrs show in living and dying who God is and what the world is like. They not only *communicate* what Christian faith is about but their non-self-centeredness in their life and death is also an *indication* or an *argument* for the truth of Christian beliefs.

In his review article, Brad Kallenberg descries a similar argumentation in all the lectures of *With the Grain of the Universe*:

> If God is not real, then Christian witness is necessarily babbling. (Or if God is not real, then Karl Barth can be reduced without remainder to Reinhold Niebuhr.) But Christian witness is intelligible on its own terms to those who seriously seek to know. (Or, Barth does not reduce to Niebuhr.) Therefore, there is a reality outside the purview of natural theology as well as outside all other anthropocentric disciplines, and "this everyone understands to be God." (206)[30]

But, Hauerwas also admits that in a way his argumentation is "hopelessly circular" (231).[31] This circularity is a result of the epistemology of witness. Hauerwas holds that all he can do is point to witnesses like Karl Barth and Saint Maximilian, and explain that their witness is neither self-justifying nor self-referential. Indeed, we can also conceive Hauerwas as a witness using trinitarian speech and pragmatic analyses to bear witness of the witness by

30. Kallenberg remarks, "Hauerwas employs Aquinas's 'little coda' on page 26 of *With the Grain*. However, it should be clear by now that for Hauerwas's Aquinas, the term 'everyone' referred to ordinary Christian believers but certainly not the *unstoried* and *traditionless* modern individual" (206n, his emphasis).

31. Griffiths remarks, "It is no criticism to say that the central thesis displayed in these Gifford Lectures is almost tautologous and that it seems obviously true" ("Witness," 69).

these witnesses. Yet, it is up to his readers whether they believe this witnessing. Of course there are always reasons to refuse it, to speak not of martyrs but of masochists, to read the *Church Dogmatics* as a neo-orthodox polemic. And Hauerwas can only answer by retelling these stories, by persisting to bear witness to these witnesses.[32]

3.4 An Obscure Mennonite Theologian and a Non-Constantinian Pope

In the next sections of the final Gifford lecture, Hauerwas elaborates on his appeal, explaining further what faithful and truthful witnessing entails. Hauerwas does not wish to suggest that all Christians, or even the majority, actually live as faithful and truthful witnesses. He admits there are many false and unfaithful forms of Christian speech and action. But the final lecture does suggest that Christians have been called to be witnesses and that they could answer this call since the Holy Spirit has created communities in which they are being trained in truthful and faithful witnessing. Yet, Hauerwas also realizes that trained witnesses fail and that even the lives of saints are not sin-free. Indeed, even the most experienced witness needs constant communal training to remain humble and to descry the lies in his speech and the falseness in his life.

But Hauerwas does not speak extensively about this training by Christian communities since he has done this in many of his other works. Instead, he prefers to summon witnesses who have been trained by their communities: an "obscure Mennonite theologian" (230) and a "non-Constantinian Pope" (226).

> John Howard Yoder and John Paul II represent the recovery of the politics necessary for us to understand why witness is not simply something Christians "do" but is at the heart of understanding how that to which Christians witness is true. If lives like theirs did not exist, then my argument could not help but appear as just another "idealism." (217)

Hauerwas introduces Yoder and John Paul II as witnesses bearing witness to a witnessing church, a church challenging the presumptions of modernity. In their writings, both Yoder and the late pope stress that if Jesus Christ is the one and only Lord of the church, the church can adapt itself neither to

---

32. Hauerwas quotes Barth: "We can only repeat ourselves" (*Church Dogmatics*, II/1, 250). Again we can say that this can be read not just a characterisation of Barth's but also of Hauerwas's own work.

the politics of violence by the nation state, nor to the culture of death in Western society. John Howard Yoder and John Paul II are witnesses because they have dedicated their lives to the alternative politics of peace and truth by the church. Together they show that the words "faithful" and "truthful" are not empty adjectives. Truthful are those words that unmask the powers that be by professing obedience to the cross. Faithful are those actions that resist the indifference of modern society by self-giving love.

By summoning his third and final witness, Hauerwas tries to prove that this church to which Yoder and the late pope bear witness is real. This witness is Dorothy Day, founder of the Catholic Worker, both a pious Catholic and a radical pacifist who committed her life to the daily works of mercy.

> Because Dorothy Day existed, we can know that the church to which John Paul II and John Howard Yoder witness is not some ideal but an undeniable reality. Moreover, such a church must exist if indeed the cross and not the sword reveals to us the grain of the universe. (230)[33]

4. TWO LATER ESSAYS

After the publication of *With the Grain of the Universe* in 2001, the theme of Christian witness appears in many of Hauerwas's essays. I will discuss two texts in which Hauerwas does not just repeat the argument of the Gifford Lectures, but elaborates on some aspects of his understanding of witness.

4.1 Witnessing Contingency

Hauerwas discusses witness in an essay for a Festschrift for Victor Preller.[34] Preller was one of the first scholars to interpret Aquinas not in neo-scholastic terms, but with the help of the philosophy of language. In this essay, Hauerwas mentions similarities between Preller's reading of Aquinas and his own reading of Wittgenstein. According to Hauerwas, Aquinas and Wittgenstein have a similar approach: their work does not obscure the frightening character of all that is by reductive explanations, but it *shows* the world in its bare contingency.[35]

---

33. In the next section, Hauerwas adds, "I am sure that the brief allusion to Dorothy Day can only confirm the judgment of some people that the argument I have tried to make in these Gifford Lectures is nothing more than a nice example of special pleading. For those inclined to so dismiss my argument, I have no decisive response other than to ask if they represent practices that can produce a Dorothy Day" (231).

34. "Connections."

35. In Hauerwas's reading of Preller, Aquinas formulates his proofs of God not so

The essay refers to Wittgenstein's description of the normal human condition as "aspect blind." Man's natural reaction to the diversity of the world is to control it by demonstrating that things have to be as they are. This is how people become blind to the contingency of our existence. Hauerwas considers Wittgenstein's work as an attempt to rediscover the frightening beauty of the particular. Moreover, he suggests that the exercises developed by Wittgenstein to see the particular are not unlike the exercises Christians must do "to see in the sheer thereness of what is: God's work" (80). Hauerwas honors Preller since he has learned from him that Aquinas offers such an exercise: an exercise to acknowledge that we are creatures who received our ability to speak as a gift. This acknowledgment does not immediately lead to the conviction that the triune God created the world. However, it does suggest that if we fail to live in humility—a mistake made by Christians and non-Christians alike—we get a distorted idea of how things are.

Then Hauerwas makes a fascinating remark:

> Put in the terms I use in *With the Grain of the Universe,* any account of Christianity that does not make witness constitutive of the practice of faith cannot be true. Not to be true not only means to be unfaithful to Christian practice, but also means to belie the contingent character of all that is. Witness witnesses our contingency. But Christians believe that God has given us life-forming practices that enable us to live without seeking false comforts in a world of contingency we do not and cannot control. That we must be trained to be human, that we must be trained to communicate with one another so that we make the connection between ourselves and others, and this and that, indicates that the God we worship is the same God who has created the sun, the stars, and this petunia. That Preller helps us in *Divine Science and the Science of God* to recognize why all that is does not exist by necessity enables us to see that all that is witnesses to the God who created what is. (80)

This phrase is more than a repetition of the central claim in Hauerwas's Gifford Lectures. Hauerwas gives some fresh insights. Firstly, he uses the verb "to witness" not only for human speech and action: all that is, witnesses to God.[36] He suggests that once we have become witnesses, our witness is

---

much to formulate positive knowledge of God, but rather to show man's scant understanding of God, himself, and the world. In Hauerwas's reading of Wittgenstein, the fact that we cannot grasp the world in terms of "being" or "existence," points at the contingency of all that is. What we call the "world" is not necessary but miraculous, it is made up of connections between contingencies. In his later work, Wittgenstein points to the beauty of the particular. His investigations show that there is no deeper reality than the everyday reality.

36. This idea, that all that is witnesses to God, cannot be found in *With the Grain*

confirmed by the witness of creation. Secondly, this section helps to see how Christian faith deals with the contingency of existence: Christian practices enable man to live without self-deception, without seeking false comfort in a world we cannot control.[37] Thirdly, and most importantly, is how the relation between witness and contingency is displayed. Hauerwas suggests that any denial of the constitutive role of witness is false, not only because it is unfaithful to Christian practice, but also because it belies "the contingent character of all that is." Put another way: that nothing is necessary but witness follows not only from the particular shape of Christian faith but also from the typical character of all that exists. Thus, witness witnesses our contingency.

4.2 World Upside Down

Some years later, together with Charles Pinches, Hauerwas wrote an article for a Festschrift for Fergus Kerr.[38] In this essay, he again takes up the theme of witness. Many of the issues of *With the Grain of the Universe* are repeated. Hauerwas and Pinches speak of witness as a way of speaking truthfully and acting faithfully in a contingent world and discuss the necessity of witnessing for knowing the character of the world, ourselves and God.

> The speaker and what is spoken cannot be separated if Christians' claims about God and God's world have the purchase of truth. "Witness" is the crucial grammar that upholds and enfolds these claims. (136)

What is new is that the article contains explorations from the New Testament. Hauerwas's conception of witness is related to the gospel of Matthew and to the book of Acts. The essay indicates that there are sound biblical arguments for making the connection between speaker and what is spoken. One argument can be found in Matthew 10, in the story of the calling and sending of the twelve disciples. Hauerwas and Pinches indicate that the disciples must spread good news that the Kingdom of Heaven is near, by preaching *and* by doing: "cure the sick, raise the dead, cleanse the lepers, cast out demons" (Matt 10:8).

---

of the Universe. In his Gifford Lectures, Hauerwas only remarks that *for Barth*, creation testifies to its creator.

37. In "Hooks" Hauerwas gives an example of this self-deception: "The 'discovery' of necessities is but the philosophical expression of the need to have armies to protect us from the stories others have to tell" (90).

38. "Witness."

> The disciples of Jesus are sent out as bearers of news; they have received a message to spread, but they themselves are also the exemplification of what they have to say. However, this is not really their doing. That is to say, whatever actions are theirs as faithful disciples, and to whatever degree their lives bear truthful witness, this is always also the result of a gift they have been given. This is why the news or story they have to tell turns out always to be inseparable from what has happened to them. The story they tell is about them insofar as they testify in the telling to what happened to them. But it points past them, or through them, to the God they believe they have met in Christ Jesus. (137)

According to Hauerwas and Pinches, the twelve disciples must be conceived as witnesses bearing witness through their speech, acts and lives. On the one hand, this witness is about them: they bear witness to what happened to them, to the gift they received. But they also bear witness to Jesus Christ as the giver of this gift.

In their discussion of Acts, the authors mainly refer to the pericopes about Paul.[39] They are particularly interested in Paul's speeches about his vocation: "Paul is witnessing about becoming a witness" (140). And, they show how, not unlike the witness by the twelve disciples in Matthew, Paul's witness about becoming a witness refers to Jesus Christ who called him as his witness. Furthermore, by witnessing to Jesus Christ as his Lord, Paul refers to a comprehensive truth, the truth that Jesus Christ is not *his* Lord, but the Lord of heaven and earth.

> The truth to which Paul and others witness in Acts is comprehensive: it renarrates the whole of human life, indeed, all that is, in the light of the God who is—now fully known through Christ. (144)

The disciple claims to his audience that all that is must be understood from this truth, that Jesus is Lord. In his speeches, Paul tries to renarrate his own life and the lives of his audience in the light of this truth. By telling this story, he challenges pagans and their understanding of the world: the pagan world is turned "upside down."

---

39. For their reading of Acts Hauerwas and Pinches are indebted to Rowe, *World Upside Down*. For a further discussion of the book of Acts, and Rowe's reading of it of see "Disciplined Seeing." There Hauerwas remarks about Paul's vocation: "He asked, 'Who are you, Lord?' The incredulity of the question indicates that Paul must lose his vision before he will see, and that he will testify to what he has seen only when he has been able to identify the voice that summons him, and the light that blinds him, with the one who came to the people of Israel preaching peace, who healed the sick and fed the hungry, and who was later put to death on a tree" (51).

As we have seen above, in the last lecture of *With the Grain of the Universe* Hauerwas speaks of witnesses as a people involved in a politics of living faithfully, truthfully *and* peacefully. In their essay, Hauerwas and Pinches speak of a politics of witness, a politics which includes both truthful speech and faithful, peaceful action. But the authors emphasize that this politics of witness begins with speech.

> The new politics is a politics of speech—and so also of act. But it begins in the speech of the church which is a story we Christians believe is not just ours but everyone's. (138)

As the stories in Matthew and Acts indicate, this story begins in a simple way with the meeting of the disciples with Jesus Christ. But this story is also very complex and involves many subplots. The story does not only talk about the first disciples but also about all those women and men past and present who are convinced by the witness of these witnesses. Indeed, this story is not just about Christians and the church, but about everyone and everything and it suggests that "all that is exists as a witness to God" (138).

Finally, as an aside, Hauerwas and Pinches make a remark which is interesting for this study:

> The existence of the church is itself the determinative (although not the only) witness to an alternative politics to that of the old age. (138)

In a footnote, the authors explain what they mean by "although not the only." There is a "witness outside the church" (138). But instead of further elaborating what such a witness outside the church entails, they refer to a book, *Christianity, Democracy, and the Radical Ordinary* written by Hauerwas and the non-Christian radical democrat Romand Coles. Although this reference seems a bit awkward, it is in fact very clear. Hauerwas and Pinches suggest that Romand Coles, and others who are involved in radical democracy in a similar way, are not just allies, but witnesses bearing witness of an alternative politics of the old era. To put it in pneumatological terms: though in his ethics and theology Hauerwas focuses on the work the Holy Spirit does *within* the church, he is not unreceptive to how the Spirit works *outside* the church.[40]

---

40. In *The Peaceable Kingdom* Hauerwas remarks, "That is why as Christians we may not only find that people who are not Christians manifest God's peace better than we ourselves, but we must demand that they exist" (101).

5. WITNESS AND STANLEY HAUERWAS

The last part of this chapter is a short theological biography. In this section I will try to explain how the work and life of Stanley Hauerwas relate to the idea and the practice of witness. First, I will overview his work and life, and then I will show that witness is in fact the leading notion of Hauerwas's work *and* life.

5.1 Stanley Hauerwas[41]

To his own surprise, Stanley Hauerwas was declared "America's Best Theologian" by *Time* magazine in 2001.[42] In the introduction to his memoirs, *Hannah's Child*, Hauerwas writes,

> Those who know me, moreover, did not miss the irony of the occasion. After all, I have made a career criticizing the accommodated character of the church to the American project. I am then rewarded for being the great critic of America by one of the standards of American life? We live in a strange world. But, what the hell, I've tried to make the most of it, that is, I've tried to use this form of secular power for God's good purposes. (ix)

This quotation is a fine illustration of Stanley Hauerwas's personality: a swearing theologian; a critic of America with a sense of humor; a scholar relating his own work to God's good purposes; a professor with a preference for self-mockery. There are many anecdotes being told about this Duke Professor with his unacademic style. In lecture rooms and conferences halls, his one-liners are quoted and his Texan accent imitated. But Stanley Hauerwas is more than a theological entertainer. Hauerwas uses his rhetorical gifts to promote a serious ethical and theological agenda.

Stanley Martin Hauerwas was born on the 24th of July 1940 in Pleasant Grove, Texas. He grew up in a working-class family, his mother was a housewife, his father a bricklayer. The Hauerwas family attended Pleasant Grove Methodist Church and at age 15 Stanley gave his life to the ministry. As Hauerwas tells us in his memoirs:

41. For the biographical information in this section I am indebted to Cavanaugh, "Stan" and Thiessen Nation, "Stanley Hauerwas." Furthermore, I am indebted to *Hannah's Child*, Hauerwas's own memoirs.

42. Elshtain, "Theologian." In *Hannah's Child* Hauerwas remarks: "It is true that when David Reid, at the time the publicist for Duke Divinity School, came to tell me that I was to be so named my first response was, ' "Best" is not a theological category.' My response was not an attempt to be humble. I do not think you can try to be humble. I was simply responding to the absurdity of it all" (ix).

> So finally one Sunday night, after singing "I Surrender All" for
> God knows how many times, I went to the altar rail and told
> Brother Zimmerman that I wanted to dedicate my life to the
> Lord. I thought if God was not going to save me, I could at least
> put God in a bind by being one of his servants in the ministry. (3)

Hauerwas went to college to become a minister, but never left the academy. After receiving his BA in philosophy from South Western University
in Georgetown, Texas, he went off to Yale Divinity School. Within six years
he received a BD from Yale Divinity School, a MA and MPhil in philosophy
from Yale University and a PhD in Christian ethics from Yale University.

Some of his interpreters consider Hauerwas to be a representative of
the "Yale School." But Hauerwas himself underlines that in the 1960s at Yale
no one had the idea that the PhD students and their teachers represented
a particular "school."[43] It cannot be denied, nevertheless, that Hauerwas is
shaped by his Yale education: "There is no question that one can see the
lasting imprint, however creatively reworked by Hauerwas, of a number of
his teachers at Yale."[44] Typical of the Yale education was that students were
taught to read Barth *and* Wittgenstein. Through this reading, Hauerwas
learned to see religion not as a universal phenomenon but as a particular
practice with a particular speech: "Though he may have gone to Yale to determine if Christianity were true, he discovered at Yale that Christianity is
in fact verified or falsified in places like Pleasant Grove."[45]

Stanley Hauerwas married Anne Harley in 1962 and they had a son,
Adam. In his memoirs, Hauerwas speaks frankly about his difficult marriage
to Anne who was suffering from mental illness. After more than twenty
years they divorced. Some years later Hauerwas married Paula Gilbert, an
ordained Methodist minister. In 1970, after two years teaching at Augus-
tana College in Illinois, he went to the Roman Catholic University of Notre
Dame to teach Christian ethics. At Notre Dame, he was strongly influenced
by Roman Catholic theology, especially by the Roman Catholic vision of the
church, with its urge for continuity and unity, good order and authority, and
moral living as an alternative to liberalism. Since 1984, Hauerwas has taught
Christian ethics at Duke University.

Hauerwas grew up in a Methodist congregation. For most of his life,
he taught at a Methodist university, and he married a Methodist minister.
Nevertheless, he does not consider himself to be a Methodist ethicist or
theologian. Hauerwas is not writing for Methodists or from a Methodist

43. *Wilderness Wanderings*, vii.

44. Thiessen Nation, "Stanley Hauerwas," 29.

45. Cavanaugh, "Stan," 20.

perspective, but considers himself as a Christian ethicist and theologian who is writing for the whole church. In fact, he's always been very critical about contemporary Methodism. For Hauerwas the United Methodist Church (UMC) suffers from forgetfulness. In an attempt to accommodate itself to the truths and values of the modern liberal society, he argues the UMC has forgotten what Methodism is about: to remind all Christians of what it means to be the church. In the introduction to *The Peaceable Kingdom* he remarks,

> Of course the fact I am biographically a Protestant is not irrelevant to the way I work. I have no desire to rid myself of my particular background as an evangelical Methodist. Rather it is my conviction that Methodism, like other Christian traditions, with its limits and possibilities, helps awaken all of us to being members of Christ's whole church. Thus, even if I am critical of my tradition, I am rightly so only so long as that criticism serves to direct Protestants and Catholics alike to the one Lord who reigns over all people. (xxvi)

Hauerwas is attracted by those ecclesial traditions that realize that being Christ's whole church requires a different politics than accommodation: for instance, the Mennonite congregations with their commitment to nonviolence and the Episcopal churches with their weekly celebrations of the Eucharist. Hauerwas calls himself a "high church Mennonite"[46] and his work can be read as an attempt to explain that this self-characterization is not contradictory.

Hauerwas's favorite genre is the essay. Most of his books are collections of essays that were written for various occasions and published before in magazines or volumes with other authors. His essays are on both practical ethical issues—such as abortion, euthanasia, the mentally handicapped, the nation state, violence, and war—as well as on more theoretical ethical themes, such as character, virtue, and narrative, or Aristotle and Aquinas. Moreover, Hauerwas is not the kind of ethicist writing exclusively on ethical themes. Since he believes that practice cannot be separated from story and vice versa, many of his essays refer to theological, biblical and doctrinal themes. In all his essays, the church is pictured as the place where theory and practice, and theology and ethics come together. Hauerwas's most important essays are collected in *The Hauerwas Reader* (2001).

---

46. *A Community of Character*, 6.

Some of Hauerwas's books are more coherent than others, such as *The Peaceable Kingdom* (1983) and *With the Grain of the Universe* (2001). A remark in the introduction to the latter provides an insight into how *With the Grain of the Universe* relates to his other works:[47]

> This is not the "big book" that many of my friends and critics have suggested I should write. Indeed, if this book is different than my past work, I hope the difference is simply that here I make clear why I do not think theologians, particularly in our day, can or should write "big books" that "pull it all together." Any theology that threatens to become a position more determinative than the Christian practice of prayer betrays its subject. At best, theology is but a series of reminders to help Christians to pray faithfully. So if this book does anything different than my past work, it does so only to the extent that it displays why my work cannot be held but be as occasional and unfinished as Barth's *Church Dogmatics*. (10)

After he published his Gifford Lectures, Hauerwas wrote about a wide range of subjects. He published a theological commentary on Matthew, a collection of essays about "the state of the university," and a book with Jean Vanier, founder of L'Arche community.[48]

And in 2010, *Hannah's Child* is published. Reflecting on the book's character, Hauerwas remarks,

> I would like to think that this book might fall into the category of "testimony," but I am not confident that what I have done deserves that description. When I was a child I often heard testimonies in church. They usually came during services on Sunday night. A member of the congregation would suddenly "feel moved" to declare to those assembled what God had done in her life. Such heartfelt testimonies made by unsophisticated people in straightforward language impressed me then and impress me now. I trusted their testimonies. (286)

This explains why Hauerwas but scarcely uses the term "testimony" as it reminds him of his own revivalist tradition. For Hauerwas "witness" sounds less pietistic and therefore more to the point. However, this remark also indicates that he has not forgotten his roots. On the contrary, by referring to his memoirs as "testimony" he reclaims his own revivalistic tradition.

---

47. See for a similar observation the introduction of *The Peaceable Kingdom*, xvi.

48. *Matthew*, 2006; *The State* 2007; *Living Gently*, 2008.

5.2 Living in a World without Certainties

Though witness is the central theme of Hauerwas's Gifford Lectures, it does not appear frequently in all his work. According to the subject index of *The Hauerwas Reader* terms such as "virtue," "character," "story," and "narrative" appear more often in Hauerwas's essays than "witness" (or "testimony"), and particularly in his early essays the term is scarcely used.[49] Nevertheless, I will argue below that Hauerwas's work has always presupposed the idea *and* the practice of witnessing witnesses.[50] I will indicate this by explaining Hauerwas's work as a series of answers to one leading question: *How can we live truthfully in a world without certainty?*[51] As will become clear, according to Hauerwas the ultimate answer to this question is: *through witness.*

From Wittgenstein, Hauerwas has learned that we live in a world without certainty, a contingent world, a world with no natural moral rules or universal ethical laws. In this world without certainty we need tools, we need guidance, or as Hauerwas writes in his early essays, we need "vision" since we can only act in a world we can see.[52] Hauerwas has found that vision is not only necessary for physical action—for example, to lay bricks—it is also crucial for moral action. For him, morality is not simply a matter of how we respond to particular situations. In order to know what we should do, we have to know what the world in which we act is like, we have to know who we are, and who others are. Thus, we need moral vision. Furthermore, his early articles already express the importance of narrative: moral vision can only be acquired through stories. As Hauerwas writes in *Vision and Virtue*,

> Metaphors and stories suggest how we should see and describe the world—that is how we should "look-on" our selves, others, and the world—in ways that rules taken in themselves do not. Stories and metaphors do this by providing the narrative accounts that give our lives coherence. (71)

49. In *Vision and Virtue* (212) Hauerwas comes to speak of witness in his essay on Yoder's *The Christian Witness to the State*. Though he mentions the term witness he does not reflect on it.

50. Kallenberg, "Strange New World" has been helpful for understanding how *With the Grain of the Universe* relates to Hauerwas's other work. For an overview of this other work, see Wells, *Transforming Fate*.

51. See *The Peaceable Kingdom*: "The task of Christian ethics is not to relieve us of the ambiguity but to help us understand rightly what it means to live in the world we do—that is, to live truthfully in a world without certainty" (16).

52. To put it more precisely, Hauerwas learned this from Iris Murdoch who learned this from Wittgenstein. See Kallenberg, "Strange New World," 198.

According to Hauerwas, the moral life is a "struggle and training in how to see" (ibid., 20). And therefore, people need stories to give coherence to their lives. Moreover, we are not instructed by just any story but by particular stories. For instance, if all the stories we know are told in the soap operas we watch on TV, we will reflect on ourselves and others as characters in a soap whose relationships spring from fickle feelings of desire and discontent. But if we have learned from our pastor that God is an absolute ruler who has appointed human rulers to govern man, we will judge our own lives and those of others in terms of obedience and disobedience.

Brad Kallenberg points out that for Hauerwas ethics is a "therapeutic discipline."[53] Hauerwas schools his readers to see the difference between false and truthful stories. False stories, those based on distorted ideas about man or God, do not produce moral vision but rather self-deception, enforced coherence, and an easy sense of security. Truthful stories acknowledge the contingency of the human condition with its conflicts between passion and reason. These stories show a way for us to live coherently amidst the diversity and conflicts of our moral existence. A crucial insight of Hauerwas's early writings is that we are only capable of moral action and moral growth by finding our particular role within the story. Truthful stories invite man to follow the way and to enact a particular role within the story. In his doctoral dissertation, Hauerwas calls this particular role "character."[54] In the 1970s and early 1980s, the description of this process of finding a role within a story is more and more refined by an examination of Aristotle's and Aquinas's account of the virtues and their acquisition by moral agents.[55] Through his interaction with Alasdair MacIntyre, who was one of his colleague's at Notre Dame, Hauerwas learns that virtue ethics is a promising alternative to dominant ethical approaches.[56]

One of the constant themes in Hauerwas's work is his critique on liberal society and on how this society is defended by dominant ethical reflection. The early essays on moral vision criticize contemporary ethics for not observing man's dependence on particular stories. The dominant suggestion is that all we need for moral guidance is good principles. Hauerwas is not against principles but against abstractions. He argues that principles cannot be abstracted from stories without distortion. Later, this critique is intensified by the suggestion that the very idea that principles can and should be

---

53. Kallenberg, "Strange New World," 202.

54. *Moral Character*.

55. This theme can already be found in "Aristotle and Thomas."

56. The influence of Macintyre can be found for instance in "Courage Exemplified." See also *Hannah's Child*, 160ff.

abstracted from stories itself springs from a "thin" narrative: the tale of man without tradition trying to compose his own life. As Hauerwas writes in *A Community of Character*: "our primary story is that we have no story, or that the stories that we have must be overcome if we are to be free" (149). This analysis leads to a radical repudiation of the dominant ideology of liberalism in the United States. He then formulates theses for reforming Christian Social Ethics and the ninth thesis puts it clearly and harshly:

> *1.9. In our attempt to control our society Christians in America have too readily accepted liberalism as a social strategy appropriate to the Christian story.*
>
> Liberalism, in its many forms and versions, presupposes that society can be organized without any narrative that is commonly held to be true. As a result it tempts us to believe that freedom and rationality are independent of narrative—i.e., we are free to the extent that we have no story. Liberalism is, therefore, particularly pernicious to the extent it prevents us from understanding how deeply we are captured by its account of existence. (11–12)

According to Hauerwas both contemporary ethics and modern society are caught in a "perpetual double think."[57] Liberalism tells us that we have no story, but what it cannot acknowledge is that we did not choose this "story that we should have no story except the story we chose when we had no story."[58] And because of this misconception, liberal society and liberal ethics cannot inspire people to acquire moral vision or to live virtuous lives.

How can we live truthfully in a world without certainty? In his early work, Hauerwas formulates an answer to this question. Modern society and its propagators cannot help you in your quest, you need a truthful story, a story that does not deny the world's contingency but charts a way through it by giving you character, virtues and moral vision.

5.3 The Community of the Church

Hauerwas is aware that there are many traditions—religious and non-religious—telling particular stories, shaping characters and propagating virtuousness. But if this is the case, then how do we know if a story is true? In *A Community of Character* he writes that "the test of the truthfulness of any story does not reside in its conforming to or embodying a prior universal

57. "Christian Practices," See also Kallenberg, "Strange New World," 202.
58. "Christian Practices," 748.

norm, but rather in how we and others find their lives illuminated and com-
pelled by the accuracy and truthfulness of its particular vision" (149). And
a few lines above, we read,

> What we require is not no story, but a true story. Such a story
> is one that provides a pilgrimage with appropriate exercises and
> disciplines of self-examination. Christians believe Scripture of-
> fers such a story. There we find many accounts of a struggle of
> God with his creation. The story of God does not offer a reso-
> lution of life's difficulties, but it offers us something better—an
> adventure and struggle, for we are possessors of the happy news
> that God has called people together to live faithful to the reality
> that he is the Lord of this world.

Thus in *A Community of Character*, Hauerwas suggests that the story of God
is truthful since this story does what it should do: it illuminates and compels
the lives of Christians by telling the happy news that God has called people
together. Christian Scripture stands the test, by charting a truthful way of
living through uncertainty. But more and more Hauerwas realizes that in
some ways his argumentation remains unclear since he fails to explain to
whom the pronoun "we" refers: who are the possessors of the good news?
Where can we find this community of character?

In the 1980s, Hauerwas came to think that every argument for the
truthfulness of a story presupposes the existence of concrete communities
in which the story is embodied. "I began seeking to recover the importance of virtue and the virtues and ended up with the church."[59] This view
is expounded in *The Peaceable Kingdom*. Hauerwas argues that without
presupposing "the existence and recognizability of communities and corresponding institutions capable of carrying the story of God" (96), Christian
ethics remains vague and unintelligible. Therefore in *The Peaceable Kingdom*
he is both propagating and practicing an ethics that springs from concrete
Christian communities.

But this urge for concreteness is still directed by story. Hauerwas is
not doing "empirical ethics," he is not presenting research according to the
dos and don'ts of Christians. Hauerwas holds that these Christian dos and
don'ts can only be understood from their story, a story that begins with
God choosing Israel as his people, that continues with God sending his only
Son, and that has an open end when the disciples are filled with the Holy
Spirit and preach the resurrection to Jews and pagans. Hauerwas practices
theological ethics. In fact, *The Peaceable Kingdom* presents research after the

---

59. "The Testament," 214.

work of the Holy Spirit. Hauerwas suggests that the mission of the disciples was not without success, that there are possessors of the happy news of the gospel, that this story is embodied in the practices of the church.

And for Hauerwas the church

> is where the stories of Israel and Jesus are told, enacted and heard, and it is our conviction that as a Christian people there is literally nothing more important we can do. But the telling of that story requires that we be a particular kind of people if we and the world are to hear the story truthfully. That means that the church must never cease from being a community of peace and truth in a world of mendacity and fear. (99–100)

When Hauerwas speaks about the church, he refers to the empirical communities where the stories are told, where the sacraments are celebrated, those communities that call themselves the "church": "There is no ideal church, no invisible church, no mystically existing universal church more real than the concrete church with parking lots and potluck dinners" (107). For Hauerwas all these groups of fallible human beings *are* the church. Of course, communities calling themselves the "church" often tell and enact the stories of Israel and Jesus in a way that is partly or even completely false. But that does not mean that the church is not there, they are simply an unfaithful part of the church. But in order to understand what the church really is, one should not focus on unfaithful but on faithful ecclesial practices. Along with Aristotle, Hauerwas holds that a practice can only be fully understood if one knows its true end.

In *The Peaceable Kingdom*, Hauerwas is reminding both Christians and non-Christians of the true aim of the church—not unlike the Old Testament prophets remind Israel of its original vocation. He writes about this end in *is*-sentences:

> The church is not the kingdom but the foretaste of the kingdom. For it is in the church that the narrative of God is lived in a way that makes the kingdom visible. (97)

> That is why the story is not merely told but embodied in a people's habits that form and are formed in worships, governance and morality. (98)

> Put starkly the first social ethical task of the church is to be the church—the servant community. As such the church does not have a social ethic; the church is a social ethic. (99)

These is-sentences tell how it should be, how it could be, and how it sometimes actually (factually and empirically) is. Moreover, Hauerwas is not addressing a specific kind of church, but he writes for the whole church, for the
one and only catholic church.

The specific, almost magniloquent language of *The Peaceable Kingdom*
betrays the influence of John Howard Yoder. Hauerwas has been reading
Yoder since the early 1970s, and became more and more convinced by Yoder's theological ethics.

> However, Yoder was a pill I had no desire to swallow. His eccle-
> siology could not work apart from his understanding of Jesus
> and the centrality of nonviolence as the hallmark of the Chris-
> tian life. (xxiv)

But Hauerwas did swallow the pill; he and Yoder even became friends.[60]
Hauerwas is convinced by Yoder's ecclesiology and by his claim that since
the church is a community of peace, violence is not an option for Christians.
With Yoder, Hauerwas holds that peacefulness is not an additional feature
of the church, it is one of the most central characteristics of what being the
church entails. The church embodies the gospel by becoming a community
of peace, by showing the world what God's coming kingdom looks like.
Moreover, like Yoder, Hauerwas stresses that the community of peace is not
an apolitical "spiritual" body. On the contrary,

> Christians are engaged in politics, but it is politics of the
> kingdom that reveals the insufficiency of all politics based on
> coercion and falsehood and it finds the true source of power
> in servanthood rather than dominion. . . . The church is a pol-
> ity like any other, but it is also *unlike* any other insofar as it is
> formed by a people who have no reason to fear the truth. (102)

For Hauerwas, the politics called "church" is an alternative to the dominant
politics of money and war. This politics gets its shape from the communal life
but also from the institutional framework of the church: in the way the church
deals with wealth or conflicts. And, though Hauerwas knows that what he
writes may seem deviant, it is not meant to be dissident. Indeed, he claims that
he is not writing something new or extraordinary, but just reminds the church
of its original orthodoxy and orthopraxy, of its original vocation.

Nevertheless, Hauerwas is also aware that in some respects he has an
unorthodox view on what orthodox Christianity is. His readers may ask:
"what has happened to the traditional Christian affirmations of salvation

---

60. *Hannah's Child*, 116ff.

and faith in all this talk of the kingdom?" (91). He answers by arguing that faith is a not a pre-moral state of being. It is a moral response which involves transformation:

> Faith is in effect, finding our true life within the life of Christ. . . . this life is fundamentally a social life. We are "in Christ" insofar as we are part of that community pledged to be faithful to this life as the initiator of the kingdom of peace. (93)

While the practice of living with Christ is at the heart of Christian faith, sanctification and justification are secondary theological notions. Sanctification is "but a way of reminding us of the kind of journey we must undertake if we are to make the story of Jesus our story." Justification is "but a reminder of the character of this story, namely what God has done for us by providing us with a path to follow" (94).

In the 1980s and 1990s, Hauerwas elaborates on the arguments of *The Peaceable Kingdom*. With William Willimon he wrote *Resident Aliens* and this booklet became a bestseller. *Resident Aliens* is a pamphlet in which the authors proclaim, without regret, that Christianity is no longer the dominant and dominating religion of the West. The era of "Constantinianism" and "Christendom" is over. The time in which the church and the state worked together to preserve the divine order has come to an end. According to Hauerwas and Willimon, this new situation gives Christians an opportunity to recover what they truly are: resident aliens, people who cannot be loyal citizens of the United States of America for their citizenship is in heaven.[61]

How can we live truthfully in a world without certainty? In *The Peaceable Kingdom*, Hauerwas gives his second answer. In a world without certainty you cannot live truthfully on your own. You need a community which is committed to a particular story. You need a community which does not fear the truth, but has developed a strategy to deal with contingency. You need the community of the church, of a people living faithfully to the story of Israel and Jesus Messiah.

5.4 The Most Basic Idea in Hauerwas's Oeuvre

From the early 1980s onwards, the term witness appears more frequently in Hauerwas's texts. Hauerwas applies the term in the same sense as Yoder. The verb "to witness" and the noun "witness" are used to describe what the church does and what it is. According to Hauerwas the church has been

---

61. See Phil 3.20: "But our citizenship is in heaven, and it is from there that we are expecting a Savior, the Lord Jesus Christ."

called to be a witness to the good news of the gospel. And this call is answered by Christians if they live a virtuous life, a life of peacefulness and patience, a life through which they show the good news of the gospel to the world.[62] But the witness is not the dominant term in Hauerwas's reflections on the character of the church. He applies other terms to describe ecclesial practices, such as "enacting the story," "embodying the gospel," "living faithfully" or "being a disciple."

But if we look retrospectively, it turns out that for Hauerwas witness has always been more than just a term to describe ecclesial practices. "Witness" appears at specific places in his texts, often when he reflects on the relation between the life of the church and the truth of Christian beliefs. The notion of witness helps Hauerwas to explain that by seeing how stories and beliefs are enacted in the life of the church, we can understand that and how biblical stories and Christian beliefs are true. In *A Community of Character*, we read,

> The task of the Christian is not to defeat relativism by argument but to witness to a God who requires confrontation. Too often the epistemological and moral presuppositions behind the Christian command to be a witness to such a God have been overlooked. The command to witness is not based on the assumption that we are in possession of a universal truth which others must also "implicitly" possess or have sinfully rejected. If such a truth existed, we would not be called upon to be witnesses, but philosophers. Rather the command to be a witness is based on the presupposition that we only come to the truth through the process of being confronted by the truth. (105)

And in *The Peaceable Kingdom* we read,

> For the necessity of witness is not accidental to Christian convictions, it is at the heart of the Christian life. Those convictions cannot be learned except as they are attested and exemplified by others. The essential Christian witness is neither to personal experience, nor to what Christianity means to "me," but to the truth that this world is the creation of a good God who is known through the people of Israel and the life death and resurrection of Jesus Christ. (14–15)

62. See, for instance, some phrases from different articles in the *The Hauerwas Reader*: "we might be a witness for the second chance that God has made possible for all people" (316). "So the world's true history is not that built on war, but that offered by a community that witnesses to God's refusal to give up his creation" (422). "the necessity of the church to grow through witness and conversion" (498).

In some ways, these quotations prefigure the argument later made in *With the Grain of the Universe*. Hauerwas speaks of Christians as a people confronted by the truth, the truth that God created this world and made himself known through Israel and in Jesus Christ. Since this truth can only be made known by a people prepared to live with this God, it requires witness. But Hauerwas does not further elaborate on this idea, neither in *A Community of Character* nor in *The Peaceable Kingdom*.

With the Grain of the Universe is unique in Hauerwas's oeuvre for its comprehensive reflection on the character of Christian witness. Yet, in his Gifford Lectures Hauerwas is not presenting novel theological insights but is reflecting on what he has found before. During the preparation of the Gifford Lectures, Hauerwas had the opportunity, or—perhaps better—he was forced to articulate, the most basic idea of his theology and ethics as an alternative to a Gifford-like natural theology. Given his former work, it's no surprise that the most basic idea in Hauerwas's theology and ethics is witness. For Hauerwas, the term witness is simply the best way to describe what the church does, and what it is. Story and practice, speech and action, conviction and community come together in the notion of witness. Moreover, "witness" points out exactly why the communal life of Christians is the necessary resource for our speaking about God and man and also for reflecting on the character of the natural.

Thus, though witness may not be the most remarkable term in Hauerwas's oeuvre, *With the Grain of the Universe* reveals that the idea and the practice of the church as a community of witnesses is *the* basic and leading idea in all of Hauerwas's ethics and theology. What was implicated in his work in the 1960s and 1970s, what was explicated now and then in his work in the 1980s and 1990s is said once and for all at the University of Saint Andrews in 2000–2001: we need the witness of the church to speak meaningfully about God, ourselves, and the world.

How can we live truthfully in a world without certainty? Hauerwas's third and final answer is: through witnessing! Look at the witnesses bearing witness in this world, witness how Christians bear testimony in their communal lives. If you let yourself be persuaded by their truthful words and faithful actions, if you are prepared to become a witness yourself, then you will find a way to live truthfully in this world. This third answer is a refinement of his second answer. It explains that the ecclesial community is a community of witnesses showing, through their speech and actions, what the world is like and how we should behave within it. Moreover, all the aspects within the first answer, the notions of story, character, virtue and moral vision, come together in the figure of the witness. For Hauerwas the virtuous people of character *are* witnesses, bearing testimony to the gospel. They show others what the world is like, they offer moral vision, their testimony *is* the embodiment of the story.

5.5 A Sectarian, Fideistic Tribalist

Hauerwas's ethics and theology have been widely critiqued.[63] Most of this criticism relates to his pronounced position on various ethical debates, but other authors have also criticized his more basic theological views. It is not necessary to give a complete overview of these critiques at this point. I will confine myself to one example—that of James Gustafson, one of Hauerwas's own teachers at Yale.[64] Gustafson's charges of sectarianism, fideism and tribalism are typical of the way Hauerwas has been criticized over the years. What is interesting for us is that both Gustafson in his critique and Hauerwas in his reaction come to speak about witness.

In his essay "The sectarian temptation" Gustafson observes that more and more Christian theologians emphasize the incommensurability of the Christian religion. Stanley Hauerwas is presented as one of the prominent propagators of the approach in which Christianity is conceived as a "cultural linguistic phenomenon." According to these theologians, Christianity tells a particular story about the world we live in, containing unique understandings of the character of God and man, and propagating a particular way of acting in the world. Although Gustafson recognizes that in a time of de-Christianization of Western culture, it is attractive to stress the distinctiveness of the Christian religion from the surrounding culture, for him this option is "a sectarian temptation" which must be resisted. This temptation

> is seductive because it can provide reasons for not engaging in the fray of intellectual life, not engaging in the ambiguities of political and moral life. One only bears *witness* to a historic tradition, and the mark of authenticity is that of fidelity to the tradition. (154)

According to Gustafson there are two forms of this sectarian refusal to engage in public life.[65] On the one hand, it can take the form of a theologi-

---

63. For an overview of this critique and Hauerwas's response, see Wells, *Transforming Fate*, 130–35.

64. *Hannah's Child*, 58ff.

65. It remains somewhat unclear in Gustafon's critique and in Hauerwas's answer, how the charges of sectarianism, fideism, and tribalism relate to each other. In my view, sectarianism can best be understood as an umbrella term. This general critique is then further specified in the critique of fideism—charging Hauerwas with isolating the truth

cal fideism misrepresenting Christian faith as a "Wittgensteinian language game" which is not open to other views. In this fideistic approach, Christian convictions become self-justifying and incorrigible because there is no meaningful dialogue between theology and other sciences. Religious knowing is isolated from other ways of knowing. But it can also take the form of a sociological tribalism which misrepresents Christianity as a social group which is distinct from the rest of society. In this tribalistic approach, ethical claims apply only to Christian believers and the moral and social issues in society are neglected. Christian practices in the church are isolated from the political, cultural, social and economic practices of Western societies.

In his reaction to Gustafson's critique, Hauerwas has two main responses to the accusation of sectarianism, fideism and tribalism.[66] First, he argues that he does not wish to isolate Christian truth claims from other ways of knowing. On the one hand Hauerwas does not believe "that religious convictions are or should be treated as an internally consistent language game that is self-validating" (10). But he also opposes attempts to build a foundationalist epistemology for Christian convictions. He denies that scientific knowledge can be used as a standard for the verification and validation of religious and theological claims. But this refusal of foundationalism does not imply that theological claims are immune from the challenges Gustafson speaks of and that conversations between natural sciences and theology are impossible.

Nevertheless, Hauerwas admits that in his view, the conversations between Christians and criticizers of Christian faith are more complex than Gustafson considers them to be: "the very content of Christian convictions requires that the self be transformed if we are adequately to see the truth of the convictions" (10). And for us it comes as no surprise that in this argument, Hauerwas mentions the vital importance of witness:

> For the convictions that Christians hold about the way things are entail the existence of a people, since what we know can be known only through witness. (11)

---

of Christian beliefs from other truths—and the in the critique of tribalism—charging Hauerwas with isolating the church from society. Tribalism can be defined as "a way of thinking or behaving in which people are more loyal to their tribe than to their friends, their country, or any other social group" (Rundell, "Tribalism"). Fideism can be described as a position "which holds that in establishing and accepting religious convictions, faith is primary and reason is either secondary or entirely dispensable" (Bunnin, "Fideism").

66. See the introduction of *Christian Existence Today*.

Thus, Hauerwas claims that if criticizers of Christian faith remain just criticizers, if they do not let themselves be taught by witnesses, they will not fully understand the content of Christian convictions.[67]

Second, Hauerwas argues that he does not want to isolate the church from society. He admits that he is critical of the liberal character of the social and political presuppositions in Western societies, but this critique does not imply that Christians should not participate in society. And again he uses the term witness:

> My call for Christians to recover the integrity of the church as integral to our political witness does not entail that Christians must withdraw from the economic, cultural, legal and political life of our societies. It does mean, however, that the form of our participation will vary given the nature of the societies in which we find ourselves. (13–14)

For Hauerwas, Christians participate in different ways. While he holds that Christians should not get involved with the state when it uses violence to maintain internal order or external security, they could and should fruitfully cooperate with non-Christians, for instance in the government, in the economy, or in the educational system. Yet there are also situations in which they must wonder if cooperation is the best form of participation, for instance when schools insist teachers and students swear allegiance to the flag. In that situation, it might be better to withdraw, to establish schools in which Christians teach their children to participate peacefully in a violent society. But, on the other side, when the distinction between public and private schools contributes to the segregation of race and wealth, Christians could have good reasons to send their children to state schools.[68]

Thus, where Gustafson accuses Hauerwas of propagating fideism—i.e. reducing intellectual reflection on Christian faith to witnessing within an isolated religious tradition—Hauerwas replies that witness is the idea which helps theology to speak of truth in a way which overcomes the dichotomy between particularism and universalism. And where Gustafson accuses Hauerwas of propagating tribalism—i.e. transforming the church into a tribe of witnesses—Hauerwas replies that witness is the practice by which

67. A profound examination of the charge of fideism given by Kallenberg, *Ethics as Grammar*, 113–159. Kallenberg discusses all-important criticizers and formulates an answer to their critique from Hauerwas's perspective.

68. An insightful discussion of the charge of tribalistic sectarianism is given by Rasmusson, *Church as Polis*, 231–47. Rasmusson mentions the various criticizers and in the next chapters of his book he formulates an answer to this critique.

Christians participate in society in faithfulness to the gospel. Towards the end of this book, in chapter 5, I will formulate my final considerations regarding the issues of sectarianism, fideism, and tribalism.

Now that Hauerwas and his account of Christian witness has been introduced, we will continue our research in chapter 2 by examining how this relates to other understandings of witness and testimony.

Mapping the Meaning of Testimony and Witness

WITNESS IS A KEY term in the ethics and theology of Stanley Hauerwas. But nowhere, neither in *With the Grain of the Universe* nor in his other work, does Hauerwas reflect on the terminology he uses. He gives no definition of witness, no model of witnessing, but applies the term witness and its derivatives intuitively.[1] Yet a theological reflection on the term witness, as well as its synonyms and derivatives, is indispensable for this study. For a thorough examination, we must understand what concepts and practices these terms refer to and what is distinctive about Hauerwas's use of them.

This chapter is about the meaning of witness. It explains the various contexts in which the terms "witness," "testimony" and their derivatives are used, compares the different meanings and definitions, and examines how biblical and Christian conceptions of witnessing and testimony relate to other, non-Christian conceptions. By mapping the meaning of "witness" and "testimony," I will conceptualize Hauerwas's position. As will become clear, Hauerwas's account of witness is not unproblematic. The problem is not so much his position within the field of thought on witnessing and testimony, but that he does not fully mark out the position he takes in this field. The focus in this chapter is strictly on language and not ideas. I will not ask how Hauerwas's considerations regarding the necessity of lived lives correspond with ideas which can be found in Scripture, tradition and non-Christian sources. My main question is: how does Hauerwas's use of witness relate to the use of this term in other discourses? There is a great methodological

---

1. Though in "Witness" (136) Hauerwas remarks that witness is the grammar which holds speaker and what is spoken together, he does not explain what he means by "grammar."

benefit to this approach. Since the focus is exclusively on discourses in which the term witness is used, we can discuss very different sorts of discourses and thoroughly examine how they relate to Hauerwas's account.

This chapter consists of eleven sections. Section 1 discusses the etymologies of witness and testimony and deals with everyday, legal, and religious definitions. Since all conceptions of witnessing and testimony (including Scriptural and Christian) are strongly determined by legal accounts of witness, Section 2 focuses on the legal view of witnesses and their testimony in the past and present. Then we step back in time to explore the ancient sources of our understanding of witnessing and testimony. Section 3 deals with the ancient Greek understanding of testimony and Sections 4 and 5 look at the accounts of witnessing and testimony in the Old and the New Testament respectively. Section 6 is about the relation between witnessing and martyrdom and Section 7 gives an outline of other understandings of witnessing and testimony in the Christian tradition. Section 8 examines the notion of "testimony of life," and Section 9 discusses literature of testimony by survivors of catastrophes. Sections 10 and 11 respectively discuss philosophical and theological reflections on testimony.

Much of the information in this chapter comes from dictionaries and, because Germans are arguably the most competent dictionary writers in the world, I will refer extensively to German literature. Although the eleven sections contain a lot of information, the mere gathering of information is not the intended goal of this chapter. Its aim is rather to examine how understandings of witnessing and testimony in different times and contexts relate to each other.[2] Through this exposition, we will come to understand what kind of position Hauerwas takes. All the sections will end with a conclusive remark which compares findings to Hauerwas's account of witness. At the end of this chapter, these conclusions will be collected to give a first evaluation of Hauerwas's understanding of the character of Christian witness.

1. THE TERMS "WITNESS" AND "TESTIMONY"[3]

According to *The Oxford English Dictionary* the etymology of the noun "witness" moves from an abstract meaning to a concrete meaning.[4] The noun witness derives from the noun "wit" or "gewit"—denoting "the faculty of thinking and reasoning"[5] and the "mind as the seat of consciousness." Its

2. Peters gives an analysis of witness and testimony which is somewhat similar to the analysis in this chapter: "Witnessing," 707–23.

3. This section largely relies on the different articles in Simpson and Weiner, *The Oxford English Dictionary*.

4. "Witness, sb." in ibid., vol. xx.

5. "Wit" in ibid. See also Klein, "Wit, Witness, n."

most abstract sense can be found in Middle English: "knowledge, under-standing, wisdom." In a more concrete sense it means the "attestation of a fact, event, or statement" or "evidence," and, in a formal setting, "testimony by signature [or] oath." Although in their mass noun forms, the meanings of the English terms "testimony" and "witness" are almost identical, testimony has a different etymological background: it stems from the Latin *testimonium*. As its Latin original, the term "testimony" means "personal or documentary evidence or attestation in support of a fact or statement; hence, any form of evidence or proof."[6]

The noun "witness" also refers to people. A witness is someone who "gives evidence in relation to matters of fact under inquiry," specifically "evidence upon oath or affirmation in a court of justice." The noun can also refer to someone who is "present at a transaction" or "at the execution of a document and subscribes it in attestation thereof." Thirdly, we speak of people who are witnesses *of* or *to* something: people who are "present as spectator or auditor" and who are "able to testify from personal observation." In a figurative way, the noun witness can also refer to an object, a thing "that furnishes evidence or proof of the thing or fact mentioned."[7]

The nouns relating to the verbs "to witness" and "to testify" (from the Latin verb *testificare*) are often used almost synonymously. Intransitively, the verbs refer to the "speech act" of bearing witness, of giving a testimony. As a transitive verb, "to witness" is defined as "to bear witness to (a fact or statement); . . . to furnish oral or written evidence,"[8] and "to testify" means "to give proof of (a fact); to assert or affirm the truth of (a statement)." The transitive "to witness" also has another sense: "to be a witness, spectator, or auditor . . . to experience by personal . . . observation."[9]

Both *testimonium* and *testificare* are related to the Latin noun *testis*. *Testis* (which is not related to the English noun "test" or the verb "to test") stems from the Proto-Indo-European root *tréyes*: three. Originally, *testis* refers to the third, the disinterested witness, who is present at a legal transaction between two parties. In classical Latin the meaning of *testis* is broadened, and it corresponds with most of the definitions of the English noun "witness" (as a person): *testis* is someone who testifies in court, who gives verbal or Scriptural evidence and in a figurative way *testis* can also mean "eyewitness."[10]

6. Simpson and Weiner, ibid., vol. xvii, "Testimony."

7. "Witness, sb." in: ibid., vol. xx.

8. "Witness, v." in: ibid.

9. "Testify. v." in: ibid., vol. xvii. Less relevant here are the verb "to attest" ("To bear witness to . . . to testify") and the noun "attestation" ("The action of bearing witness; the testimony borne") (see ibid., vol. i).

10. "Testis" in De Vaan, *Etymological dictionary*.

All the English verbs and nouns mentioned above have equivalents in other existing European languages,[11] not only in the Romance languages, whose vocabulary directly stems from Latin, but also in German (and other Germanic languages). In English and German, we see a similar development: just as the noun witness (which originally meant knowledge) became synonymous with both *testis* and *testimonium*, the noun *Zeuge* (originally referring to someone taken to court) became the German equivalent for *testis*. In modern German, *Zeuge* refers not only to the person brought to court in order to testify, but also to the third person in a transaction, and to the observer of certain events, while the meaning of its derivative *Zeugnis* is identical both to "testimony" and *testimonium*.[12]

In my view, there are two reasons for the equivalence of the nouns *testis, Zeuge* and *witness*.[13] Firstly, the terms "witness" and "testimony" refer to something inherent in all human interaction: a person reporting to another about things they observed.[14] In some situations, this speech act is formalized: for instance, those making deals need witnesses (neutral persons present to witness the transaction or agreement); courts administering justice need testimonies (statements from those taken to court to give relevant information). The fact that witnessing is a common speech act which is formalized in various systems of law, explains why different languages have comparable terms. The second explanation is the Roman factor: not only the influence of the Latin language on other languages, but also the influence of Roman law—with its refined understanding of *testis* and *testimonium*—both on Continental and English law and judicial speech.[15] As this specific judicial speech with its strict definitions of "witness," "witnessing" and "testimony" influenced everyday language, the German and English terms became almost synonymous. As we see below, the legal version of witnesses and their testimonies is still the dominant model for thinking and speaking about witness and testimony in other contexts.

Finally, *The Oxford English Dictionary* lists a sense of the noun "testimony" that takes more distance from its Latin original: an "open attestation

---

11. Unlike other European languages, in English the verb "to witness" can refer to the act of seeing something, or even more generally to the act of observing something with the other senses.

12. "Zeuge," Bluhme, *Etymologisches Wörterbuch*.

13. This suggestion is my responsibility. I have not found support for it in the literature I studied.

14. See Peters, "Witnessing," 708. See also Coady, *Testimony*, 3–24, and Paul Ricoeur, "The Hermeneutics," 119–54. While in the current chapter I only refer occasionally to Coady and Ricoeur, in the next I take a long look at their groundbreaking analyses.

15. See Fischer, "Zeugen" and Gilissen, *Historische inleiding*, 664–671.

or acknowledgment; confession, profession." These dictionary examples all relate to Christian faith, for instance *"to seal one's testimony with one's blood,* to die as a martyr for one's religious profession."[16] This description corresponds with both a definition of the verb to testify as in "to profess and openly acknowledge (a fact, belief, object of faith or devotion, etc.); to proclaim as something that one knows or believes" as well as with a definition of the noun witness: as in someone who testifies "for Christ or the Christian faith" especially "by death; a martyr."[17] As we shall see below, this particular meaning of witness, witnessing and testimony originates in the New Testament's use of the Greek term for testimony (μαρτυρία) and its derivatives. It was only after the influence of Christianity, that the Latin words *testis, testificare* and *testimonium* gained this specific connotation.[18] These definitions do not apply to the verb "to witness" and to the noun "witness" (as the attestation of a fact). In English, these verb and noun forms have "less Christian," i.e. more neutral, connotations. Within the context of Christian faith, three different applications of concepts of witness, witnessing and testimony can be discerned.

- Firstly, Christians present themselves as witnesses bearing testimony to their faith. The Christian witness personally vouches for Christian faith. He refers to an outer or inner experience *of* faith as evidence *for* his faith. The reference to experience and the speaker's personal endorsement distinguishes testimony from profession (though the dictionary definitions indicate that the words are often used synonymously). Thus: the Westminster Confession is a *profession* of faith; the disciples in Acts give *testimony* of Jesus's resurrection. The contrast between testimony and mission is also evident. While the "missionary" is a messenger who has been sent to communicate the message of his master, the witness can personally vouch for his testimony. Thus, the disciples in Acts are typically not just messengers (*apostles*) sent by their master but also witnesses who bear witness to what their master has shown to them.

16. Simpson and Weiner, ibid., vol. xvii, "Testimony." Emphasis by dictionary.

17. The equivalents of witness and testimony in other European languages have similar meanings. Testimony is a profession spoken openly even when people do not want to hear it; witness as someone vouching for the truth of his faith, being prepared to die for it.

18. Below, in section 4, we see that in the work of the stoic philosopher Epictetus we find a notion of witness which resembles the Christian notion. Though before he was banished to Greece, Epictetus lived in Rome, his teachings are written in Greek. As far as I know, there are no classical Latin authors speaking of witness in the way Epictetus does.

- Secondly, in the Christian religion witnessing refers to martyrdom. The martyrs bear witness to Christ not by their words, but by their readiness to suffer and die for their faith.

- The third application is not mentioned in the dictionary. Theologians such as Barth, Yoder, and Hauerwas speak of the witness of the Christian life. They suggest that through all their words and acts, Christians bear witness to Jesus Christ.

To sum up: the terms witness, witnessing and testimony apply to everyday speech acts and to judicial procedures, the latter being strongly influenced by Latin language and Roman law, but they also apply to Christian speech and action. If we relate this to Hauerwas's account of Christian witness, we can conclude that he speaks of witness in a rather specific way. In his Gifford Lectures Hauerwas does not use the verb "to testify" and the noun "testimony," because for him these words sounds too pietistic or revivalistic to be suitable for his argument.[19] He prefers to use the verb "to witness" and the noun "witness," because, to his ears, witness sounds more neutral and "less Christian." However he applies these more neutral terms almost exclusively to Christian practices. In *With the Grain of the Universe* and in his other work, witness and witnessing refer to the visible and communal Christian life. And strikingly, Hauerwas does not relate his theological account of witness to everyday or legal conceptions of witnesses and their testimonies.[20]

2. WITNESS AND TESTIMONY IN COURT [21]

The oldest form of legal witness is the so-called "contract witness." Contract witnesses occur in many ancient societies: they are persons of irreproachable conduct, neutral, uninvolved, who are present at the completion of

19. As we have seen in chapter 1.5, in *Hannah's Child* Hauerwas speaks of bearing testimony through his memoires.

20. In this chapter, and in the rest of this study, I will not restrict myself to the term "witness." I will use the verb "to testify," and in my usage this verb is synonymous to "to witness." Moreover, when I refer to "that what is being witnessed" I will mostly use the noun "testimony," while in my usage the noun "witness" refers to the person who bears testimony. Yet, when I speak more generally of the theological idea that Christians must be understood as witnesses bearing testimony, I will use the noun "witness."

21. This section largely relies on three sources. The main source are the articles in *Handwörterbuch*, in particular Fischer "Zeugen," Fischer, "Zeugnis," Sellert, "Zeugnispflicht." For information about witness in systems of law from the Middle Ages to modern times, I have also consulted Gilissen, *Historische inleiding*. For information about witness in systems of law before the Middle Ages, I have consulted VerSteeg, *Law*, and Bellotto, *Witnessing*, 225–51.

transactions, agreements, marriages and other contracts. Through the presence of these witnesses, deals gain an official character. The presence of the contract witness is a guarantee that all parties commit themselves to the deal. Witnesses are present when the agreement is made, they know the conditions, and if there's a legal conflict between the parties, they are called to testify in a lawsuit, to give impartial information about the contract. In the earliest codices, these contract witnesses played a prominent role. Kings, not willing to arbitrate between disputing parties without some neutral, impartial information about the bargain, demanded the presence of witnesses whenever official arrangements were made. In literate societies, these contracts were put into writing, the names of the witnesses being mentioned in the document so that if a legal conflict arose, the contract witnesses could affirm the legitimacy of the document.[22] In modern society, documents and notaries almost completely replaced the role of the contract witness. Yet, there's one legal act at which the presence of contract witnesses is still required: a marriage ceremony.

Witnesses did not always play an important role in lawsuits. In less advanced systems of law the function of a lawsuit was to determine whether a defendant was guilty. The burden of proof rested with the defendant. If there were no contract witnesses or documents to prove his innocence, the defendant had to purge himself by undergoing an ordeal by battle, by fire, or by taking an oath. The defendant was often assisted by so-called "oath-helpers": persons who took the oath with him. These oath-helpers were not witnesses: they vouched for the innocence of the defendant without necessarily knowing the material facts of the case.[23] In more developed systems of law—such as those in the ancient states of Babylonia and Egypt, in the cities of Athens and Rome and in Europe after the fourteenth century—a distinction was made between civil law and criminal law. These criminal lawsuits gained a new function: truth finding. To have a case, a plaintiff would have to produce evidence: reliable information that could be verified. The defendant also needs evidence to prove his innocence. In criminal lawsuits both sides can produce documents, so-called "physical evidence," but the most important form of evidence is testimony, information given by people. The "oath-helper" evolved into a witness, someone who, perhaps by coincidence, had seen or heard or in some other way possessed relevant information and testified about it.[24] But while after the fourteenth century witnesses and their testimonies played a crucial truth finding role in criminal lawsuits, in civil lawsuits witness became less important. After the rule that documents

22. For instance, Hammurabi's laws (VerSteeg, *Law*, 15, 28–31). See also Bellotto, *Witnessing*, 236–38.

23. See Scheyhing, "Eideshelfer."

24. See Fischer "Zeugen". See also Gilissen, *Historische inleiding*, 664–65.

must be affirmed by living witnesses was repealed, documents became the most import form of evidence in civil law. In a civil lawsuit, parties only summon witnesses if documented evidence is unavailable or inadequate.

Testimony is "say-so evidence."[25] Judges and juries are invited to accept something as true because the witness tells them to. Both in criminal and civil cases the role of the witness is the same: delivering evidence by reporting observations.[26] In some law systems, this report cannot be given by the parties themselves but only by those who are not involved in the process. Roman law, in particular, stresses the importance of the neutrality of the witness: a *testimonium* cannot be given by the parties involved or by their relatives but only by a third party.[27]

In all systems of law the relationship between witnesses and the court is complicated. On one side, the administration of justice is dependent on witnesses. Particularly in criminal law, judges and juries need witnesses to find the truth. Witnesses have authority because they know relevant facts: eyewitnesses and earwitnesses have seen and heard things and in modern law the so-called "expert witness" often possesses knowledge based on scientific research.[28] Moreover, the witness claims integrity: he presents himself—or he is presented by one of the parties—as someone giving reliable information. But despite this claim of integrity, there is always a chance that the witness will lie to the court. On the other side, however, the court yields power over the witness. Since people are not always willing to tell the truth, all systems of law have introduced rules and procedures that aim to force witnesses to be honest. In most societies there is a legal, or at least social, obligation for civilians to testify in court under oath. The oath of the witness is an old and common procedure: witnesses are forced to swear and by doing so they not only call on divine help to speak the truth, they also call down divine punishment on themselves if they lie. As an effect of this procedure, people who refused to take an oath, such as Mennonites and Quakers, found themselves in serious trouble when they were summoned to testify.[29] In the modern law of secularized societies, witnesses can choose between an oath and an affirmation—a solemn promise not to lie but to tell the truth.[30] After swearing or affirming, the witness is questioned either by the judge or by the representatives of both parties.

25. Coady, *Testimony*, 27.

26. See Fischer, "Zeugen".

27. See VerSteeg, *Law*, 298.

28. See Coady, *Testimony*, 277–306.

29. Hauerwas has strong sympathy for the Mennonites and Quakers, but (as far as I know) he does not discuss their refusal to take oath.

30. See Erler, "Eid."

Yet, the court's power over witnesses has its restrictions. In many ancient systems of law, torturing witnesses was not allowed (except for those who were also suspects). In ancient Rome, slaves were questioned under torture but their statements were not considered as testimony: a *testimonium* is a statement from a free man under oath.[31] Modern criminal law has another important restriction. It is a fundamental right that the court cannot force a witness to give information that is self-incriminatory. In addition, witnesses sometimes have the right or the obligation to refuse testimony: for instance, spouses cannot be forced to testify against one another, and attorneys and clergy cannot be forced to speak about confidential matters.[32] Perjury, the breaking of an oath by giving a false testimony, has always been considered a serious crime. A false witness not only lies to the court, but also to God. In secularized societies, too, the breaking of an oath or affirmation is more than "not telling the truth": it is considered an action that undermines the entire legal system.[33]

In medieval and early modern Europe, certain people were excluded from testifying. The testimony of "unsuited" persons like insane people and children was not permitted. The statements of some others, such as criminals and Jews, were not considered "full" testimonies. These rules of jurisprudence originate from the Corpus Juris Civilis—the codex of Roman civil law collected by the Byzantine Emperor Justinian I. Perhaps the most important directive adopted from Justinian Laws was the two-witness rule. In the late Roman Empire and in pre-nineteenth century continental Europe, full evidence could only be delivered by two witnesses hence the phrase, *testis unus testis nullus*, "one witness is no witness."[34] By the end of the eighteenth century, ideas about evidence began to change. Both in continental and in common-law jurisdictions the maxim became *testimonia ponderanda, non numeranda sunt*—"testimonies should be weighed, not

31. See VerSteeg, *Law*, 306–11.

32. See Sellert, "Zeugnispflicht."

33. Modern law is unique in making a distinction between actual perjury, viz. deliberately giving false testimony, and making inaccurate statements unwittingly, which is conceived as a crime. See Holzhauer, "Meineid." The history of law indicates that false testimonies are not only given by witnesses who want to obstruct justice, but also by those who try to "help" the administration of justice. Some witnesses, for instance, lie in court to prevent "criminals avoiding fair punishment." In other cases, the system of law itself stimulates or forces people to bear false testimony: e.g. witch trials, and soviet show trials. In cases like these, truth finding is made subordinate to the "greater" enterprise of punishing all criminals, or of the purification of society. A colourful picture of these (and other trials) can be found in Kadri, *Trial*, 108–51, 186–225.

34. Ballentine, *A Law Dictionary*, 495.

counted"[35]—a principle that was also adhered to in the Roman republic.[36] In current law, everyone can bear witness, including children and the mentally disabled, though not under oath. The commonly held conviction is that the law cannot pre-determine the value of a testimony; only the judge or jury can assess it, and only during a lawsuit.[37] Where in civil law the testimony of one witness could be enough to decide in favor of one party, in criminal law a suspect can only be accused if the testimony of one witness is backed up by other evidence.

By questioning, the judge or attorney searches for information about facts observed by the witness, and tests whether this information is reliable—that is, not based on hearsay or unprovable assumptions. Such evidence is deemed "invalid" by US law and "insufficient" by other systems of law.[38] In the case of the expert witness, the questioner asks for a scientifically based opinion and tests whether this opinion is not prejudiced in any way. The witness is obliged to answer all questions, including skeptical, ridiculous, painful and extremely personal ones. When the witness remains silent or lies, the court can prosecute him. Having heard a witness, the court decides whether it accepts the testimony. Two different issues are at stake here. The first is the *competence* of the witness: is it probable (in civil cases) or beyond reasonable doubt (in criminal cases) that the witness has seen, heard, or knows the attested fact? Could the witness simply be mistaken? The second issue is the *integrity* of the witness: is it probable, or beyond reasonable doubt, that the witness observed or knows the attested fact? Or are there reasons to mistrust the testimony, for instance, because the witness's own interests are at stake, because he has a reputation for lying, or because the witness is prejudiced against a suspect? In the early systems of law, these issues were dealt with intuitively, in the law of late medieval and early modern Europe, rules of evidence prescribed whether a testimony was valid, and in modern law there are rules and jurisprudence regarding evidence, but ultimately it is up to the judge or jury to decide whether a testimony is accepted as evidence.

The differences between Hauerwas's account of Christian witness and judicial testimony are obvious. In court witnesses are passive—they follow procedures, answer questions—whereas Christians giving testimony are active: they testify on their own initiative, speak the truth and vouch for it. Nevertheless, there are some remarkable similarities. The testimony of a Christian is a speech act in which the truth about a disputed issue is disclosed to a public, as is the testimony of a witness in Roman and European

---

35. Ibid., 509.

36. See VerSteeg, *Law*, 297–99.

37. For the evolution of procedure of evidence see Kornblum, "Beweis."

38. See Erler, "Hörensagen."

law. The witness vouches for the truth of what he says by making an implicit or explicit claim: "believe me, for what I say is relevant, I have the authority to say it since I am an honest human being and my assertions are based on personal experiences." Notably, in *With the Grain of the Universe* Hauerwas does not pay attention to these similarities between judicial testimony and Christian witnessing. His account remains separate from the legal understanding of witness and testimony.

3. WITNESS AND TESTIMONY IN ANCIENT ATHENS[39]

The Greek nouns μαρτυρία ("testimony") and μάρτυς ("witness") and the verb μαρτυρέω ("to bear witness or to testify") stem from the proto-Indo-European root *smer* "to be mindful." Originally, these words were judicial terms, but just like the equivalents in other languages, they are also used in other contexts. The derivative μαρτύριον refers to the content of a testimony, or to the evidence of an object, and outside the judicial context means "evidence."[40]

The laws of Athens stated that third parties should be present at legal events such as marriages, the liberation of a slave, or a commercial transaction. In court, both parties would bring witnesses, adult male citizens who could not speak for themselves, but could only affirm the statements of the pleas of the plaintiff or the defendant. Having heard both sides, the jury voted without deliberation on the defendant's guilt or innocence. Since testimonies were not tested, either by cross-examination or by questions from the jury, it often happened that both parties simply told conflicting stories that were affirmed by contradictory testimonies. Perjury was officially prohibited but hard to prove. To win a case in Athens, producing evidence was insufficient, one needed good rhetoric: a plea that convinced the jury.[41]

Both Plato and Aristotle reflect on this Athenian judicial practice. Plato writes about the epistemological difference between the eyewitness and the judge who hears a (truthful) testimony: the former knows, the latter only has a true opinion.[42] Aristotle is as critical as his teacher. He distinguishes between technical evidence, proof arrived at by careful rhetoric, and non-technical evidence, proof outside the argument itself. Testimony is non-technical evidence: the credibility of it does not speak for itself but depends on the witness's credibility. Paul Ricoeur explains that Aristotle's rhetoric is

39. This section largely relies on VerSteeg, *Law*, Scholz, "Zeuge, Zeugnis" Coenen, "Witness, Testimony," and Trites, *The New Testament*, 4–16 (chapter 1: "The Witness Terminology of Secular Greek").

40. Coenen, "Witness, Testimony," 1038.

41. See VerSteeg, *Law*, 208–17.

42. See Scholz, "Zeuge, Zeugnis," 1319.

ruled by logic. Therefore, testimony "occupies necessarily an inferior place, for it shows the dependence of the judgment and of the judge to something exterior: on the first level, the things spoken by another, and on the second, things seen by him."[43] In fact, Plato and Aristotle are not only critical about the epistemological status of testimonies in court, but about all information garnered from reports by others. For both philosophers, true knowledge is the deeper understanding of reality, which we gain through the proper interpretation of all that's around us. If knowledge is conceived as a general and stable *knowing why*, information from testimony can hardly acquire the status of true knowledge since it is a particular and also fallible *knowing that*.[44]

Section 1 indicated that in modern European languages, there's an extra meaning of witnessing and testimony which is closely related to Christian faith and in particular to the New Testament. According to L. Coenen, this extra meaning of witness is not unfamiliar to classic and koine Greek. Indeed, even before Aristotle, a proximate and additional use of testimony had established itself, whereby μαρτυρία "was no longer intended to substantiate something objectively given, but instead expressed moral or philosophical convictions."[45] Though Socrates is the most famous example of a man openly acknowledging his beliefs in an extremely repressive situation, in his writings about Socrates, Plato does not call his teacher a witness.[46] However, there is a Greek philosopher who thinks of himself as a witnessing philosopher: Epictetus. This stoic philosopher, living in the first century, conceives Socrates as the archetype of the true philosopher. Although he has *not* been influenced by early Christianity, for Epictetus, philosophers such as Socrates (and himself) have been called to be a witness to the divine truth. As he writes in his *Discourses*: "In what character do you now appear? As a witness summoned by God."[47] The genuine philosopher speaks the truth about God to the powerful, even if they do not want to hear this testimony. He is prepared to accept the consequences, and to suffer and die for his testimony.[48]

43. Ricoeur, "The Hermeneutics," 128.

44. Scholz, "Zeuge, Zeugnis," 1319.

45. Coenen, "Witness, Testimony," 1039.

46. See Trites, *The New Testament*, 12–13. See also Coenen, "Witness, Testimony," 1039 and Ricoeur, "The Hermeneutics," 129.

47. Epictetus, *Discourses* 1.9, 1102. A similar remark can be found in book 3, "for he [Zeus] neglects not one of the smallest things; but to exercise me, and make use of me as a witness to others" (*Discourses* 3.23, 2108).

48. Trites writes that according to Epictetus "the stoic–Cynic philosopher bears witness not only with his lips, but also with his life" (*The New Testament*, 13). It is true that philosopher bears witness with his body, "I and my body bear witness to this"

To summarize: this section reveals a connection between the legal account of witnessing and testimony in law on the one hand and the philosophical reflection on the witness and his testimony on the other. Moreover, there is a strong resemblance between the ancient Greek understanding of witness, witnessing and testimony and the definitions explained in Section 1. And the meanings of μαρτυρία and μάρτυς correspond mutatis mutandis with the Latin and modern definitions of testimony and witness respectively. More surprising is Epictetus's understanding of witnessing. We can conclude that, although the idea and practice of bearing witness through life and death to a divine entity is strongly propagated by Christianity, it is *not* an exclusively Christian invention. Indeed, there are some interesting resemblances between Hauerwas's understanding of the Christian witness and Epictetus's understanding of the philosophical witness. The first-century stoic philosopher and the twenty-first-century Christian theologian agree that a witness is summoned by God to proclaim a controversial truth, and is prepared to suffer for his testimony. This also raises an important question: would Hauerwas agree with Epictetus that philosophers such as Socrates are genuine witnesses or would he say that only Christians are true witnesses?

4. WITNESS AND TESTIMONY IN THE OLD TESTAMENT[49]

In biblical Hebrew, the noun עֵד denotes persons bearing witness. The verb עוד *(hif)* has both a judicial meaning, "to summon witnesses" or "to witness," and an extra-judicial application in which it refers to authoritative declarations. The noun עֵדוּת is usually translated as "testimony." The etymology of these terms is uncertain.[50] The Septuagint translates them quite consistently as μάρτυς, μαρτυρέω and μαρτυρία. Witnesses play a crucial role in Israel's lawsuits. In the Torah, the witness is someone reporting perceived facts, but unlike the (quasi-)neutral third in Roman law, the עֵד speaks the truth about a wrongdoer and his wrongdoings for the higher sake of God's law and God's justice. To begin a case, the witness to a crime, either a victim or a bystander, has to rise up in the presence of the people and the leaders and witness against the wrongdoer, i.e. make an official accusation based on arguments and the evidence of his own perception (Deut 17:2–13). After deliberating on both the accusation and the evidence (Deut 19:18), the elders or judges

---

(*Discourses* 3.22, 2078). However the phrasing "witness with life" cannot be found in the references to Epictetus's *Discourses*.

49. This section largely relies on Simian-Yofre, "עוד'wd," and Schwemer, "Prophet, Zeuge."

50. Simian-Yofre, "עוד'wd," 1108–10.

pass judgment, and if the case is too complicated it can be taken to a higher court (Deut 17:8). In Mosaic Law, one witness is not always sufficient for a conviction (Deut 19:15). In cases of murder (Num 35:30) and idolatry (Deut 17:6), for instance, two witnesses have to stand up and testify against their neighbor. When the charge of the witness is accepted, the witnesses execute the punishment (Deut 17:7) thus bearing full responsibility for the outcome of their testimony.[51]

In Mosaic law, bearing witness means testifying against others, and this is conceived not so much as a complaint by an injured party but as a legal act that protects the order of the Torah against violations (Lev 5:1; Deut 17:2–7). Therefore, the presumption of truth favors the accusing witnesses: when two or three people witness against their neighbor, and the court finds no reason to doubt the truthfulness of their testimony, the case is settled and the accused will be sentenced.[52] Since judicial procedure depends on the honesty of these witnesses, Mosaic Law strictly forbids false testimonies. As the ninth commandment states, "You shall not bear false witness against your neighbor" (Exod 20:16, see also Exod 23:1–3 and Deut 5:20). As in other ancient systems of law,[53] those who bear false witness against their neighbor get the punishment they wished for their neighbor (Deut 19:19).

In several texts of the Old Testament, we read about contract witnesses (Ruth 4:9–11; Isa 8:2; Jer 32) and also of objects as witnesses to a contract: a heap of stones, for instance, refers to the agreement between Jacob and Laban (Gen 31:44–52, see also Gen 21:30; Jos 22:27). When one of the parties breaks the contract, the objects can witness against them. Thus, heaven and earth (Deut 4:26) or the song of Moses (Deut 31:19) will testify against Israel when the people are unfaithful to their covenant with Yahweh.

Finally, in Exodus, Leviticus and Numbers, the noun עֵדוּת—which is traditionally translated as testimony—is used frequently in texts about the ceremony in the tabernacle, often in status constructus: "the tabernacle of the Testimony" (Num 1:50, New King James Version), "the ark of the Testimony" (Exod 25:22 NKJ), "two tablets of Testimony" (Exod 31:18 NKJ) and in phrases like "And you shall put into the ark the Testimony which I will give you" (Exod 25:16 NKJ). In this case, עֵדוּת means "written document" and the word denotes the two tables on which the words of the covenant are written. The term is applied here since the words of the covenant are evidence of God's faithfulness to his covenant—and they testify against Israel when it becomes an unfaithful partner. In Deuteronomy and elsewhere in the Old Testament we find the plural of עֵדוּת together with related terms, for

51. See ibid., 1113.
52. See ibid., 1122.
53. See VerSteeg, *Law*, 30, 68, 134–35, 299.

instance: "the testimonies, and the statutes, and the judgments" (Deut 4:45). Here, the word means something like "covenant regulation."[54] Psalm 119 mentions the term 23 עֵדוֹת times. In this Psalm, the covenant regulations of the Lord are praised together with his word, his law, and his commandments: "Blessed are those who keep His testimonies" (Ps.119:2 NKJ).

In the Prophets (Nevi'im) and Writings (Ketuvim), it turns out that Israel is not always true to the covenant. One example of this unfaithfulness is the misuse of Mosaic legal procedure. Proverbs not only praises the "truthful witness" for saving lives (Prov 14:25) but also warns against the "worthless witness" who "mocks at justice" (Prov 19:28) who "will not go unpunished" (Prov 19:9). Psalm 27 and Psalm 35 are about a lawsuit in which "false" (Ps.27:12) or "malicious" (Ps.35:11) witnesses stand up and testify against the psalmist. 1 Kings 21 tells the story of Queen Jezebel settling a trial in which two scoundrels give a false testimony against Naboth which leads to his execution.

In the prophetical literature the verb עוּד is used many times in an extra-juridical sense. Yahweh "testifies against" (Neh 9:29 NKJ) his people (see also Jer 6:10, 11:7; 42:19); he sends his prophets to warn them to be faithful to him and his demands (2 Kings 17:13). Some texts speak of Yahweh's prophets being killed because of their testimony: "they slew thy prophets which testified against them" (Neh 9:26 NKJ, see also 2 Chron 24:19). In some other texts, Yahweh is a witness: "my witness is in heaven" (Job 16:19), a witness who knows of the sins of men (Jer 29:23), and witnesses against sinners (Mal 3:5) or also against his own unfaithful people (Mic 1:2; 1 Sam 12:5). Twice Israel is called a witness. In the book of Joshua we read of Joshua saying to Israel: "You are witnesses against yourselves that you have chosen the Lord, to serve him;" "We are witnesses," they reply (Josh.24:22). In Isa 43 and 44, Yahweh begins a trial against the nations, and he does not keep to the rules regarding evidence in Mosaic law but summons Israel as a silent but *positive* witness for his case (Isa 43:10–12; 44:8).[55] These fascinating prophecies of Isaiah will be discussed extensively in chapter 4.

This section indicates that the Old Testament has a typical understanding of testimony. The law that the witness to a crime bears the responsibility to charge, to testify against the criminal, is not common to Greek, Roman and modern accounts of witness. In fact, the Old Testament proves that the notion of the witness as a third party producing evidence is not a "natural idea," but a typical characteristic of classical and modern legal processes. However, the concept of witness in Hebrew law is not completely different to that of other legal systems. Both the עֵד and the *testis* give evidence by referring to their own observations. Moreover, as with the Latin terms,

---

54. Simian-Yofre, "עוּד'wd," 1126.

55. In Job 21:11, the verb עוּד refers to an act of giving a *positive* testimony.

Hebrew words are used both in legal and non-legal contexts. But since the legal contexts differ, the non-legal use of the Hebrew term also differs: when the prophets are witnessing, they do not report neutrally about their observations, but bring a charge against Israel based on their observations. Ultimately, we can conclude that the way Hauerwas speaks about witnessing in *With the Grain of the Universe*—witnessing as showing what it means to be human, what the world is like, who God is—is not the same as the Old Testament's understanding of witnessing and testimony.[56]

5. WITNESS AND TESTIMONY IN THE NEW TESTAMENT[57]

There is no textual evidence that the meaning of witnessing and testimony changed in the intertestamental period. The book of Jubilees calls the prophets witnesses, not because of their violent death but because their prophesies are a testimony against Israel.[58] In the books of Maccabees, suffering and dying are important motives. The prophets take up the wrath of God towards Israel, they suffer and die instead of the people. However, the authors of the books of Maccabees do not apply the Greek noun μάρτυς or its derivatives to describe the dramatic life and death of Israel's prophets.[59] It is only in the New Testament that a connection is made between suffering, dying and bearing testimony.

The first section pointed out that some definitions of testimony and witness are typically Christian: testimony as an open attestation, a confession or profession; a witness testifies of his faith through speech and acts, through suffering and dying. This section will indicate that this understanding of witness, witnessing and testimony can be traced back to the New Testament. Yet for Paul, the New Testament's earliest and most productive writer, witness is not an important motif.[60] In fact, Paul scarcely uses the term μάρτυς or its

56. To be sure, Hauerwas's highlighting of the theological impact of the lived life of God's people resembles much of what is proclaimed in the books of the Old Testament. After all, the Torah is about how men could live truthfully and faithfully as Yahweh's covenant partners, while the prophets criticize Israel for being untruthful and unfaithful. However, except for Isaiah 43 and 44, the terms "testimony" and "witness" are not used in the writings of the Old Testament to explain what it means to live as Yahweh's covenant partners. In my analysis, the focus is on how these terms are used.

57. This section largely relies on three sources: Coenen, "Witness, Testimony," Schwemer, "Prophet, Zeuge," and Trites, *The New Testament*.

58. See Schwemer, "Prophet, Zeuge," 323–50.

59. See Coenen, "Witness, Testimony," 1042.

60. I realise there are many themes in Paul's writing which come very close to the

derivatives in his letters.[61] Although in some instances[62] μαρτύριον refers
to "the gospel, the proclaimed message of salvation in Christ,"[63] Paul does
not reflect on the character of testimony. For him, μαρτύριον is just another
term referring to moral or philosophical convictions which, as we have seen
above, is a common application in classical and in koine Greek. This is true
even for Romans 9, where Paul declares that his conscience is "also bearing
me witness in the Holy Spirit" (Rom 9:1 NKJ).[64] As will become clear below,
witness becomes a key theological motif elsewhere in the New Testament,
for instance, in the Lucan and Johannine literature.

According to the synoptic gospels, Jesus was tried under Hebrew law
(Mat 26:57–68; Mark 14:53–65; Luke 22:66–71).[65] The gospels tell how the
judges in the Sanhedrin look in vain for a lawful μαρτυρία—a testimony
against Jesus, confirmed by two or three witnesses. But they do find a legal
basis on which to convict him: Jesus admits to the court that he is the Son
of Man and for the Sanhedrin this answer alone suffices to convict Jesus of
blasphemy. Matthew, Mark, and Luke depict Jesus as a divine envoy who is
killed for admitting that he is "the son of the Blessed One" (Mark 14:61).
But none of the synoptic authors suggest that this prophesying prophet can
be also understood as a witnessing witness giving a positive testimony of
his convictions. Although Mark and Matthew write in Greek, when they
speak of testimony and witnessing they follow the rules of Hebrew law: the
witness bears testimony *against* someone.[66] In the gospel of Luke, however,

---

meaning of witness and testimony in Hauerwas's work: 1. Paul has been called by Jesus
Christ to be an apostle to the gentiles; 2. he works as a missionary who is sent to accom-
plish a mission; and 3. this vocation qualifies his entire life. See L.J. Lietaert Peerbolte,
Paul the Missionary, 177–256. I will not further discuss this resemblance. Instead I will
concentrate on those New Testament books in which the terms "witness" and "testimony" are key theological motives.

61. Paul speaks, for instance, of God as his witness (Rom 1:9; Phil 1:8), he witnesses
for the integrity of other people (1 Cor 8:3; Col 4:13), he refers to the two–or–three
witness rule of the Torah (2 Cor.13:1) and he suggests that we would bear false witness
to God if we do not believe the resurrection of the dead (2 Cor 15:15). See further
Coenen, 1043.

62. See 1 Cor 1:6: "the testimony [μαρτύριον] of Christ has been strengthened
among you." See also 1 Cor 2:1 and 2 Thess 1:10.

63. Coenen, "Witness, Testimony," 1043.

64. See also Rom 2:15 and 2 Cor 1:12.

65. According to Stambaugh (*The New Testament*, 30–36) in the Roman Empire in
the days of Jesus and the disciples, Roman law applied to Roman citizens, whereas local,
traditional laws applied to non-Roman inhabitants of the provinces. In Judea, the local
Jewish government that was appointed by the Romans administered justice over the
Jewish citizens according to the laws of Moses.

66. For negative testimony, see for instance Mat 18:6 or Mark 6:11 and also Luke
9:15.

we also find another sense of witnessing. At the end of his gospel, Luke tells about Jesus's last speech to his disciples. Jesus speaks of his disciples as witnesses (μάρτυρες) to his suffering, death and resurrection: "You are witnesses of these things" (Luke 24:48). This conception of μάρτυς coincides with what we've seen above in Section 3 in our discussion of how the ancient Greeks understood witness and testimony: the disciples are witnesses giving *positive* evidence.

In his gospel, Luke rarely uses the term or its derivatives in this way, but in Acts he does. The positive conception of witness is frequently used to describe the ministry of the disciples.[67] The first reference to the disciples as positive witnesses is in Acts 1, in a pericope corresponding to the end of Luke 24. Jesus says to his disciples: "But you will receive power when the Holy Spirit has come upon you; and you will be my witnesses in Jerusalem, in all Judea and Samaria, and to the ends of the earth" (Acts 1:8). In one way, the disciples are witnesses, for they have seen and heard: they have witnessed the risen Lord (Luke 24:48). Yet, through the power of the Holy Spirit, they are also capable of *bearing witness* to what they have seen and heard (Acts 1:8). In Acts, Luke tells the story of the apostles as witnesses driven by the Spirit, giving testimony (μαρτύριον) from Jerusalem to Rome. Finally, in Acts, the meaning of witnessing is never completely separated from its judicial sense: the disciples give positive *evidence*. When Paul or Peter speaks, they are not just proclaiming the gospel, they are witnesses bearing testimony to Jesus's resurrection for Jews and gentiles, and for Jesus himself who sits at the right hand and will come to judge the world (Acts 10:39–42; 26:22–23).

Bearing testimony is "giving positive evidence" in the Johannine and Lucan literature. In the gospel of John, the noun μαρτυρία and the verb μαρτυρέω are used frequently and refer to the positive testimony that Jesus is the Christ. The contrast with Luke-Acts, however, is significant. In the Lucan literature, the disciples are witnesses, but Jesus himself is *not* portrayed as a witnessing agent. In the gospel of John, all the testimonies, either by witnessing agents (John 1:7) or by Scripture itself (John 5:39), are dependent on the final and most authoritative testimony given by Jesus. Jesus is the ultimate witnessing agent, he speaks of himself as the one who knows that he is the Christ, and as the one who bears testimony to this truth: "Even if I bear witness of Myself, My witness is true, for I know where I came from and where I am going; but you do not know where I come from and where

67. Also see Luke 21:13: "This will give you an opportunity to testify." According to Coenen ("Witness, Testimony," 1043) it is not clear whether the idea that the disciples will give a positive witness before kings and governors is a typical Lucan invention, or an idea which can already be found in the parallel text in Mark 13:26.

I am going." (John 8:14 NKJ). Jesus's testimony is not accepted by Jewish leaders, only by his disciples. Jesus promises his disciples that when he is gone to his Father, he will send his Holy Spirit to help them to bear witness to the testimony of their master. In the letters of John, we find a similar use of μαρτυρία and μαρτυρέω.[68]

There is, however, also a striking similarity between the Lucan and Johannine literature. The testimonies of the Johannine Jesus and the testimonies of the Lucan disciples are controversial and often spark conflicts with those who listen to them. In the fourth gospel, those who do not accept Jesus's testimony seek to kill him, and when Jesus dies on the cross, they think they have succeeded. In Acts, Stephen is pictured as a Christ-like figure dying for his proclamation of the resurrection, and in retrospect, Paul calls Stephen a witness. The idea that witnessing to the truth is controversial and leads to suffering can also be found in the book of Revelation. In the second chapter, we read how Jesus himself speaks to John of Patmos about the disciple Antipas as "my witness, my faithful one, who was killed among you, where Satan lives" (Rev 2:13). Moreover, in his vision, John of Patmos sees the great whore who was drunk with "the blood of the saints and the blood of the witnesses to Jesus" (Rev 17:6). Just as the prophets of the Old Testament were killed for their prophecies of the truth, these witnesses are killed for their testimonies about Christ. Indeed, in Revelation 3, Jesus is portrayed as *the* archetype of a witness, he is *the* "faithful and true witness" (Rev 3.14).[69]

This short overview indicates that in a large part of the New Testament, the positive conception of testimony is dominant. In the Lucan and Johannine literature (including Revelation), Jesus, the disciples and the elders are not portrayed as accusing witnesses, but witnesses giving a positive affirmation. Apparently, the authors saw no problem with speaking of testimony in a way that is foreign to Hebrew law. Without doubts or reservations, these authors apply a conception of the witness and his testimony common to Greek law and philosophy. Thus, we cannot say there is a unique New Testament understanding of witness. The content of the witness's testimony is characteristic of the New Testament, not the conception of the witness and his testimony. And despite all the differences, one could say that the claim of these testimonies is the same: Jesus is the Christ.

68. See for instance 1 John 1:2 and 3 John 1:12.

69. In Hebrews, we read of the heroes of the Old Testament and how through faith they were capable of doing marvellous things, how they suffered and how they died. Twice we read that these women and men received an approval by God himself: by faith "the elders obtained a good testimony" (Heb 11:2, NKJ see also 11:39). And somewhat later these heroes are described as a crowd, a "cloud of witnesses" (Heb 12.2) encouraging present Christians to persist in faithfulness.

There are many resemblances between the disciples in Acts, John and Revelation and the witnesses in *With the Grain of the Universe*. Just as the disciples are in Acts and John, the Christians in Hauerwas's work are considered to be witnesses gifted with the Holy Spirit and called to proclaim their truth regarding God and man. In the New Testament this testimony that Jesus is the Christ evokes serious conflicts with those that hear it and these witnesses are prepared to suffer and die for their testimony. As we saw in chapter 1, Hauerwas discusses at length in two essays how his reflections on the character of Christian witness relate to how Acts speaks of the witnessing of the apostles. But remarkably, neither in this essay nor in other texts, does Hauerwas refer to the gospel of John or the book of Revelation.

6. WITNESS AND THE TESTIMONY OF THE MARTYRS[70]

Stories about those who refuse to renounce their convictions in front of hostile authorities are told by Greeks and Jews, for instance, Plato's apology of Socrates or the books of Maccabees. Characteristic of the book of Revelation is its strong emphasis on the relation between faithful witnessing and suffering (though a similar connection can be found in the work of Epictetus). In the light of Revelation, the first generations of Christians saw themselves as disciples of Jesus, a witnessing people, preferring suffering and death to denying the testimony of Christ. Some of them were actually prosecuted for proclaiming the gospel or for confessing they were Christians in court. These women and men—both those who were killed in the prosecutions and the survivors of the tortures—were honored by the title of *confessor* or μάρτυς.[71] Martyrdom is important for the early church. Christians believed that the ultimate form of faithfulness was answering Jesus's gift of his body and blood with the gift of their own. Many longed for it and, though they were not permitted to actively seek martyrdom, some even chose to give themselves up to the authorities. Others, however, did not remain faithful under the prosecutions and their apostasy led to heated discussions about whether they could return to the church.

The prosecutions by the Roman Empire were meant to silence Christians, but the effect was the opposite. People were impressed by the testimony of the *confessors* and μάρτυρες and many of them converted to Christianity. Tertulian writes in his apology: "The oftener we are mown down by you, the more in number we grow; the blood of Christians is seed."[72] Through

70. This section largely relies on Gerlitz, "Martyrium."

71. See ibid., 208–10.

72. Tertulian, "Apology," 82.

the impact of Christian martyrdom on late antique society, the meaning of μάρτυς altered. In the second half of the third century, in Greek and Latin, the term—that simply meant "witness" in the classic Greek of Plato and Aristotle and in the koine Greek of the New Testament—became used to describe people persecuted to death for being Christian. Whereas in the books of the New Testament suffering and dying is the ultimate consequence of proclamation of the gospel by the μάρτυς, since the third century, the genuine μάρτυς or *martyr* is a person suffering and dying for their faith in Christ. Moreover, the stories of the martyrs were written down, and the new literary genre of the martyrology appears. For the church, these martyrologies were a useful instrument for propagating Christian faith.

The term martyr has been adopted in all European languages to describe a person suffering and dying for his convictions. In other places and times, both the notion of martyrdom and the genre of the martyrology have been reinvented. See, for instance, how in the Reformation and Counter-Reformation, Protestants and Roman Catholics wrote martyrologies about how "their" martyrs were killed by violent oppression by adherents of the "false religion."[73] Since the rise of the nation state, the notion of martyrdom and the genre of martyrology has been secularized and is used to justify the violent death of soldiers and other victims of war and despair. These people are portrayed as martyrs giving their lives for their country.[74]

As we saw in chapter 1, Hauerwas has a specific view on martyrdom. He argues that Christian martyrdom must be thought of in relation to non-violent ethics and a non-Constantinian politics. Thus, for Hauerwas, just as for the early church, a martyr is not a soldier dying in the wars of an empire, but a Christian suffering for his refusal to fight for the Pax Romana or Pax Americana. Yet, though Hauerwas conceives martyrdom as the ultimate consequence and even the most determinative display of witnessing, unlike many propagators of martyrdom in the early Church, he does not separate martyrdom from the witness's life. Indeed, from Hauerwas's perspective, the violent death of Christian martyrs can only be understood correctly in relation to the faithful life of their communities.

73. See Gerlitz, "Martyrium," 216.
74. See ibid., 200.

7. WITNESS AND TESTIMONY IN THE CHRISTIAN TRADITION[75]

Section 5 has indicated that there is no such thing as a unique New Testament concept of witness and testimony. In many New Testament texts the terms witness, witnessing, and/or testimony are applied to describe the ministry of Jesus Christ and/or his disciples. As we shall see below, in the Christian tradition, texts in John, Acts, and Revelation have instructed Christians about the character of God's revelation, the nature of Jesus Christ and the purpose of the Christian life.

Before discussing the Christian tradition, we will examine the other Abrahamic religions. Both Jews and Muslims speak of themselves as witnesses to God. For Jews one of the most significant verses in the Thora is Deut 6:4: "Hear, O Israel: The Lord is our God, the Lord alone." This verse is the beginning of the prayer Shema Yisrael and the basis of Israel's confession that Yahweh is the one and only God. In Masoretic manuscripts, two letters of Deut 6:4 are enlarged, the Ayin and Daleth, together these letters form the word עֵד (witness). Jewish commentaries explain that anyone who hears this verse is being called as a witness to it.[76] The Koran describes how in the last judgment the believers and unbelievers will be called to bring witnesses in favor of their case.[77] Furthermore, God himself is described as a witness—*shahīd* is one of God's "beautiful names." In later Arabic the word *shahīd* takes on a new meaning: martyr.[78] Finally, in Islamic tradition the word *shahāda* refers to the Islamic credo: "I testify that there is no god except God and I testify that Muh.amed is the messenger of God."[79]

As we discussed in the previous section, John and Luke speak about the testimony of the Scriptures, and Psalm 119 praises the testimonies of the

---

75. This section largely relies on Von Lüpke, "Zeuge, Zeugnis." For my understanding of the theology of the church fathers and reformers, I am indebted to Reeling Brouwer, *Grondvormen*.

76. This tradition can be traced back to Rabbi Jacob ben Asher (1269–1343). Rayner, *Jewish Religious Law*, 95. The rabbinic commentary Pesikta de Rav Kahana (before the seventh century) notes on Isaiah 43:12 "You are my witnesses, and I am God" (Isaiah 43:12) Rabbi Shimon ben Yochai taught: "Only when you are my witnesses, I am God, but when you are not my witnesses, it is as if I am not God" (Neusner, *Pesiqta deRab Kahana*, 12:6).

77. Radscheit, "Witnessing and Testifying," 494.

78. In Arabic, a similar development as in Greek can be noted. According to Rippin this change of meaning can be traced back to Christian influence on Islam: "the development from witness to martyr derived from Christian Syriac usage of the cognate *sāhda* in translating the Greek *martus*" ("Witness to Faith," 488).

79. See ibid., 488.

Lord. From these texts stems the idea that God himself is witnessing in Scripture. Moreover, Christians thought that these testimonies hold knowledge, not only about God, but also about the character of human beings, nature and history. Both Augustine and Aquinas depict a harmony between general knowledge coming from inference, observation and memory and specific knowledge coming from God's testimony in Scripture. For Augustine, God reveals himself in time by creating temporary events that witness to eternity, and the Bible is the most important expression of this self-revelation. The goal of creation is to answer this divine testimony by bearing witness to the One through whom creation exists. Augustine struggles with the skeptical tradition of Greek philosophy. In his early work, he argues that communication through signs cannot constitute true knowledge. But he could not deny that in Scripture, God's testimony is communication through signs. Augustine argues in his later work—in a way not unlike the anti-reductionist epistemologists that we'll discuss below in Section 10—that human beings have to rely on reports from others. In contrast to modern anti-reductionism, however, Augustine calls the act of trusting another's words "belief," and he argues that it's not irrational to believe, either in the testimonies of others or in God's testimony in Scripture.[80]

With regard to weighing up other people's reports, Aquinas's position is similar to Augustine's. But Aquinas has his own way of assessing the relation between general knowledge and the knowledge from the testimonies in Scripture. According to Thomas, it's possible to acquire some knowledge of God and the world through his general revelation to which creation testifies. But to know God and the world completely, we need the testimony of Scripture, and in particular the ultimate witness given by Christ. Those who believe answer this specific testimony by imitation of and participation in the ultimate witness of Christ.[81]

In the Reformation, the testimony of Scripture becomes the main argument against the habits and teachings of the papal church. The harmony between the divine testimony in Scripture and what is known generally collapses. The reformers prefer evidence from God's own testimony to general knowledge from reason. For Luther every man is a sinner, a false witness not capable of hearing the testimony of God in creation. Man can only be saved when he lets himself be persuaded ("über*zeugen*") by the word of God in Scripture. Calvin, in reaction to the appeal to the Holy Spirit by the Radical Reformation, refers to Romans 9:1 and develops the teaching of the inner witness of the Holy Spirit. He argues that in his word God bears witness of

80. See Von Lüpke, "Zeuge, Zeugnis," 1325.
81. See ibid., 1326.

himself and this word will only find faith in the heart of men if it is sealed with the inner testimony of God's Holy Spirit. Thus, the inner testimony of the Spirit affirms the outer testimony of Scripture.

In the centuries after the Reformation, the idea of God testifying in Scripture, and Scripture testifying to God, becomes problematic. With the rise of science and Enlightenment philosophy, the status of knowledge from Scripture has come under attack. A thorough critique comes from Hermann Reimarus who argued that a human testimony of divine revelation through miracles cannot be accepted as persuasive for all. For Reimarus the inner testimony of reason does not need an outer confirmation by an authoritative text.[82] A parallel development can be discerned in the pietistic movements of orthodox Protestantism in which testimony is conceived as an outer expression of an inner pietistic experience. This tradition will be further discussed in Section 9.

This section points out that testimony, witness, and its derivatives belong to the vocabulary of Christian faith and have been used to describe divine speech acts and human answers. Moreover, Hauerwas's conception of witness as a human answer to God's call corresponds with traditional Christian accounts of witness. Likewise, important strands in the Christian tradition affirm that witnessing truthfully and faithfully is only possible with the help of the tutelage of the Holy Spirit. But where the figure of the witness and the notion of testimony are at the heart of the theology of Luke and the Johannine authors, it seems that for Augustine, Aquinas, Luther and Calvin, testimony and witness are terms only belonging to Christian vocabulary. It was only after the Reformation that the special character of the witness and the notion of testimony were reinvented.

8. WITNESS AND THE TESTIMONY OF LIFE

Hauerwas speaks of witness in a particular way. In his work, witness not only refers to specific utterances or actions, but more generally to an *ethos*, to a particular way of living. This section examines the roots of this specific notion of what could best be described as "the testimony of life." While the idea that what we believe and proclaim cannot be separated from how we live can be found on almost every page of the Old and New Testament,[83] the

---

82. See ibid., 1326–28.

83. See for instance Brueggemann, *Theology Old Testament*, 695–705, and Rowe, *World Upside Down*, 139–76. Brueggemann and Rowe will be further discussed in · Chapter 4.

Bible does not describe this particular way of living as a "testimony of life."[84] This specific understanding of witness as an ethos can be found in the Free Church tradition.

In the service of the first European Anabaptists and their heirs in Northern America, giving testimony was a vital part of the liturgy. According to the *Global Anabaptist Mennonite Encyclopedia* in the congregations of the American Mennonite (Mennonite Church) and Amish Mennonite groups, it was customary for the ordained men to "sit on 'the long bench' behind the pulpit on the pulpit platform throughout the service and at the close of the sermon to have each in order of seniority, from a seated position, give a brief 'testimony' to the sermon."[85] Indeed, "giving testimony" has become a well-known ritual in Free Church liturgy. During the service, the pastor invites the members of the congregation to stand up and share their testimony with the other members. This testimony will often refer to personal experiences in the life of the speaker or witness.[86] Often this testimony is a verbal expression of the inner emotions of the speaker or sometimes it's a story about life and how the witness has dealt with a certain issue. It is not difficult to see why this ritual became a part of the Free Church tradition. In the services of the Free Church, the presence of Christ is neither guaranteed through the sacrament of the priest, nor through the reading and preaching of Holy Scripture. The community believes that when they come together, Christ will be there. Through the "ritual" of testimony the belief that he really is present is affirmed.

But testimony is more than just an element in the service. In the Free Church tradition, the lived life of a Christian is itself considered as a testimony. This specific conception of witness and testimony can be traced back to seventeenth century Quakers. In a letter from 1683, William Penn and his friends write: "this was ye testimony of life in our living assembly through many faithfull Brethren yt god was wth us and is wth us."[87] In this letter, the meaning is inverted: the term "testimony of life" does not refer to a statement about how an individual lives his life but to a lived life which by itself bears testimony that God is with the brethren. Likewise, in their declaration to Charles ɪɪ from 1660, the Quakers present themselves as a people who "testify to the world, that the spirit of Christ, which leads us into all Truth,

84. Speaking of the works of Jesus that testify of him, the gospel of John comes close to this idea (John 5:36). Strikingly, although in the gospel Jesus is unique for witnessing through his actions, his disciples bear witness only through what they say. See further chapter 4.2.3.

85. Bender, "Testimony."

86. See Peters, "Witnessing," 709.

87. Penn, "An Epistle from Friends."

will never move us to fight and war against any man with outward weapons, neither for the kingdom of Christ, nor for the kingdoms of this world."[88] Moreover, they describe this way of living peacefully as their "testimony to the whole world." Another Quaker calls himself "a witness for the truth."[89]

In the early twentieth century, mainstream Protestants begin to speak of the Christian life as a life of witnessing. Witness terminology appears in theology (which will be discussed below in Section 11) and in missiological literature of the mainstream churches. Through the influence of Karl Barth, the third International Missionary Conference (Tambaram, 1938) speaks of mission as witness by Christians.[90] While in Tambaram's documents witnessing is considered as proclamation or evangelization, in later documents witness refers to how Christians live with others.[91] Referring to the various activities through which churches and individual Christians relate to "the outside"—that is, to those from other religions and secular society—it becomes almost synonymous with "mission."[92] In the 1960s, Roman Catholics begin to use witness terminology. In the Second Vatican Council, witnessing is an activity of the church, particularly of lay people in the church.[93] As *Lumen Gentium* states, Christians "make Christ known to others, especially by the testimony of a life [original Latin version: "testimonio vitae," a.b.] resplendent in faith, hope and charity."[94]

We can conclude that, though Hauerwas prefers to speak of "witness" and "witnessing" instead of the revivalist terms "testimony" and "testifying,"

88. Fox, *A declaration*. According to Hamm (*Quakers*, 101–8) in the ethics of the Quakers, the idea of testimony of life still plays an important role. They understand themselves as a people bearing testimony through a specific way of living. See for instance the "testimony of simplicity".

89. The 17th-century English Quaker Willam Mather describes himself as "A witness for the truth, as it was in the beginning" (*A brief character*).

90. See Molendijk, *Getuigen*, 13–18.

91. See ibid., 37–110.

92. See Jansen, *Talen naar God*, 88–95. Jansen concludes that though witness terminology plays a significant role in the articulation of missionary activities of the church, what is lacking in this literature is a thorough theological reflection on what witness is. The conception of witnessing and testimony remains abstract, and is separated from both its everyday and its judicial meaning and from the biblical understanding.

93. See Molendijk, *Getuigen*, 111–40.

94. Second Vatican Council, *Lumen Gentium*, section 31. The term "ecclesia testimonium vitae" can also be found in *Evangelii Nuntiandi*, an Apostolic Exhortation by Paul VI, section 43. Witness terminology can also be found in the ecumenical documents on mission. See Molendijk, *Getuigen*, 163–73. Recently the Pontifical Council for Interreligious Dialogue, the World Council of Churches and the World Evangelical Alliance published *Christian Witness in a Multi-Religious World*. This document addresses practical issues associated with Christian mission in a multi-religious world.

he is an heir to the Free Church tradition. Although Hauerwas has not examined the origins of his understanding of witness, there is continuity between his conception of the witness of life and the Quaker conception of the testimony of life.[95] For Hauerwas, Christians have been called to be witnesses of peace, and they show what peace is through their way of living. In a similar way, the early Quakers do not just speak of peace, but show what peacefulness means through their "testimony of life." Indeed, Hauerwas and the Quakers agree that witnessing itself is a peaceful form of communication. Moreover, with respect to the testimony of life, there is a connection between the early Quakers, the bishops of Vatican II, and Hauerwas. While living in different times and belonging to different ecclesial traditions, they agree on what role Christians should play in society. Christians must not try to re-Christianize society through a Constantinian politics of making Christianity the dominant religion in society. The notion of testimony of life helps them formulate this alternative politics. Yet there remains some obscurity in Hauerwas's account of witness. He does not explain *why* a particular way of living must be conceived as an authoritative testimony. He rejects "the Free Church option," that through the inner conviction of a pious soul, a particular way of living becomes an authoritative testimony. And his account is also different from "the Roman Catholic option" which holds that a particular way of living cannot be authoritative by its own but needs to be affirmed by the official teachings of the church. But if he rejects these two options, what does make witnessing through life an authoritative testimony? In this respect Hauerwas's account of witness remains somewhat unclear.

9. WITNESS AND THE TESTIMONY OF SURVIVORS

In our late modern societies, many groups and individuals use witness terminology to describe their role in the public domain. This is particularly true for people who witness catastrophes. Some of these witnesses are "thirds" who, by accident or on purpose, are present when a catastrophe occurs—for example, journalists[96] and human rights campaigners[97] who witness an injustice or disaster and bear witness so the whole world knows about it. Moreover, both in court and in the media, we meet witnessing victims: those personally affected by catastrophe. These witnesses feel that

95. Though Hauerwas mentions the example of the early Quakers, and their non-violent ethics (*Reader*, 427, 453, 614, 615), he does not discuss their understanding of the testimony of life.

96. See Plaisance, "The Journalist." See also Thomas, "Witness as Communication," 107–9.

97. See for instance the tagline of Human Rights Watch on Facebook: "Tyranny has a witness."

for the sake of justice, and truth, they cannot remain silent but must speak about what has happened to them—for example, genocide survivors[98] and victims of abuse.[99] Here we will discuss one example of the witnessing survivor: the witnesses who survived the Shoah.

In the first years after the Shoah, most of the Jews who returned from the Nazi concentration camps remained silent. They were incapable of speaking about what they witnessed. But some of them bore witness and wrote down their testimonies.[100] In short, sober sentences they describe what they saw. They write about the murder of their loved ones, about the industry of killing, about their own suffering, and about the complete coincidence that they survived. As Eli Wiesel remarks: "If the Greeks invented tragedy, the Romans the epistle and Renaissance the sonnet, our generation invented a new literature, that of testimony."[101] And as time went on, these witnesses gained audiences and Western societies began to realize what happened in the concentration camps. More and more witnesses felt that the world should know what happened to them and broke the silence. In the 1980s, thousands of interviews with survivors were recorded on video, so that the world could see the faces and hear the voices of these witnesses, even after their death.[102]

During the previous decades, a great deal of scholarly literature has been produced about the Shoah testimonies.[103] All these commentators seem to agree that the testimony of the survivor requires special attention. It is more than an illustration of the historiography of the murder of the Jews. Though careful historical research of the murder of the Jews is necessary, this research cannot grasp the deepness of the horror and the absolute strangeness of it.[104] If we want to know what the Shoah is, we must begin by listening to the witnesses, to those who were present. There are no third persons to this catastrophe, no neutral eyewitnesses who could give a

98. See for instance the website "Stories of the Cambodian Holocaust," with testimonies by survivors from the killing fields, the Cambodian genocide of 1975.

99. See for instance the website of the "Child Witness to Violence Project."

100. Levi (*The Black Hole*, 25) published his testimony from Auschwitz already in 1947. But it only received attention after it was reprinted in 1958. See also *If This Is a Man*.

101. Wiesel, "The Holocaust," 9.

102. See for instance the website of the "Fortunoff Video Archive for Holocaust Testimonies."

103. An overview can be found in Friedman, *Holocaust Literature*.

104. The psychiatrist Dori Laub (Felman and Laub, *Testimony*, 62) tells about a session with a survivor who was an eyewitness to a revolt in Auschwitz. He indicates that this woman does not just report of an historic event, she bears testimony to how the unimaginable act of rebellion breaks through the monotonousness of horror.

trustworthy report about what happened in places like Auschwitz. According to Dori Laub there are only offenders who were neither allowed nor willing to speak; or bystanders, who have lost their innocence through the very fact they remained bystanders; or victims, most of them killed before they realized what happened.[105] Indeed, Primo Levi emphasizes that, as a survivor, he is not a real witness. Survivors are exceptions who "by luck" were not immediately sent to the gas chambers. According to Levi, the real witnesses are those who died in Auschwitz. But, of course, they did not come back. Therefore Levi can do no more than bear witness to the impossibility of speaking about what Auschwitz really is.[106]

Hauerwas has written about Auschwitz, in particular about the guilt of Christians in relation to the Jews, but not about the relation between Christian witness and Shoah witnesses.[107] Yet, there are some remarkable similarities. Like the Shoah witness, the Christian witness which Hauerwas describes knows of something special, and feels a strong obligation to speak about it: the whole world must know what they know. What these witnesses bear witness to, however, is as different as day and night. For a full understanding of these similarities and differences further examination is required.

10. WITNESS AND TESTIMONY IN CONTEMPORARY PHILOSOPHY [108]

Contemporary philosophical reflection on the character of witness and testimony takes place in two different discourses: one debate is about the epistemological status of witnessing, the other considers the significance of the language of testimony in the crisis of modernity. But before discussing how Hauerwas's account of witness relates to these debates, we must first examine the debt he owes to the philosophy of Ludwig Wittgenstein.

In a groundbreaking study, Brad Kallenberg indicates how deeply Hauerwas has been influenced by Wittgenstein: "he has been enabled to think *through* Wittgenstein *by means of* the particular language of Christianity."[109] Kallenberg mentions three insights which Hauerwas gained from Wittgenstein. Firstly, Hauerwas has learned from Wittgenstein that to make good judgments, we need vision, and this vision can only be acquired through training in particular language games. Through this insight Hauerwas came

---

105. See ibid., 75–92.

106. See Levi, *The Drowned*, 83–84. See also the discussion of Levi in Agamben, *Remnants*, 33ff.

107. See "Remembering as a Moral Task."

108. This section largely relies on my own examination of the different authors. Futher, I have consulted Von Lüpke, "Zeuge, Zeugnis."

109. Kallenberg, *Ethics as Grammar*, 8. Emphasis by Kallenberg.

to see that a moral life is a life of transformed vision. In his work he tries to explain how the story of the gospel offers such a vision. By enacting this particular story, Christians acquire the skills which are needed to distinguish right from wrong. Secondly, Hauerwas has learned from Wittgenstein that language games are embodied in particular forms of life. Through this insight Hauerwas realized the importance of "concrete communities." In his work he argues that the meaning of Christian faith can only be grasped through participation in the particular form of life called "church." Thirdly, Hauerwas has learned from Wittgenstein how our understanding of reality depends on language. We need words to see the world as it is, but we also need the world to know the true meaning of those words. Through this insight, Hauerwas realized the importance of particularity. According to Hauerwas the practice of Christian faith heals us from our aspect-blindness and offers us words through which we see the world as it is, and not as it appears.

It's interesting to note that Hauerwas's preoccupation with witness cannot be traced back to his study of Wittgenstein. Wittgenstein rarely speaks about witness and testimony[110] and the remarks he has made do not seem to have influenced either Hauerwas's thoughts on witness or Kallenberg's study on Hauerwas.[111] As we have seen above, Hauerwas's interest can be explained culturally as deriving from the influence of the Free Church tradition and, as we shall see below, it can be explained theologically as coming from the influence of John Howard Yoder and Karl Barth. Yet in *With the Grain of the Universe* and his other work, Hauerwas uses Wittgenstein's insights to explain what we mean when we speak of Christians as witnessing witnesses. One important lesson Hauerwas learned from Wittgenstein is that language games "show."[112] He applies this insight to Christian faith,

110. The terms "testimony" and "witness" or (*Zeuge, Zeugnis* and *zeugen*) do not appear in Wittgenstein's first work, *Tractatus. Logico–Philosophicus*. In the posthumously published *Philosophical Investigations*, Wittgenstein makes some remarks about witnessing. He opposes the empiricist idea that when we say "I see red" we actually mean "I bear testimony of my observation of redness." According to Wittgenstein it makes sense only in very specific cases to say that we bear testimony of this or that observation. However, Wittgenstein does not give a coherent view on the different aspects of the character of witnessing. See Wittgenstein, *Philosophical Investigations*, 243–44 (section 386), 319–20 (416). See also *On Certainty*, 3–4 (8), 111–12 (441), 126 (485).

111. As we have seen in chapter 1, in his review essay on *With the Grain of the Universe*, Kallenberg does discuss the significance of witness in Hauerwas's theology. Yet he does not discuss how Hauerwas's account of witness relates to Wittgenstein.

112. See for instance the following quote from *On Certainty* cited by Hauerwas ("Witness," 135): "a language–game must 'show' the facts that make it possible. (But that's not how it is)," (162 [section 618]).

speaking of Christians as a people who are involved in specific language games and argues that what Wittgenstein means by "showing," resembles what Christians mean by "witnessing."

Yet in my view this approach has shortcomings. Wittgenstein does not offer Hauerwas the tools which are needed to formulate precisely what kind of speech witnessing is. Because Hauerwas lacks these tools, he cannot explain *in what way* showing is like witnessing, *what kind of* showing witnessing is, and *why exactly* the language of witnessing is relevant if we are to speak about the truth of Christian faith. As we have already seen in this chapter, in this respect his reflections on Christian witness remain unclear. His account is abstracted from the everyday and legal understanding of witness and testimony and he does not explain why witnessing through life can be considered authoritative testimony. Thus, I will continue this section by giving a short overview of available philosophical reflection on witness. In the next chapter I will examine whether some of the discussed philosophers offer the tools which are needed to describe Christian witnessing more precisely.

Philosophers interested in epistemology have discussed testimony for centuries. Classical epistemology discerns four sources of knowledge: perception, inference, memory and testimony (the latter being a report from others about observations, inferences or memories). The epistemological status of testimony has been under constant philosophical debate. On the one hand, philosophers see that man often relies on reports by others. Most of the time we believe what others tell us, and learn from their testimonies. Yet philosophers wonder whether information derived from testimony is as reliable as that which we get through our own observation and inference. There are three exemplary answers to this question. A first group of philosophers denies that we can gain reliable knowledge from reports by others. These philosophers have a far-reaching skepticism with regard to "everyday knowledge": we in fact know much less than we think we do. The second group consists of so-called "reductionists," who are prepared to recognize testimony as a source of knowledge, but only in so far as it can be reduced to other more fundamental sources. The third group, the "anti-reductionists," acknowledges testimony as an independent source of knowledge, having the same epistemological status as other sources.

As we have seen above, the first position is shared by Plato and Aristotle. Their views have strongly influenced Western thinking about the status of knowledge. Most early modern thinkers are reductionists.[113] A prominent and clear-cut reductionist is David Hume. Resembling a jurist who makes

---

113. Coady (*Testimony*, 120–30) mentions one exception: the eighteenth–century Scottish philosopher Thomas Reid.

rigid rules for the acceptance of evidence, Hume lays down strict criteria to determine whether a testimony can be considered true: a report is true when it is in correspondence with what we already know from observation and reason. For Hume, this means, for instance, that biblical reports about miracles are unreliable and therefore unacceptable. Contemporary epistemologists have realized that Hume's reductionism is problematic: in the process of acquiring knowledge we are more dependent on others than Hume realized. Some epistemologists recognize this and still hold a modest reductionism. Others defend the anti-reductionist position.[114] Recently C. A. J. Coady emphasized that knowledge necessarily has a social dimension: "our trust in the word of others is fundamental to the very idea of serious cognitive action."[115]

The similarities between the conceptions of witnessing and testimony in modern law and philosophical epistemology are not just coincidental. These conceptions are both strongly influenced by an Enlightenment understanding of rationality in which the deciding factor for the acceptance of a testimony is not the authority of the witness but the consideration of the rational subject. Christian perceptions of testimony are not completely different from the way the term testimony is used within the field of epistemology. After all, as we have seen in Section 1, contrary to the profession of faith, testimony is based on *personal experience*. Therefore C.A.J. Coady conceives Christian testimony as a genuine form of testimony.[116] But of course, the problem regarding Christian testimony is the status of this personal experience. The question any epistemologist would ask theologians such as Hauerwas is: to what experience do Christian witnesses refer, and why is this experience authoritative? In the next chapter we will use Coady's analysis of testimony to further examine this question and formulate an answer.

The other debate on the character of witness and testimony referred to at the beginning of this section, originates in the early nineteenth century. Søren Kierkegaard is the first to emphasize the significance of the idea of testimony.[117] Through the writings of his pseudonyms, Kierkegaard empha-

114. See for instance Fricker, "Varieties."

115. Coady, *Testimony*, vii. Coady criticizes both Plato's skepticism (3–24) and Hume's reductionism (79–100). In some respects, epistemological and legal approaches of witness correspond. Like law, epistemology is not interested in witnesses themselves, nor in the story they have to tell, but in the evidence produced by them. Just like jurisprudence helps the judge to decide whether to accept a testimony, epistemology is there to help scientists, scholars, and other professionals, to make rational decisions with regard to information derived from reports by others.

116. See ibid., 52–53.

117. See Kierkegaard, *Søren Kierkegaard's Journals and Papers* 4, 768–70.

sizes that questions about truth cannot be answered by Hegelian philosophy nor by traditional doctrinal theology but only by a more subjective discourse. As he is for Epictetus, for Kierkegaard Socrates is the paradigmatic example of the true philosopher. In his life and death he showed what it means to live for the truth.[118] But unlike Epictetus, Kierkegaard knows how in the New Testament Jesus and the disciples are pictured as witnesses bearing testimony of a controversial truth. In his religious discourses he discusses Christ's testimony to the truth before Pilate. Kierkegaard claims that Christians are called to follow the way of Jesus, even if others are offended by it. If they answer faithfully to this vocation, they will become, like Jesus, witnesses of the truth. To his disappointment, however, Kierkegaard sees no preparedness to be a witness in the Danish state church, no willingness to be a martyr. Indeed, Kierkegaard is outraged when the late Bishop Jakob Mynster is remembered as a witness to the truth in a speech by his former teacher Hans Martensen. In articles written for a Danish newspaper he attacks this characterization of Mynster and argues that what the New Testament means by witnessing—undergoing suffering, humiliation, and martyrdom—is the complete opposite of what this man stood for.[119]

Post-World War II continental philosophers such as Emmanuel Levinas, Paul Ricoeur, Jacques Derrida, and Giorgio Agamben began to use the terminology of testimony in a way that differed from the epistemological approaches.[120] These philosophers belong to a group of intellectuals who

118. See Kierkegaard, *Kierkegaard's Journals and Notebooks*, 4, 420.

119. See Kierkegaard, *The Moment and Late Writings*, ix–xxxi.

120. In the next chapter Ricoeur and Agamben will be further discussed. Levinas discusses testimony his essay "Truth of Disclosure and Truth of Testimony." He speaks of testimony in his opposition against Greek thinking (and its repetition in Heidegger's philosophy—a philosophy which, according to Levinas, could too easily be misused to legitimate the totalitarian politics by the Nazi's). Due to its focus on "enclosing being," Greek thinking cannot but treat testimony as inferior and second–hand. Levinas develops an alternative way of thinking, a philosophy which is aware of what is beyond being, the Infinite. While it refuses to enclose itself completely, the Infinite breaks into being and makes the subject responsible for the other. According to Levinas, through this awareness of responsibility, the subject bears testimony to the glory of the Infinite. Indeed, this special testimony is articulated in everyday language. We bear witness to the infinite when we do not hide ourselves from the face of the other, but respond to him or her by saying "Hello" or "here I am" (97–128). For Derrida (*The Instant*), testimony speaks about what is secret. When I bear witness, I make an assertion about something that is known to nobody else but me. Typical for testimony is that the witness refers to the secret, but does not disclose it: the secret becomes public without ceasing to be secret. And, since that which a witness witnesses remains secret, it is impossible to prove "beyond reasonable doubt" that a testimony is true. Derrida is aware that this view of testimony contrasts both with the epistemological philosophy and with legal traditions discussed above in Section 3. Epistemological and legal rules of evidence demand that one must distinguish between literature and testimony, between

saw themselves as being confronted with the moral and intellectual crisis of modernity, a crisis which manifested itself in the testimonies of the Shoah. In their philosophical searches, they come to speak of the figure of the witness and the notion of testimony. Indeed, like Kierkegaard, they apply the terminology of testimony to speak of a controversial truth.

Though Hauerwas is not directly influenced by this continental debate on the character of testimony, his project has similarities with those of the aforementioned philosophers. As we saw in chapter 1, for Hauerwas the practice of Christian witness offers a way to speak and act truthfully in a world without certainty. Therefore he can be classified as a criticizer of modernity who applies the terminology of testimony to speak of a truth which is forgotten or neglected in modernity.

11. WITNESS AND TESTIMONY IN CONTEMPORARY THEOLOGY [121]

In the work of some twentieth-century theologians we can find a conception of witness which is close to that of Kierkegaard's. First, I will discuss Karl Barth and then I will explain how American theologians such as John Howard Yoder, James McClendon, and Stanley Hauerwas can be also conceived as heirs of Barth and Kierkegaard.

In an essay from 1934, Barth already speaks about the Christian as a witness.[122] Just as Kierkegaard uses the terminology of witness in opposition to Hegel, Barth uses it in a theological discourse that distances itself from liberal Protestantism and its theologies. The Christian as witness does not speak about his inner experiences but bears testimony to how God reveals himself to man. We find the notions of witness and testimony at two crucial moments in his *Church Dogmatics*. Firstly, in his doctrine of the Word, Barth uses the term testimony to explain how Scripture relates to revelation.

---

fiction and truth. But according to Derrida, this distinction is not obvious; in fact it is itself fictional. Derrida is fascinated by how this difficulty to distinguish between fact and fiction manifests itself in (quasi)autobiographical texts—and he discusses a story by Maurice Blanchot which is included in his book. If we accept the uneasiness of this indistinctness, we will find how Blanchot testifies of something which cannot be known otherwise: in the case of Blanchot it is like the moment of death, always in abeyance. See also "Poetics and the Politics."

121. This section largely relies on my own examination of the different authors. I have used two additional sources: Assel "Zeugnis, Zum Begriff" and Scheuer and Fonk, "Zeuge, Zeugnis, Zeugenschaft."

122. Barth, *Der Christ als Zeuge*. See also *Witness to the Word*, Barth's lectures on the first chapter of the gospel of John at Münster in 1925 and at Bonn in 1933.

Scripture must be understood as a fallible human text, yet as such it is a testimony to the fact that God speaks his Word to man.[123] Through the help of the Holy Spirit the church understands Scripture as a testimony to God's revelation and bears witness to it.[124] Secondly, in his doctrine of reconciliation, Barth ascribes the term witness to Jesus Christ. Jesus Christ is not just the *Lord* who becomes *Servant*, or the *Servant* who becomes *Lord*, he is also the truthful *Witness* who makes himself known to man through his testimonies and who calls them to become his witnesses.[125] What it means to follow Jesus and to live as a witness is further elaborated on in the posthumously published fragments of the ethics of reconciliation.[126]

John Howard Yoder is a student of Barth and a representative of contemporary Mennonite theology. Yoder criticizes how dominant Protestant and Roman Catholic theology both past and present legitimize the use of state violence. In his early but significant book *The Christian Witness to the State*, he explains how pacifist Christians could relate to the modern nation state.[127] While Yoder opposes the idea that Christians have the duty or responsibility to serve the nation state in fighting war and enforcing order, he also believes that Christians should not withdraw from society. The term "witness" helps Yoder to articulate the role of the church in relation to the state. While along with the Free Church tradition Yoder speaks of witness as a particular way of living. Along with Kierkegaard and Barth, Yoder applies the notion of witness to refer to a controversial truth. The church has been called to live peacefully, and through their politics of peace, Christian communities bear witness to God, the true source of all peace. At the same time, the church has the prophetic task of addressing the state, particularly on issues relating to power and violence. The church must remind the state that it has no self-evident authority to use violence but that only the absolute minimum of violence is excusable.

James McClendon, a Southern Baptist, is strongly influenced by Yoder. Like Yoder, McClendon, holds that, though the church is not at home in this world, neither should it withdraw from the world. As a representative of the Free Church tradition, witnessing for McClendon is a way of living. For him, the vocation to be a witness implies that Christians share their lives

123. See for instance § 19–1 "Scripture as a Witness to Divine Revelation," in *Church Dogmatics*, I/2, 457–72.

124. See for instance § 20, "Authority in the Church," in *Church Dogmatics*, I/2, 538–660.

125. See the title of Chapter XVI, "Jesus Christ, The True Witness," in *Church Dogmatics* IV/3.

126. Barth, *The Christian Life*.

127. Yoder, *The Christian Witness*, 4.

not only with each other but also with others. McClendon elaborates on this in *Witness*, the third volume of his *Systematic Theology*.[128] While the first volume, *Ethics*, is about how the church must live, and the second volume, *Doctrine*, is about what the church must teach, *Witness* offers a theology of culture.[129] The leading question in McClendon's theology of culture is how the church, a people who know that ultimately they are not at home in the world, can nevertheless find a place in the world. In this quest of finding their place Christians are confronted with different phenomena such as religion, science, culture and philosophy. In the tradition of Kierkegaard, Barth, and Yoder, McClendon shows how Christian witnesses can remain faithful and not let themselves be bedazzled by religious, scientific, cultural or philosophical ideologies. McClendon nevertheless also points to the beauty of art and music and the truth of specific religious, cultural and philosophical insights, suggesting that to remain faithful to their vocation as witnesses, Christians must also be receptive to the culture in which they find themselves.

While Section 9 has indicated that—due to his emphasis on the significance of witnesses of life—Hauerwas can be regarded as an heir of the Free Church tradition, this section indicates that he is also an heir of what can be described as the Kierkegaardian-Barthian tradition. With regard to his understanding of witness, Hauerwas is indebted to Barth, directly through his study of *Church Dogmatics* and indirectly through his reading of and friendship with Yoder.[130] We can conclude that in the work of the American theologians Yoder, McClendon and Hauerwas, the Free Church tradition and the Kierkegaardian-Barthian tradition have come together in a new approach to Christian witness.

12. CONCLUSION

By setting out the different meanings of witness and testimony, this chapter conceptualizes Hauerwas's position. His account of witness is not far removed from the understandings of witness and testimony in Scripture, in tradition and in recent philosophy and theology.

- Hauerwas's notion of Christians as a people who have been called to be witnesses to the world, can be found in the writings of some of the authors of the New Testament and other Christian theologians in the past, and particularly in the work of contemporary theologians such as

128. McClendon, *Systematic Theology 3: Witness*, 1–47.

129. McClendon, *Systematic Theology 1: Ethics*, *Systematic Theology 2: Doctrine*.

130. See chapter 1.5.3.

Yoder and Barth. Speaking of the philosopher as a witness called by a divine decree, the Greek philosopher Epictetus resembles in some way these biblical and Christian authors.

- Hauerwas's idea that the Holy Spirit enables the church to witness truthfully and faithfully can also be found in Scripture and tradition. Moreover, the notion of *testimonium vitae* can be found in the Free Church tradition and in twentieth-century reflections on mission by Protestants and Roman Catholics alike.

- Moreover, the everyday, legal, biblical, Christian, literary, philosophical, and theological accounts of witnesses and their testimony concur with Hauerwas that witnesses are agents who claim to speak the truth in a situation of disagreement, dispute or conflict. Not only Christian writers, but also others such as Epictetus, conceive martyrdom as the ultimate consequence of witnessing faithfully and truthfully.

Nevertheless, we have also seen that Hauerwas does not give a thorough justification of why he deems the term witness so suitable for describing the character of the Christian life. Firstly, though he discusses Acts, he neither refers to the gospel of John nor to the book of Revelation, nor to the prophecies in Isaiah 43 and 44. In chapter 4 of this study I will discuss these books and examine how Hauerwas's understanding of witness relates to how these Bible books speak about witness and testimony. Secondly, this chapter has established that there is no exclusive Christian approach to witnessing but that legal and other conceptions have been integrated into Christian discourse about the figure of the witness and the conception of testimony. Hauerwas does not thematize this: *With the Grain of the Universe* refers neither to semantic and semiotic analyses nor to legal or philosophical reflections on the witness and his testimony. Since Hauerwas does not fully explain why Christian life could best be described as a testimonial practice and to what extent this testimonial practice resembles practices of witnessing outside the Christian community, his account of Christian witness remains in some ways vague and abstract. In the next chapter, I will examine whether it can be concretized and clarified.

CHAPTER 3

Concretizing and Clarifying Hauerwas's Account

STANLEY HAUERWAS STRESSES THE importance of concrete witnessing. In *With the Grain of the Universe*, he argues that Christians are called to bear witness through what they say and what they do, and that these concrete testimonial practices are necessary for salvation and for the right understanding of the character of God, ourselves and the world. But as we have seen in the previous chapter, Hauerwas's account of witness remains somewhat vague and abstract. He does not explain *how* we must see truthful and faithful Christians as witnesses or *in what way* their utterances, actions and lives could be understood as testimonial practices. Now the crucial question is what this conclusion means. If it indicates that it is impossible to describe Christian speech and action as a practice of witnessing, then in the end Hauerwas's plea for the necessity of witness could be dismissed as empty ideology. But there is another way of looking at it. It could be that Hauerwas's account is in need of further explanation. In that case, we could perhaps do what Hauerwas fails to and elaborate on the view of Christian speech and action as a genuine practice of witnessing.[1]

In this chapter, I argue for the latter. I will indicate that it's indeed possible to concretize and clarify Hauerwas's account of witness and to speak about Christian life as a testimonial life and of the Christian community as a community producing witnesses. However, these explorations will also reveal that in some respects Hauerwas's understanding of witness is one-sided. As we will see, some of these shortcomings can be corrected in this chapter. Others are more complex and will be further discussed in the next two chapters.

1. In this chapter I will often use the term "practice." I understand practice as "the actual performance of an activity in a real situation" (Rundell and Fox, "Practice").

The previous chapter established that, though it is typical for Christians to understand themselves as witnesses bearing testimony, there is no specific Christian conception of witnessing and testimony. Biblical authors and Christian theologians adopt everyday, legal and other conceptions of the witness and his testimony. In this chapter I will examine three philosophical approaches to these conceptions of witnessing. To be sure, it is not my intention to make a full comparison between Hauerwas and the three philosophers which will be discussed. I will "use" some of their insights as a heuristic instrument which will help me in my attempt to concretize and clarify Hauerwas's account of Christian witness. Thus, the role of philosophy in this chapter is quite similar to the role it plays in much of Hauerwas's own work.[2]

The previous chapter indicated that there are many philosophical conceptions of the witness and his testimony. Roughly speaking there are three approaches: analytical philosophers speak of testimony as a source of knowledge about facts; in the phenomenological and hermeneutical tradition, the witness testifies of a truth beyond the factual; and for post-structural philosophers, testimony is what remains after the crisis of knowledge. As we will see in this chapter, all these philosophical approaches are helpful but in rather different ways.[3] In the first section, the investigations of the analytical philosopher C.A.J. Coady are used to concretize Hauerwas's considerations on the ecclesial community of witnesses. In the second, the semantics of the hermeneutical philosopher Paul Ricoeur uncover that Hauerwas's approach is inadequate without a complementary display of the practice of individual witnessing and extraordinary testimonial acts. And in the third section, Giorgio Agamben's post-structural reading of the literature of survivors is applied to clarify how Hauerwas's conception of witness relates to this special form of testimony. In these sections, a short introduction to the philosophical analysis is succeeded by a larger segment in which Hauerwas's account of witness is concretized and clarified.

Finally, this chapter has significant theological implications but it does not contain systematic theological evaluations. A full systematic analysis of Hauerwas's understanding of Christian witness can only be given in chapter 5 of this study after an examination of the biblical understandings of testimony in chapter 4. The present chapter is no more than a thought exercise with two leading questions: what does this practice of witnessing which Hauerwas speaks of look like? And: can the obscurities of his concept be clarified?

2. See the introduction of this study.

3. A similar approach can be found in Brueggemann's, *Theology of the Old Testament*. In his introduction Brueggemann (119–20) discusses the character of testimony with the help of Coady, Ricoeur and scholarly literature on Auschwitz testimonies.

1. C. A. J. COADY—AUTHORITY, EXPERTISE, AND COMMUNITY

In 1992 C. A. J. Coady published *Testimony: A Philosophical Study.*[4] With this book, the Australian philosopher aroused interest among philosophical epistemologists in a topic that was scarcely discussed before: the epistemological status of testimony. His insights are useful for evaluating Hauerwas's understanding of Christian witness. This section consists of three parts. The first discusses Coady's understanding of testimony as speech act. The second deals with the witness's expertise and the transference of testimonies from one witness to another. And the third part considers an issue brought up by one of Coady's critics: the acceptance of testimony by the audience. Each part begins with a short introduction to the issue under discussion and is followed by an analysis of the corresponding aspects in Hauerwas's account of witness.

1.1a Coady's Analysis: The Speech Act of Testimony

Coady argues that witnessing is a specific speech act. It belongs to the more general category of asserting: the act of informing an audience that something is the case. There are roughly two different ways of presenting information. On the one hand the informant makes an assertion by presenting arguments that something is the case (arguing) or is not (objecting). Here the audience considers whether the arguments are persuasive, and if they are, they will accept the supplied information. On the other hand, the informant informs an audience by presenting himself as a witness: "one having a particular kind of authority to speak to the matter in question" (43). This is the essential characteristic of the speech act of testimony: the witness claims authority. Implicitly or explicitly the witness vouches for the correctness of the assertion: "I can inform you that *p*, since I have good reasons for knowing that *p*." The audience has to consider whether the witness is who he says he is, whether he has the authority he claims to have. If they think he has such authority they will accept his testimony, if they think he lacks authority they will reject it.

The following definition is essential for Coady's understanding of testimony:

4. In this section references to Coady will appear in the text.

A speaker S testifies by making some statement p if and only if:

1. His stating that p is evidence that p and is offered as evidence that p.

2. S has the relevant competence, authority, or credentials to state truly that p.

3. Ss statement that p is relevant to some disputed or unresolved question (which may, or may not be, p?) and is directed to those who are in need of evidence on the matter. (42)

Testimony is a statement *about* certain facts which is also evidence *for* those facts. The first of the above criterion can only be grasped when we look at the second: this "statement about" is also "evidence for," since it is spoken by a person. According to Coady "testimony is 'say-so' evidence" (27). We are invited to accept this statement because it is spoken by a person with competence, authority and/or credentials. This is evident in the formalized setting of the courtroom: a testimony is evidence because the speaker has the authority and credentials of a sworn witness and the competence of someone who speaks about facts he observed. But according to Coady, in non-legal situations testimony is also say-so evidence. A journalist writing a report presents himself as an authority able to give a reliable interpretation of what he saw and heard. A bus driver calling the name of the next stop may know something his passengers do not. Finally, the third criterion emphasizes that testimony is a statement made to inform the audience. The speaker asserts something new, something the audience did not know before. If the audience already knows what a person tells, he is not a witness for them. For regular passengers in the bus, the bus driver's call is not a testimony since they know the route by heart.

1.1b Coady's Analysis and Hauerwas's Account

For Hauerwas, witnessing is more than speaking. It involves deeds. In fact, it involves the lives we live. Though Coady's focus is almost exclusively on testimony as a verbal utterance, there is something quite relevant in his analysis. Coady's definition indicates that Hauerwas's reflections on witness as the communication of Christian beliefs *and* as an argument for Christian faith are not as strange as they might appear. For Coady, witnessing is a speech act in which an agent makes an assertion *and* claims to have authority and competence to inform correctly. The very fact that a statement is given by a person is brought forward as an argument for the correctness of this statement. The testimony is spoken by a *witness*, an authoritative person.

Furthermore, Coady's analysis helps to clarify Hauerwas's conception of the act of witnessing. If a Christian says to his non-Christian neighbor "God forgives all sins" or "conflicts should not be solved by repayment and revenge but by forgiveness and reconciliation" he informs his neighbor about a particularly Christian way of speaking about God and man. And he does this while presenting himself as a witness with authority: he knows of forgiveness and reconciliation because he read of it in the Bible and/or because he himself experienced the liberating power of human and divine forgiveness and reconciliation. Moreover, Christians witness to each other. Preachers bear witness in their sermons of what they found in Scripture. Christians who experienced the importance of forgiveness and reconciliation in their lives witness to fellow Christians for whom forgiveness and reconciliation is just another dogma. In all these cases, the speech act of testimony is both a form of communication *and* evidence for the correctness of the statement. Of course this analysis is but the beginning of the evaluation of Hauerwas's account of witnessing. The bare fact that some Christians tend to put themselves forward as witnesses—women and men with sufficient competence, authority, or credentials to speak about the true character of God, man, and the world—does not mean that they actually *have* authority, that they *are* competent speakers. This issue will be discussed in the following sections.

1.2a Coady's Analysis: Expertise, Transference and Community

Many reports are not observations but reports of observations by others. In everyday communication we are often "hearsay witnesses" saying that p without observing p ourselves. In fact in many situations we say that p without any reference to the original observation by the original witness. Coady considers these reports of observations by others as genuine testimonies. He argues that in many cases the information can transfer from the original observer to others without a loss of reliability. By reporting reports, we create chains of witnesses: a reports to b, b reports to c, c reports to d, etcetera.[5] According to Coady, the hearsay witness at the end of the chain can often be conceived as an authoritative witness.

5. Coady (199–223) discusses John Locke who suggests that in the process of transferring information, the reliability of the report decreases. According to Locke, due to human failures and imagination the quality of the information at the end of the chain

Thus, for Coady testimony is an essential part of human communication. In fact, in almost every form of contact we are dependent on information given by authorities. A father explaining to his daughter the difference between horses and donkeys is an authority to his child, testifying about what he knows of animal life. But when his daughter tells him there is no milk in the fridge, she is an authority witnessing of her observations to her father. According to Coady testimony is vital, even in the scientific community where first-hand observations are held in such high esteem.[6] There is a "testimonial aspect" in all those forms of human communication in which information is transferred by an implicit or explicit reference to the specific expertise of the speaker.

As we saw in the previous chapter, reductionists such as David Hume claim that it's irrational to trust witnesses without critical deliberation. Testimonies can only be accepted if they can be traced back to an original observation by a rational observer. For Coady this reductionism makes no sense. He argues that the idea of knowledge, of "serious cognitive activity," presupposes a "basic trust in the word of others" (vii). Testimony is more than a vehicle for information, independent from observation, inference, and memory: testimony is a genuine source of knowledge. See for instance the expert witness in court. The authority of this witness does not stem from an observation of relevant facts but from a specific, scientific expertise. The expert witness testifies of what he knows, he gives a view based on scientific knowledge (27, 35, 277–303). But his expertise cannot be traced back to a single "original observation." The appropriation of scientific expertise begins with instruction from professors who teach their students to observe properly and to interpret their observations. The same is true for the father teaching his daughter the difference between horses and donkeys. One can only distinguish horses from donkeys through instruction by others, by learning words such as "horse" and "donkey," "big" and "small," "ear" and "hoof."[7] Therefore, Coady argues that a basic trust in testimonies from others is vital in order to know any subject.

---

is diminished. Coady proves that degeneration is not inevitable. Some persons in the chain could give an interpretation which the original observers could not give. In fact, through linking reports with other data, through reflection and discussion, it is possible to increase the quality of the information. Moreover, if there is more than one original witness to a fact, those collecting several testimonies might be better informed than the original witnesses.

6. According to Coady (8–13), authority is extremely significant in science. Specialist research in a particular subject can only be tested by the specialists in that subject. Other scientists must base their opinion both on the authority of the researcher (is it a PhD–student or a professor from a renowned university?) and on the authority of his colleagues (what do the other experts say in their reviews?).

7. To be sure, Coady does not want to propagate gullibility. Of course fathers and

Finally, in one section of *Testimony* Coady comes to speak about the religious account of testimony. For us this short analysis is very interesting. In religious contexts, the verb "to testify" is used "to specify the way a man's life or his deeds or some particular act (which can be an act of professing his belief) are to be treated as pointing to some transcendent reality." Coady suggests that his definition of testimony is still at work here, "although in a more heightened, dramatic, and mysterious form." When martyrs die for their beliefs, this is at least evidence or testimony *that* they believe. Moreover, "people who speak of the witness or the testimony of martyrs or the lives of men dedicated to certain ideals intend to convey by that language the idea that the words and deeds of the men (or women) in question stand to the "realities" they believe in, rather as reports stand to the realities they are about (all quotations 52)." At least for religious people, the words and deeds of martyrs and other witnesses are testimonies *to* what they believe. And Coady continues:

> It is one thing, however, to hold that the "religious" use of "testimony" or "testify" is intended to conform to, or legitimately extend, the sense of such terms, as defined by the speech-act model, it is another to hold that these intentions are successful, and another again to accept any of these testimonies as true. Whether this way of talking is ultimately intelligible will depend very much on the special competence and authority that it presumes the witnesses to have and, granting intelligibility, there is then the question of how we are to weigh the evidence presented. (52–53)

1.2b Coady's Analysis and Hauerwas's Account

Coady speaks of "religious context" in general, but his examples betray that he actually has Christian testimony in mind. Indeed, his remarks match with Hauerwas's account of Christian witness. As we have seen, Hauerwas suggests that the deeds, lives and acts of truthful Christians refer to a certain transcendent reality. Although, of course, Hauerwas would immediately add that one cannot bear witness to "a transcendent reality" in general, but only to a specific God, and that Christian testimonies involve claims not just about this God, but also about the character of man and the world.

---

experts fail and lie. There may be good reasons to be critical and to test the reports of others. But according to Coady one can only detect false reports "against the background of a subsequently discovered even greater or more significant corpus of correct reports" (95–96).

Moreover, from Hauerwas's point of view, Coady is correct when he says that for Christians the words and deeds of truthful and faithful witnesses *stand to* the realities they believe in. In Hauerwas's terms: witnesses *show*.

Coady's questions with regard to "religious testimony" are also relevant. Do Christian witnesses actually have competence and authority? And if so, how much weight can we give to their testimony? A complete answer to these questions requires a full theological understanding of witnessing and testimony and such an answer will be attempted in the final chapter of this book. Here Hauerwas's understanding of witness will be explained with the help of Coady's conceptions of testimonial competence and authority. And we will see that, from Hauerwas's point of view at least, some Christians have the competence to speak authoritatively about Christian convictions.

For Hauerwas, the competent and authoritative witnesses of the church are not necessarily the clergy or theologians. Witnessing is not dependent on ordination or academic education. Witnesses who have authority and competence are those women and men who have tested Christian beliefs in their lives, and have found that these beliefs make sense: people who bear crosses reveal the grain of the universe. From Coady's perspective, the faithful and truthful witnesses playing such an important role in Hauerwas's theology can be considered as "expert witnesses"—witnesses whose authority does not stem from a particular observation but from specific expertise. Hauerwas's witnesses have expertise since they have tested Christian convictions in their lives. The relevant experience of these witnesses is not the inner religious feeling, but the outer "pragmatic" experience that it works, that beliefs pass the test, that these beliefs show a way to act truthfully in a world without certainty.

Coady argues that we are dependent on testimonies from experts—not only in court but everywhere in our society. Hauerwas would add that we are also dependent on the expertise of Christian witnesses. Just as children need their parents' testimony to see the difference between horses and donkeys, just as students need their professor's testimony to see the difference between cause and effect, we are in need of the testimonies of Christian witnesses to see the difference between wrath and forgiveness, between fate and providence, between idols and God. In *With the Grain of the Universe* Hauerwas argues that for a trustworthy knowledge of ourselves, the world, and God, we need witnesses who have tested Christian convictions in their lives, witnesses such as John Paul II, John Howard Yoder and Dorothy Day.

According to Coady, the expertise of the witness does not spring from the brilliant mind of an individual. Expertise is a skill which is acquired through instruction by an expert. Hauerwas agrees with Coady. For him, the church is a community which trains people to become experienced witnesses. Indeed, John Paul II, John Howard Yoder and Dorothy Day can be conceived as masters who instruct other Christians in the skill of witnessing. Like other masters, these commanders of Christian witnessing encourage their pupils to imitate them and test their learning in practice. If the pupils are willing to do this, little by little they will gain enough expertise to become themselves a master in the art of Christian witnessing. For example, if we are prepared to test whether our master's testimony regarding forgiveness makes sense in our own life, if we dare to forgive "those that trespass against us," then we ourselves will be capable of giving an authoritative testimony on forgiveness.

But from Hauerwas's point of view, even the most authoritative Christian masters remain sinful. Like scientists, Christians need testimonies by other masters to verify their own reports. What is more, Hauerwas claims that the sins of the faithful even witness to the God who makes it possible for Christians to know and confess their sins. Indeed, for scientists, the negative results of an experiment may—if interpreted correctly—still give useful information. Similarly, reports about failed tests of Christian conviction in life are far from worthless. In these reports, Christians witness that they are sinners depending on a God who reveals the sin and forgives the sinner.

Coady emphasizes that many testimonies in ordinary life, in science and even in court are not based on personal experiences, but on those of others. This is also true for Hauerwas's account of Christian witness. Communal training by witnesses requires more than references to the master's personal experiences—the experiences themselves are often too trivial for an authoritative and competent testimony. Masters must refer to other witnesses who have more experience in testing Christian faith. Through these references testimonies are transferred from one witness to another: the witness bears witness of a testimony by another witness. By sharing their own testimonies and by referring to the testimonies by expert witnesses from other times and places, Christians train each other to see the world as creation, to see strangers as their neighbors, to see God as triune.

Thus, Coady's analysis of testimony helps to concretize Hauerwas's conceptions and to describe the features of a communal practice of Christian witnessing. In the life of the church, witnessing is vital. Christians witness in the catechesis to the youth and proselytes, in communal instruction, in sermons, in books, but also in informal relations. Since some witnesses have more experience in living as a Christian, and/or have the ability to interpret testimonies and link them to other testimonies or Scripture, they have more authority than others. For some, Christian faith is new. These people need training by more experienced witnesses but their testimonies are not irrelevant since they may have tested Christian faith in a new and fresh way.

Finally, for Hauerwas Christians do not only witness to other Christians. In their daily interaction with their neighbors, Christians meet people who are not sure whether they are a Christian and those who are sure they are not. The testimonies of Christians are also directed towards these people: Christians bear witness to non-Christians of their experience in testing faith. Thus, just as there is a testimonial dimension to almost every form of human interaction, Christians bear witness in many ways, indeed in almost any form of formal and informal contact with others.

Coady's analysis is not just helpful for depicting the features of a community of witnesses. His analysis proves that the practice of authoritative witnessing requires some sort of communal training. Coady's analysis indicates that Hauerwas says nothing extraordinary when he claims that individual witnesses are produced by witnessing communities. And perhaps it's even possible to conceive the Christian tradition as a chain of witnesses in which testimonies about God, man and the world are passed from one generation to another. In this chain of witnesses, the degeneration of testimonies is not unavoidable. By testing Christian faith in new times and situations, by linking these testimonies to the testimonies of earlier witnesses, by thinking over and discussing old and new testimonies, Christians continue to testify truthfully and faithfully. Through the reports of the continuing tests of Christian beliefs in the lives of Christians, both believers and non-believers learn to understand what Christian faith entails.

Yet, from Hauerwas's point of view, Coady's understanding of testimony is in some respects problematic. Though Hauerwas would admit that there is a social aspect of our knowledge and sides with Coady against reductionism, he would reject Coady's conception of what can be described as a "natural epistemological togetherness." As we discussed earlier, Hauerwas argues that the world is made up of connections between contingencies and therefore people report differently. What they report depends on how they are trained and on which conceptions and stories they use. Hauerwas shows in his work that parents, professors and popes fail and lie more often and more seriously than Coady realizes. We are too often confronted with false reports, conceptions and stories to have a basic trust in the words of others. Moreover, we are often not prepared or able to speak the truth ourselves. Hauerwas therefore suggests that only when people learn to recognize their failures and learn to confess their lies can they learn to speak truthfully. Only when people learn to deal with their "natural" prejudice and fear towards others are they able to trust the words of others. But if Coady's notion of testimonial community is too harmonious, the same is true for the portrayal of a communal practice of Christian witnessing developed here. It is too kind, too beautiful. It hides the fact that there are serious conflicts within Christian communities, conflicts between testimonies, between witnesses. It hides the fact that communities suffer from perjury and insincere testimonies. These issues will be dealt with in Section 2.

1.3a Supplements to Coady's Analysis

Testimony: a Philosophical Study is widely discussed within philosophical epistemology. Many of Coady's critics argue that the act of bearing witnessing and the process of accepting testimony are more complex than Coady suggests. In a review article, Peter Lipton indicates that a trustworthy witness is more than a competent speaker.[8] According to Lipton "the connection between epistemology and ethics is almost entirely ignored by standard epistemological literature" (7). He argues that the speech act of testimony involves a double claim which connects epistemology to ethics: the witness does not just claim to know relevant facts, he claims to give an honest report about those facts. Implicitly or explicitly the witness promises not to lie but to speak "the whole truth and nothing but the truth."

Furthermore, Lipton analyses the audience, the people listening to the witness's testimony. According to Lipton, audiences only accept testimonies if "the truth of what was said is (part of) the best explanation of (among other things) the fact that the informant said it" (27). Thus, a testimony is only accepted after deliberation and this procedure of deliberation is rather complicated. First, the audience deliberates over the content of what is being said and, in contrast to Coady, Lipton holds that many reports are refused not because the witness seems incompetent but simply because the statement seems false. Second, the audience deliberates over the person who bears testimony. Parallel to the double claim of the witness, in the deliberation of the witness's trustworthiness there are two criteria: competence and integrity. The audience wonders whether the witness is both capable of knowing what he claims to know and is willing to speak "the whole truth and nothing but the truth." Thus in its deliberations, the audience often makes complex considerations such as "this assertion sounds not unlikely but the speaker has a reputation for lying"; or "this assertion seems very strange to me, but the

---

8. Lipton, "The Epistemology." In this section references to Lipton will appear in the text.

speaker is a competent observer and an honest human being." The testimony will only be accepted when the audience believes that the correctness of the testimony is the best explanation of the fact the witness said it.

1.3b Lipton's Supplements and Hauerwas's Account

Lipton's insights help to further clarify Hauerwas's conception of witnessing. In some situations Christians might reject reports from other Christians not so much because the informant lacks authority but simply because the report seems wrong.[9] But for Hauerwas, biblical and doctrinal correctness is never sufficient. To be accepted as true, statements about Christian beliefs should implicitly or explicitly refer to relevant and authoritative experience. Quasi-objective descriptions of the nature of Christ might not be incorrect, but they cannot inherently be true since they fail to refer to experiences of the test of these beliefs in the lives of those within the Christian community. Moreover, other testimonies cannot be accepted since they refer to non-authoritative experiences, for example, the crusaders crying "Christus Victor."[10]

Lipton explains that there is a cognitive and moral dimension to the witness's authority: the witness claims to be true and honest. Though Hauerwas does not speak explicitly about the connection of competence and integrity, it is obvious that when he speaks of the witness's truthfulness and faithfulness he refers both to competence and integrity: a truthful and faithful witness is able *and* willing to speak the truth. In *With the Grain of the Universe* Hauerwas suggests that truthfulness and faithfulness are characteristics of genuine Christian witnesses: faithful are those who live in allegiance to Christ, truthful are those who are capable of speaking the truth. Thus, Hauerwas would agree with Lipton that witness and testimony connect ethics to epistemology—and this is exactly why the idea of witnessing is so inspiring for him.

But from Hauerwas's point of view, Lipton's analysis is nothing but an affirmation that though ethical and epistemological matters can be distinguished from each other, they should not be separated. According to Hauerwas, humans lack a natural capacity to speak truly *and* honestly about God, man and the world. This is why Hauerwas stresses the importance of moral and intellectual training by the church. And though in *With the Grain of the*

---

9. I'm thinking of statements such as: "the Old Testament is not relevant for Christians," or "Jesus actually preached the gospel of reincarnation."

10. Of course it is George Lindbeck who gives this famous example in his discussion of truth: *The Nature of Doctrine*, 64. Hauerwas discusses this example in *With the Grain of the Universe*, 176n.

Universe Hauerwas does not speak of this explicitly, he implicitly suggests that truthfulness and faithfulness must be considered as virtues. Truthfulness is the virtue of not deceiving oneself but of seeing the world as it is. Faithfulness is the virtue of keeping the faith despite temptations. And, of course, these skills and virtues can only be acquired by training. Though the wrong training will result in improper tests, and in untruthful and unfaithful testimonies (the crusader's cry), the right training will result in proper tests and in truthful and faithful testimonies (the martyr's prayer).

But what about all those preachers who give beautiful sermons on forgiveness or reconciliation but who find it very hard to practice what they preach, are their testimonies unacceptable because of their moral failure? And what about all those pious women and men doing good works but who find it hard to reflect on what they are doing, are their testimonies unacceptable because they lack the right words? In his work, Hauerwas shows that if these preachers and pious people were autonomous individuals, the answer to this questions would be "yes," but since they form a community of witnesses, the answer is "no." The testimonies of failing preachers and simple laymen can be accepted as true since they are corroborated by each other. In its deliberations of testimonies the community realizes that no human testimony has absolute authority. Since Christians are in constant training the acceptance of their testimonies is always conditional, it needs corroboration by other testimonies. Thus, if such preachers and pious people are prepared to learn from each other, the community's expertise and moral authority increases.

1.4 Conclusion

The analyses by Coady and Lipton have been helpful to clarify Hauerwas's account of Christian witness. Firstly, the analogy with Coady's philosophical study demonstrates that though Hauerwas applies the term witness intuitively, he has a good sense of the "logic" of testimony. Hauerwas is right to conceive witnessing as a form of communication *and* as an argument for what is communicated. This is typical for testimonial statements. Secondly, Hauerwas is right to connect witness and community. According to Coady the very idea of testimony presupposes a community in training. Thirdly, Lipton's article suggests that honest and competent witnesses are moral and cognitive authorities, and this is what Hauerwas suggests with regard to Christian witnesses. But perhaps the most important conclusion of this section is that Coady and Lipton's insights help to concretize Hauerwas's conception of witnessing. Though Hauerwas's own account of witness remains somewhat vague and abstract, this section demonstrates that it is possible to clarify his conceptions and view Christian speech and action as a genuine practice of witnessing. We have learned that authoritative and competent witnesses are women and men who have tested Christian beliefs in their lives and found that these beliefs make sense, and that the church is a community in which witnesses bear witness to each other and to others of their experiences in testing Christian faith.

Yet, there are at least two clear differences between the epistemological approaches of Coady and Lipton, and Hauerwas's account of Christian witness. Firstly, for Coady and Lipton, witnesses report "verifiable information," i.e. data concerning observed facts. In their view, testimony is evidence that something is the case. Yet for Hauerwas witnesses do not so much report data but rather communicate a particular vision. In his view testimony is evidence yet it does not prove that something is the case but that this particular vision makes sense.

Secondly, Hauerwas holds that Christian speech cannot be abstracted from Christian action and that witnessing involves both speech and action. In some ways Coady's analysis affirms Hauerwas's first claim. Coady suggests that speech *is* human action. The speech act of testimony is a specific type of human interaction in which information is transferred from one subject to another. Testimony is a specific verbal practice which can only be understood within the broader context of human interaction. But Coady's conception of testimony as a speech act is not an affirmation of Hauerwas's second claim. And although Coady affirms that in the "religious" conception of testimony words *and* deeds of particular men and women testify to the "realities" they believe in, his analysis does not help us to see how this is true or in what sense human actions or human lives testify. Yet, as we know by now, this second claim is crucial for Hauerwas's account of witness. For Hauerwas, witnessing is more than reporting the test of Christian convictions in life. It is a way of life. In the next section this claim is evaluated with the help of Ricoeur's semantics of testimony.

2. PAUL RICOEUR. INDIVIDUALITY AND PASSION FOR TRUTH

In 1972 Paul Ricoeur published the essay "L'herméneutique du témoignage."[11] A translation of this essay, entitled "The Hermeneutics of Testimony," was published in the anthology *Essays on Biblical Interpretation*.[12] Ricoeur's essay is unique for its combination of semantic analysis, biblical exegesis and

11. Ricoeur, "L'hermeneutique du temoignage."

12. In this section references to Ricoeur will appear in the text.

philosophical reflection.[13] In this section I'll only focus on those parts of Ricoeur's essay which are helpful to concretize and clarify Hauerwas's understanding of the practice of Christian witness.[14]

The first part of this section considers Ricoeur's semantic explorations. The second part discusses some other relevant explorations in the essay. The same as in the previous section, each part begins by introducing some aspects of the philosopher's approach followed by an analysis of some parts of Hauerwas's account of Christian witness. More than Coady's, Ricoeur's approach reveals inadequacies in Hauerwas's account. Therefore, with the help of Ricoeur, I'll propose some supplements to and corrections of Hauerwas's account.

2.1a Ricoeur's Analysis: Conflicts and Devotion

Some of Ricoeur's thoughts on the character of testimony resemble Coady's. Like Coady, Ricoeur speaks of testimony as an act of reporting. It "transfers things seen to the level of things said." The speaker and the audience have a particular communicative relation: the "witness has seen but the one who receives the testimony has not seen but hears. It is only by hearing the testimony that he can believe or not believe in the reality of the facts that the witness reports." Like Coady, Ricoeur says that the witness's testimony refers to facts, but unlike Coady, he holds testimony to be "quasi-empirical" (all quotations 123). For him, testimony is more than the plain, verbal transmission of information from one knowing subject to another.

According to Ricoeur, a report is a testimony when it interprets an event, proving an opinion or truth. "Testimony wants to justify, to prove the good basis of an assertion which, beyond the fact, claims to attain its meaning" (124). Of course there are situations in which our reports are just assertions about observations: for example, when someone is not around, we may say "he is not here." But as Ricoeur indicates, many reports are not just conveying information about observed facts. Often the speaker immediately gives a specific meaning to his observation, and as he narrates his findings he justifies what he says: "I have looked everywhere for him, but I cannot find him. He must be lost!" For Ricoeur, testimony is a hermeneutical speech act, in which the speaker interprets what he observed and justifies his interpretation.

13. In the next chapter I will discuss the exegetical section of Ricoeur's essay.

14. For an overview of how this essay relates to Ricoeur's other work see Mechtild Jansen, *Talen*. Jansen shows how *témoignage* and *attestation* are crucial terms both in Ricoeur's philosophical work and in his theological essays.

Ricoeur explains that this "quasi-empirical" sense of testimony is complemented by a "quasi-juridical" sense. In his essay, he treats legal testimony as a model for other forms of testimony, just as Coady does. Both philosophers describe testimony as a form of evidence. But what is de-emphasized by Coady is stressed by Ricoeur: testimony is given in a lawsuit between parties; testimony is evidence for or against parties and their claims. This does not just apply to judicial testimony but to all forms of testimony: testimonies are needed in situations where people disagree because there is no immediate certainty about an issue. And because there is disagreement on many issues, there are many occasions where witnesses testify. Indeed, in all those "situations in which a judgment or a decision can be made only at the end of a debate or confrontation between adverse opinions and conflicting points of view" (125).

Testimony refers to actual, experienced events and it is a particular interpretation of these events. According to Ricoeur, witnesses are often aware of this. The witness knows that other interpretations are possible and that conflicts between interpretations may occur and nevertheless he gives the audience *his* testimony. Moreover, inside and outside the courtroom the witness offers his report with a specific aim. A testimony is given in order to be judged. Though outside the courtroom the moment of judgment is not so well-defined, it is inevitable. The witness gives his testimony to the audience in order to receive a judgment. Therefore testimony presupposes a certain amount of trust. The witness gives his own testimony, his interpretation of what he observed, hoping that the audience will believe or at least respect what he has to say.

But Ricoeur reminds his readers that witnesses do not always speak the truth. Inside and outside the courtroom, witnesses commit perjury. According to Ricoeur, false testimony cannot be reduced to error: "false testimony is a lie in the heart of the witness" (128). It is a perverse intention, undermining the exercise of justice. And Ricoeur wonders, if the false witness is a serious offender, "what is a true witness, a faithful witness?" He answers by explaining that a true and faithful witness is not merely "an exact, even scrupulous narrator" but someone who has passion or "personal devotion" for the truth and for speaking the truth. If this witness bears testimony, he is not just giving a particular interpretation of an event. Implicitly or explicitly he seals his testimony with a personal attestation: "I say this since I believe that this is the truth and I want you to know it." Thus, for Ricoeur, testimony is more than a report about experienced events with quasi-legal features. Testimony is also an act of attesting to a personal concern for the propagation of the truth.[15]

15. In the work of a journalist all three aspects of testimony can be discerned. The

Ricoeur adds: "The witness is capable of suffering and dying for what he believes." The witness may become a martyr. Yet, martyrdom cannot directly be derived from the everyday and legal accounts of testimony. In court, the life of the accused is at stake, not the life of the witness. But in some situations the witness becomes the accused, because "society, common opinion, the powers that be, hate certain causes, perhaps the most just ones." Sometimes witnesses must be silenced, if necessary forever, exactly because they have a just cause, because they tell the truth. And Ricoeur continues:

> A great historic archetype arises here: the suffering servant, the persecuted just, Socrates, Jesus. . . . This is what we mean by the word witness. The witness is the man who is identified with the just cause which the crowd and the great hate and who, for this just cause, risks his life.

Making the link between the witness and the martyr is, however, not without danger. Martyrdom is neither argument, nor proof, it refers to "a test, a limit situation." Indeed: "The argument of the martyr is always suspect; a cause which has martyrs is not necessarily a just cause" (all quotations, 129).

According to Ricoeur, every testimony has two opposite poles: a confessional or "reflexive" pole and a narrational or "referential" pole.[16] On the one hand, we have seen that all testimonies refer to the world outside the subject: testimonies are narrations of reality given to an audience. Even the so-called "inner testimony of conscience" refers to something outside the subject, namely to a more than subjective morality. But every testimony is also given by a particular "I," a witness reflecting on himself in the very act of bearing testimony. The "I" is not anyone, the witness cannot be replaced by someone else. In the testimony the subject attests to itself. This particular person not only claims to have authority—he claims to have integrity and truthfulness, he claims to be an honest subject.

---

journalist's job begins by collecting facts. Reporters try to be there, to be eye–witnesses of the event. Their names are mentioned in the newspaper, their faces are visible on television. But journalism is not just about the transmission of information, it is about telling stories. The journalist tries to grasp the meaning of his observations, he gives a particular interpretation of the facts, knowing that others "who were there" tell other competing and sometimes conflicting stories. The journalist gives a report in order to be judged, by his editor, by his public, by his colleagues, and while he renders testimony, he vouches that his story is true and faithful. Journalism is vulnerable to many seductions, but the major corruption seems to be that journalism becomes uncritical drivel to please the public or shareholders—here journalists render false testimony. However, there are also journalists for whom telling the truth is a vocation, who have a passion for the truth, and their work attests of this inner devotion to tell the people what they need to know, even if they don't want to hear it. These journalists are prepared to suffer for what they believe. And indeed there are journalists who have died for the truth.

16. Jansen (*Talen*, 82) speaks of a referential pole.

Finally, Ricoeur gives some further analysis of phrases such as "the testimony of this act" and "the testimony of his life." In these phrases the definition of testimony is inverted: testimony is not a report about observed facts but an exterior, visible action attesting to an interior and invisible conviction or faith. But Ricoeur shows that this inversion of definitions does not indicate a rupture between the various meanings of testimony. There is a "fixed point around which the range of meaning pivots." This fixed point is the witness's devotion or engagement. Through the witness's engagement, reports attain meaning, and give a particular interpretation of the observation. Through the witness's engagement, actions attain meaning and testify to the faith of the actor: "It is this engagement that marks the difference between the false witness and the faithful and true witness" (all quotations 130).

2.1b Ricoeur's Analysis and Hauerwas's Account

In this subsection, Ricoeur's insights will be used to explain and supplement Hauerwas's account of Christian witness. First I'll explain how Hauerwas relates witnessing as a specific speech act to witnessing as a way of living. Then I'll use Ricoeur's understanding of legal testimony to clarify some aspects of Hauerwas's account of witness. Finally I'll argue that in some respects Hauerwas's account of witness is one-sided and must be supplemented with Ricoeur's reflections on the witness as devoted subject.

2.1b.1 *The Testimony of Life*

In the previous section, Hauerwas's understanding of witness was explained as an act of reporting the tests of Christian convictions in Christian life. Ricoeur's semantics indicate what was presumed in the section on Coady: the witness communicates his experience of testing Christian faith through interpretative narrations. This insight helps to describe more precisely what Hauerwas suggests when he speaks of witnessing as a practice of speaking truthfully. When the witness speaks about how he tested specific conviction in his life, he narrates, he tells a story in which he reflects on himself, his interaction with others, on the world he lives in, and on the God he worships. And the more expertise a witness has, the more he is capable of narrating his experience with the help of biblical images and stories, doctrinal reflections, and testimonies by authoritative witnesses past and present.

But, as we know, for Hauerwas witnessing is more than a verbal practice. In *With the Grain of the Universe* he speaks of Christians bearing witness through speech *and* action, through their entire way of living. Ricoeur's approach corroborates Hauerwas's understanding of witness as action and as a specific way of living. However, it also indicates that the relation between these various conceptions of witnessing is more complicated than Hauerwas seems to realize. Here I will use Ricoeur's approach to explain what kind of relation is presupposed in Hauerwas's approach to witness.

In *With the Grain of the Universe*, witness is more than just a metaphor for describing the lives and acts of Christians and the church. Hauerwas's considerations on witnessing as acting and living require the idea and the existence of a particular way of speaking. Indeed, as the discussion of the book of Acts in one of his essays indicates, these considerations are in fact unintelligible without the stories of the disciples who are called as witnesses to proclaim the gospel, and without Christian witnesses in the past and present who continue to tell the good news to the world. We could say that for Hauerwas this specific testimonial speech reveals the true character of the entire ecclesial and Christian life. Hauerwas holds that truthfulness and faithfulness is not only required in specific speech acts but in everything Christians do. Christians are called to live faithfully and truthfully and by answering this call they become witnesses shaping their lives as a testimony, a *testimonium vitae*.

Thus, witnessing is not just a verbal statement by which Christians tell of how they tested their convictions in their lives. Testing Christian convictions is itself a testimonial act. Though not every Christian is an adequate tester, not every Christian lives as a faithful and truthful witness, Hauerwas suggests that there are experts who have enough competence and authority to enact Christian convictions in their lives. These people bear witness not only and not primarily when they speak about their lives, but through living as Christians, for instance in their prayers, in their service to their neighbors, in raising their children, in work and financial transactions. Their lives can be conceived as testimonies in which they show what the world is like, who God is, and what it means to be human. Thus, Hauerwas would agree with Ricoeur when the latter says that despite the clear distinction between witnessing as reporting and witnessing as acting and living, there is no rupture but a fixed point around which all the various conceptions of witnessing pivot. But where Ricoeur suggests that this fixed point is to be found in the witness's individual devotion, the implicit suggestion in Hauerwas's work is that it is the church that constitutes this fixed point. For Hauerwas, ecclesial communities are to be understood as initiators and propagators of both faithful speech acts *and* of truthful and faithful lives.

But one could get the impression that in Hauerwas's conception of witness the life of the witness has the highest priority. It seems that he implicitly inverts the relation between verbal witness and witnessing in life, suggesting that the verbal practices of witnessing must be understood as an *element* of the communal *testimonium vitae*. As a result, there's a tendency in *With the Grain of the Universe* to blur the typical characteristics of witnessing as a particular speech act. I think that this tendency is not unproblematic. It obscures the fact that verbal witnessing is not just one of the many ways by which Christians bear witness, but the archetype of all other forms of witnessing. I'll elaborate further on this critique in chapter 5.

2.1b.2 *Conflicts between Witnesses*

The previous section indicated that Coady has no eye for the conflict between witnesses. His sketch of witnessing communities is too harmonious. Ricoeur's semantics offers a correction to Coady's approach. Ricoeur points out that testimonies are usually given in situations of disagreement and imminent conflict. In this respect, Ricoeur's understanding of testimony fits better than Coady's with Hauerwas's conception of Christian witness. Like Ricoeur, Hauerwas argues that witnessing is inevitable, since regarding questions about what is true and good, immediate certainty and general agreement is impossible. Stories and visions diverge and conflicts often seem unavoidable. In his work, Hauerwas indicates that the divergence between Christian faith and the dominant stories and views in Western culture will lead to conflicts about what is good and true. For him the view of man as an autonomous individual, the world as a playground, and self-expression as the highest goal in life is incompatible with the view of man in communion with God and others, the world as God's gift of creation, and a life of worship as the highest goal. Strikingly, Hauerwas does *not* speak about disputes between witnesses. He applies the term witness almost exclusively to Christians and when he does speak of witnessing outside the church it is of a positive witness which affirms the witness inside the church.[17]

However, the former chapter indicated that though the notion of the witness and his testimony is crucial for Christian self-understanding, neither Scripture nor tradition suggests that bearing testimony is an exclusively Christian practice. I suggest that if we look at non-Christians from the perspective of the community of Christian witnesses, they could also be conceived as witnesses. Just as Christians bear witness in their lives to the story told in the Bible and the beliefs transmitted by tradition, non-Christians bear witness in their lives to the stories they tell and beliefs they have. In other words: Christians do not find themselves in a non-testimonial society, but in what can be described as "a multi-testimonial society." If we accept

17. See chapter 1.5.1.

this suggestion, then the disagreement Hauerwas speaks of, the conflict between stories and visions, can be understood as a conflict between witnesses. In some way it resembles a legal conflict. Just as in a lawsuit, whereby parties bring witnesses whose testimonies are evidence for their case, in the multi-testimonial society, Christians, members from other religions and all kinds of non-religious people, bear testimony through their lives. And just as in the lawsuit whereby the testimonies of different parties can agree but also disagree, in the multi-testimonial society testimonies of life also agree and disagree.

We must not forget that for Hauerwas the conflict between stories and visions is not only present in the relation between Christian communities and late modern society but also within the lives of Christian witnesses. Testing Christian convictions is often a struggle. It's hard to forgive one's neighbors, not just because man has a natural inclination for retribution, but also because of the dominance of stories of violence and revenge. It's not easy to conceive the trees and the birds as signs of creation, not only because the normal human situation is aspect-blind, but because Western man is used to looking at nature as the outcome of a harsh process of the survival of the fittest. Moreover, bearing witnessing to this test is also a struggle. The witness is searching for suitable words, concepts, images, and stories. Speaking truthfully and faithfully is difficult, not only because the constant danger of pride and hypocrisy, but also, as we saw in chapter 1, because of the dominance of false stories about autonomy or self-exploration. The previous section emphasized the necessity of cognitive and moral training by a master. The conflicts and struggles within the life of the witness make this training even more urgent. The powers of sin are too strong for people to acquire competence and integrity by themselves. Therefore, Hauerwas argues that truthfulness and faithfulness can only be acquired in communion with fellow Christians.

2.1b.3 *Individual Devotion*

But even communities fail. In all ages, the church has been tempted by what Ricoeur calls "false witnesses": people who are not interested in telling the truth, but distort it for their personal well-being and success. Like the false prophets in the Old Testament, false witnesses use familiar words, conceptions and convictions but covertly change their meaning and coherence. And since the communication of Christian faith is dependent on witnesses, the effects of this perjury can be disastrous. Indeed, what Ricoeur describes in his analysis will occur in communities which are being fooled by false witnesses: those who have a just cause—the true prophets, the faithful witnesses—are being silenced for telling the truth. Indeed, the history of the church shows that like other communities, Christian communities yield to this temptation and shut out truthful and faithful witnesses.[18]

Though in *With the Grain of the Universe* Hauerwas doesn't speak about the communal exclusion of truthful witnesses and the propagation of false witnesses and false testimonies, he doesn't ignore the possibility that Christian communities let themselves be fooled by false witnesses and exclude true witnesses. In other texts, he speaks of the temptation of deception and self-deception.[19] According to Hauerwas, just as all other humans, Christians and Christian communities tend to deceive others and even themselves. Indeed, without stories about confession, without people enacting these stories, deception is human fate. Thus, from Hauerwas's point of view, the "remedy" against the human leaning towards telling or believing false and deceptive stories is communal training in which men learn to confess their lies and sins.

Yet, I think Hauerwas must also admit that just as legal procedure cannot eliminate all forms of perjury, communal training cannot eliminate all hypocrisy. As a society dependent on the honesty and competence of witnesses, Christian communities are vulnerable to failure, untruthfulness and unfaithfulness and will always be liable to excluding witnesses who have a just case, who tell the truth. Moreover, this witness Ricoeur speaks of, this figure testifying against the common sense of his community, cannot be fully unfamiliar to Hauerwas. After all, he has dedicated his own life to the proclamation to his fellow Christians of a politics of peacefulness, and the denunciation of sins such as patriotism or violence. But, surprisingly, in his work Hauerwas does not reflect on this aspect of Christian witnessing. In my view, this is a serious oversight. Hauerwas's account of Christian witness is therefore one-sided and must be supplemented by a reflection on the witness witnessing against the community, the witness preferring communal exclusion to discrediting his testimony.

Though Hauerwas neglects this theme, the idea and the practice of witnessing against the community is anything but strange for Christians. As Ricoeur indicates and the second chapter of this book affirms, the notion of the witness to the truth suffering from communal exclusion does not only appear in philosophical reflection—for instance, the picture of Socrates by Epictetus or Kierkegaard—but also in Christian literature—for example, the

18. In chapter 5.1 I will discuss the life of Fedde Schurer as an example of this exclusion of truthful witnesses.

19. "Self-Deception and Autobiography."

perception of Jesus in the Johannine literature, again by Kierkegaard. Moreover, the Christian tradition tells many stories of Christian women and men past and present who were devoted to telling the truth and resisted oppression by hypocritical church leaders. Though some of them were judged by ecclesial or secular courts, they did not withdraw their testimony but remained faithful and were prepared to suffer and die for the truth.

From Ricoeur's perspective, these stories of women and men who are not willing to adjust their testimony to avoid conflict with the community indicate a crucial characteristic of the witness: the truthful and faithful witness is a keeper of the truth. Moreover, Ricoeur suggests that the truth is kept through the witness's personal devotion for the propagation of the truth. This idea that the witness must be conceived as an individual with a personal concern for his cause is affirmed by some of the explorations in the second chapter. In court, the witness takes an oath: he vouches for the truth of what he says. And in all systems of law it is impossible to swear for someone else. The witness's oath is a personal oath. The swearing witness is an "I." When he bears testimony, he implicitly or explicitly says: "Believe me, I have the authority, competence, and integrity to tell the truth, I vouch for what I say." Ricoeur shows how anyone claiming to speak the truth outside court, implicitly takes a similar individual oath not to belie his testimony. Therefore, the truthful and faithful witness must be understood as an individual, an "I," sealing his testimony with a personal attestation.

In Hauerwas's reflections on the witness's faithfulness and truthfulness, this analysis of inner devotion by the individual witness is lacking. Since Hauerwas is to show that Christian witness is different from a storyless and individualistic expression of religious feelings, he avoids all references to the inner life. But this avoidance is problematic. From Ricoeur's perspective, truthfulness and faithfulness are more than skills and virtues which can be learned through training by a master. Ricoeur's analysis suggests that the inner life of the single witness cannot be ignored and that the adjectives "truthful" and "faithful" refer to this inner devotion of the witness. Being truthful means that the witness is filled with truth, he is grasped by it, and his testimonies are an expression of this inner disposition to bear witness to it. Being faithful means that the witness has a strong inner conviction, a passion for the truth which is immune from repression. In my view, this inner devotion of the individual for the truth is vital for the truthfulness and faithfulness of the Christian community as a whole. Without the passion of prophets, the community will not know the truth. Without the devotion of saints, the community forgets what holiness entails.

But I think the notion of the Christian witness against the community does not necessarily contradict the notion of the Christian witness within the community. Ricoeur's semantics can be interpreted as a useful and necessary supplement to Hauerwas's account of witness. Hauerwas rightly argues that witnessing truthfully and faithfully is impossible without a practice of communal training in which the witness is instructed in faithfully testing Christian convictions and in speaking truthfully about this test. But Ricoeur makes clear that once a witness has acquired expertise, he may notice false convictions and vicious practices, not only in the lives of those who do not consider themselves Christians, but also in the lives of those who present themselves as truthful and faithful Christians. Indeed, the witness may find that in some respects the communal life of his fellow witnesses is untruthful and unfaithful. At this very moment, witnessing to the truth requires an inner devotion for the truth. Devoted witnesses are those women and men who dare to witness against the corruption of their peers, those who proclaim that the community is at odds with their beliefs.

Finally, Hauerwas and Ricoeur agree that the ultimate consequence of witnessing is martyrdom. As we have seen, the testimonies of faithful communities living and speaking truthfully in an indifferent society, *and* the testimonies of individuals living and speaking truthfully for transgressing communities, reveal the shortcomings of these societies and communities. Often these testimonies are irritating and threatening, especially for the society's leaders, and sometimes these leaders will attempt to silence witnessing communities and individual witnesses by sabotaging the testimony or by excluding the witnesses. Ultimately, the truthful speech, faithful action and testimonial lives of witnesses could be answered with violence against them. Those who remain faithful and truthful will become martyrs and bear testimony through life and death. Thus, both Hauerwas and Ricoeur would conclude that, although a cause which has martyrs is not necessarily a just cause, the ultimate consequence of having a just cause is indeed martyrdom.

2.2a Ricoeur's Analysis: The Testimonial Act

There are some other helpful insights in Ricoeur's essay. In the introduction, Ricoeur speaks of testimony as a moral act: testimony as the action of saying "here I am," the action of being present, here and now. According to Ricoeur, this testimonial act differs from both the symbol and the example. On the one hand, testimony is more than a symbolic gesture. The symbol depicts possible ideas and ideals, but it lacks historicity. Testimony gives the symbol "a caution to the truth" (122). What was only imagined in the symbol becomes real in concrete human action. But, on the other hand, testimony is more than an exemplary deed. Though the example is historic, it is but an illustration, an application of the rule. The exemplary actions of moral heroes are nothing but a confirmation of that which is already known "by reason alone." In confrontation with evil, heroic examples are powerless, since evil is not an exception from but a failure of the norm. According to Ricoeur, evil can only be overcome by testimonial acts. These acts are contingent but not impeded by contingency. They are historic deeds which cannot be explained by the actor's interests or self-preservation. Testimonial acts attest that the unjustifiable is overcome here and now:

> the avowal of evil waits for our regeneration more than the examples of sublimity. It waits for words and especially actions which would be absolute actions in the sense that the root of the unjustifiable will be there manifestly and visibly uprooted. (121)[20]

In the third section of his essay, Ricoeur discusses how the ordinary understanding of testimony is interrupted by testimonies of the absolute which can be found in the book of Isaiah and in some of the New Testament books. I will discuss this section in chapter 4. In the last part of his essay, Ricoeur comes to speak about the hermeneutics of testimony. He discusses the complex relation between absolute testimony and relative interpretation. With the help of a hermeneutics of testimony, Ricoeur tries to understand how "the manifestation of the absolute is indefinitely mediated" (145). While this hermeneutical approach of testimony is original and profound, this section is not so helpful for our attempt to concretize and clarify Hauerwas's account. Yet, one of Ricoeur's observations in this section is relevant for our analysis:

> What we can recognize in testimony . . . is that it is the expression of the freedom that we desire to be. I recognize as existing what is only an idea for me. What I recognize outside myself is, in its effectiveness, the movement of liberation that I posit only as an ideal. (151)

Thus, according to Ricoeur, we can be touched by testimonial acts. We declare: "this is an act which confirms that something we could only vaguely imagine is actually real." And so testimony creates an "open chain of interpretants" (145). As observers, we are first witnesses of how someone does what has to be done and secondly we react by bearing testimony to this act.[21]

---

20. For this idea of the absoluteness of testimony Ricoeur is indebted to Jean Nabert. See Ricoeur, "L'hermeneutique du temoignage," 143. See further Jansen, *Talen*, 76–78.

21. Ricoeur refers to the Christian tradition to illustrate this: "It is in this way that the primitive church continuously interpreted the "testimony of Christ," to pick up on a Johannine expression, with the aid of names and titles, figures, and functions, received for the most part from the Hebraic tradition, but also from the mystery religions

In her study on Ricoeur, Mechteld Jansen indicates that in his later work testimony remains an important theme.[22] In his philosophy, Ricoeur offers resistance to two tendencies in modern thinking: to the hyper-certainty of Descartes which claims that knowledge can and must constitute its own foundation and to the hyper-suspicion of Nietzsche that opposes every claim to the truth. Ricoeur wants to speak but without the false pretensions of an all-knowing *cogito* and the terms "testimony" and "attestation" help him in this quest. Testimonial language offers a possibility to speak truthfully about ourselves and the world we live in. Just as the testimonial act itself cannot be reduced to human self-preservation, testimonial language cannot be brushed away as merely opinion. For Ricoeur, testimonies are spoken with the certainty of belief. Though we admit that we cannot objectively ground what we say about ourselves and about the world, though we know that there are reasons to be suspicious, we believe that we must say what we say which is why we vouch for the truth of it. And, through this testimony, the subject attests to himself saying "you must believe me."

2.2b Ricoeur's Analysis and Hauerwas's Account

There is an interesting parallel between Ricoeur and Hauerwas. They find themselves confronted with a similar ethical problem. They have both learned that the world in which human agents act is a contingent world, a world without certainty. They agree that we cannot fly away from this real world into an idealistic or symbolic sphere—we *must* act in this contingent world. But traditional moral principles do not help us to do this. Principles are derived from ethical systems which in fact belie the contingent character of all that is. Hauerwas and Ricoeur respond to this problem in a similar way. They both indicate that there are real people who dare to act, without denying the world's contingency. While in his essay, Ricoeur points to the testimonial acts of resisting evil, Hauerwas points to the people living as witnesses to the peaceable kingdom. Thus, while Hauerwas and Ricoeur are

---

and from Gnosticism. In calling Jesus Son of Man, Messiah or Christ, Judge, King, High Priest, Logos, the primitive church began to interpret the relation of meaning and event. The importance of this is that interpretation is not external to testimony but implied by its initial dialectical structure" ("L'hermeneutique du temoignage," 145).

22. See Jansen, *Talen*, 69–71. Jansen particularly refers to Ricoeur, *Oneself as Another*.

often conceived as representatives of different schools,[23] they both emphasize that witnesses and their testimonies are vital for living truthfully *and* for
thinking meaningfully about ourselves and the world we live in.[24]

I think there are two more lessons which Hauerwas can learn from
Ricoeur's approach to testimony. First, as we have seen above, for Ricoeur
the testimonial act is not an everyday act but an extraordinary act. It happens now and then that the unjustifiable is overcome through an absolute
act. If this is true, then our obligation is not so much to become *actors* doing these acts, but to become *viewers* seeing these acts. Witnessing is firstly
an act of *seeing* and secondly an act of *proclaiming* what one has seen. As
we've seen in chapter 1, in his early work Hauerwas has emphasized the
significance of moral vision, but remarkably enough, in his later work he
doesn't relate this to his understanding of witnessing. What we can learn
from Ricoeur is that a truthful and faithful witness could be conceived not
just as someone who bears testimony through his everyday speech and acts:
the witness is also a careful observer. Witnessing is looking and seeing the
extraordinary character of specific actions, carried out not by ourselves but
by our fellow human beings. From this perspective, Christian witnesses can
still be conceived as "expert witnesses." But this is not the expertise of testing
Christian convictions in one's own life, but that of looking carefully, and
observing how others say what has to be said and do what has to be done.

Ricoeur's stress on the extraordinary character of testimony has another implication. Hauerwas argues that good communal training shapes
witnesses who are capable of saying truthful words and doing faithful acts.
This could easily be understood as implying that this communal training is
not just a necessary but also a sufficient condition for witnessing truthfully
and faithfully. However, if he wishes to maintain that we live in a contingent
reality, this cannot be true. In a world without certainty one does not know
beforehand what to say and do. We speak and act without knowing for sure
whether we are doing right or wrong. And even those who have been trained

23. Dan R. Stiver gives a helpful characterization of the schools in American narrative theology: The 'Yale School' focuses "on 'The Story,' that is, the biblical story. . . . The
'California School' inspired by James McClendon focuses on 'Your Story and My Story,'
that is, on biographies and autobiographies." While Hauerwas is strongly influenced
by his Yale education (see chapter 1) there are also many similarities between him and
McClendon (see chapter 2). Ricoeur, however, is regarded as a representative of the
third school. "Ricoeur is a central figure in what is often called the Chicago school of
narrative theology, which is seen as connecting theology not so much to The Story or
My Story but "Our Story," that is, the broader cultural narrative in which our identities
are formed." But Stiver immediately adds: "In actuality, however, Ricoeur's work relates
to all three" (*Theology After Ricoeur*, 115).

24. Stiver (*Theology After Ricoeur*, 206–7) makes a similar suggestion.

in the skills and virtues of truthfulness and faithfulness make serious and tragic mistakes. Even they are not immune to failure and sin, they may also become false witnesses who commit perjury. While Hauerwas has good reasons to stress the importance of training, I think that perhaps one of the most important lessons that the master must teach is the awareness that he and his trainees remain susceptible to untruthfulness and unfaithfulness. If a master fails to mention this, then his training could become an obstacle to seeing the world as it is. This training will create proud witnesses who do not witness of the world's contingency but of their own overconfidence. Moreover, Hauerwas can learn from Ricoeur that speaking truthful words and doing faithful actions are extraordinary deeds. Indeed, just as the act is more than a symbol, more than an example, it cannot be reduced to the social process of training.

Thus, in two ways, Ricoeur's idea of testimony as an extraordinary deed puts into perspective Hauerwas's understanding of witnessing as living truthfully and faithfully. First, Christians must not be preoccupied with the testimony of their own lives. Witnessing is also looking carefully and seeing what others do, be they Christians or non-Christians. Second, Christians must not be preoccupied with training. Training is no more than creating opportunities for truthful words to be spoken and for faithful acts to be done.

2.3 Conclusion

This section has been helpful in terms of analyzing Hauerwas's account of Christian witness. Ricoeur's understanding of witnesses and their testimonies has been applied to clarify and concretize some aspects of Hauerwas's account. The analysis explains the complex relation between witness as verbal testimony and witness as *testimonium vitae* and affirms Hauerwas's suggestion that witnesses are involved in conflicts about what is true and good. Furthermore, we have found that Ricoeur agrees with Hauerwas that the idea and the practice of witnessing are relevant for ethical reflection on life. Yet, Ricoeur's reflections on testimony also reveal some shortcomings in Hauerwas's theology. He fails both with his reflection on the individual witness with his inner devotion, and with his reflection on witnessing as seeing special testimonial deeds. Moreover, Ricoeur's understanding of testimony as an extraordinary act puts into perspective Hauerwas's strong emphasis on the witness's training. Finally, because Hauerwas implicitly inverts the relation between verbal witness and witnessing in life, he blurs the typical characteristics of witnessing as a particular speech act.

We have almost reached the goal of this chapter. I have indicated that although there are some shortcomings, it's indeed possible to concretize and clarify Hauerwas's account of witness and to speak about Christian life as a testimonial life and of the Christian community as a community of witnesses. It is tempting to finish here and to turn to the next chapter to see how Hauerwas's account of Christian witness relates to Scripture. But stopping here would be premature. It would be neglecting the fact that there are understandings of witnessing and testimony that do not chime so well with Hauerwas's account.

3. GIORGIO AGAMBEN. THE SURVIVOR AND THE *MUSELMANN*

As we found in chapter 2, the terminology of witness is used by victims of iniquities, and we have briefly discussed the literature of Shoah survivors. Here we will further examine how Hauerwas's account of Christian witness relates to this specific form of testimony. Our guide in this section is Giorgio Agamben's *Remnants of Auschwitz*. From the wide range of secondary literature on this issue, Agamben stands out for his original and profound analyses of the Shoah testimonies as a specific from of witnessing. *Quel che resta di Auschwitz* was published in 1998 as part III of his *Homo Sacer* series[25]—the English translation is from 1999. This section is divided into two parts. The first introduces Agamben's book and the second clarifies how Agamben's interpretation relates to Hauerwas's account of Christian witness.[26]

3.1a Agamben's Analysis: Witnesses of Auschwitz

Remnants of Auschwitz can be read as a philosophical interpretation of the Auschwitz testimonies by the Jewish-Italian chemist Primo Levi. In his books, Levi speaks of what he has witnessed in the concentration camp. But this witness is not the complete testimony given in the name of justice or truth by the *testis,* the neutral third.[27] Levi speaks of what he has seen as a *superstes,* a survivor. Agamben argues that the value of the survivor's testimony is in what is absent. Levi writes,

25. Agamben, *Quel che resta di Auschwitz.*

26. *Remnants of Auschwitz* is not undisputed. De la Durantaye, *Giorgio Agamben,* 268–272. According to Leland, Agamben's critics are objecting to "the idea that his understanding of this historical reality can *also* be used to illustrate very different situations—in other words, can be used as a paradigm" (272).

27. See chapter 2.2.

> I must repeat: we, the survivors, are not the true witnesses. . . .
> We, the survivors, are not only an exiguous but also an anoma-
> lous minority: we are those who by their prevarications or abili-
> ties or good luck did not touch bottom. Those who did so, those
> who saw the Gorgon, have not returned to tell about it or have
> returned mute, but they are the "Muslims," the submerged, the
> complete witnesses, the ones whose disposition would have a
> general significance. They are the rule, we are the exception.[28]

For Levi the complete witnesses of Auschwitz are the numb or the dead who
are called "Muslim" or *Muselmann* by other inmates in the concentration
camp. But these witnesses are mostly deceased, and the few who survive
are wordless. Levi stresses that the expertise of survivors such as himself,
survivors who are able to speak about Auschwitz, is questionable. They were
lucky to escape the penultimate stadium of the *Muselmann* and the ultimate
stadium of the gas oven. Those who are speaking of Auschwitz are not the
true witnesses, since they did not experience themselves completely what
Auschwitz was about.

Agamben makes a strict distinction between witnesses bringing
evidence in a lawsuit and the witness as survivor or *Muselmann*. If Levi's
writings are considered as quasi-legal evidence for Auschwitz or against the
Nazi's, the specific meaning of his work is lost. According to Agamben, survivors such as Levi bear witness of an absent testimony, of the impossibility
to testify. Levi's sober record about his deportation to Auschwitz alludes to
that which cannot be said. The language of Levi's reports is a language that
is without significance, that does not come close to those who are without language: the numb witnesses who experienced Auschwitz completely.
Agamben argues that if it is possible to bear testimony of Auschwitz, it occurs in the intimacy between them, between the survivor—who can speak
but who has nothing to say—and the complete witness—who has a lot to
say but cannot speak.

> Testimony takes place where the speechless one makes the
> speaking one speak and where the one who speaks bears the
> impossibility of speaking in his own speech, such that the silent
> and the speaking, the inhuman and the human enter into a zone
> of indistinction in which it is impossible to establish the posi-
> tion of the subject, to identify the "imagined substance" of the
> "I" and, along with it, the true witness. (120)

---

28. Levi, *The Drowned*, 83–84. Cited by Agamben, 33.

The contrasts with Ricoeur's account of testimony are striking.[29] For Ricoeur, meaning occurs when the witness tells his story and this meaning is sealed with a personal attestation. But according to Agamben, the witnesses of Auschwitz do not tell a meaningful story. The *Muselmann* is silent and the survivor only reports what he has seen—without vouching personally for his testimony, without pretending he is an accurate observer or a competent interpreter. The subject appears only where it disappears in the speaking for the other.

Agamben describes the experience of the Auschwitz deportees as an experience of shame, the experience that one is naked but cannot hide nor flee. The deportees were completely at the mercy of their oppressors, they were assaulted and since they could neither resist nor escape, they became witnesses witnessing of their own subjection. For Agamben, shame is a paradoxical process of simultaneous subjectification and desubjectification: "Shame is what is produced in the absolute concomitance of subjectification and desubjectification, self-loss and self-possession, servitude and sovereignty" (107). The *Muselmann*'s numbness is the ultimate result of this shame. These subjects witnessed their complete desubjectification.

Agamben wonders how Levi bears witness to the *Muselmann*'s shame and numbness. He describes the witnessing survivor as an *auctor*: someone augmenting the act or the juridical situation of another through his *auctoritas* or authority (cf. in Latin law the *auctor*, for instance a *pater familias*, authorizes, validates and legitimates legal actions by women and minors).[30]

> If *testis* designates the witness insofar as he intervenes as a third in a suit between two subjects, and if *superstes* indicates the one who has fully lived through an experience and can therefore relate it to others, *auctor* signifies the witness insofar as his testimony always presupposes something—a fact, a thing or a word—that preexists him and whose reality and force must be validated or certified. . . . Testimony is thus always an act of an "author": it always implies an essential duality in which an insufficiency or incapacity is completed or made valid. (149–50)

The *Muselmann* cannot be approached but by an *auctor*, by someone taking the position in his own language of those who have lost language. The

---

29. To be sure, Ricoeur does reflect on literature by survivors from Auschwitz, yet not in his reflections on in his writings on testimony but when he discusses the character of remembering. See Jansen, *Talen*, 107–13.

30. See Glare, "Auctor" and "Auctoritas."

survivor approaches the *Muselmann* by bracketing his own subjectivity. Or more precisely: in becoming the subject of his own desubjectification the *auctor* bears witness to the desubjectification of the *Muselmann*.

Thus, though Agamben agrees with Coady and Ricoeur that witnesses speak with authority, the survivor's authority does not spring from an expert observation or from a devoted oath but from the coincidence that he survived and from his preparedness to bracket off his own subjectivity. In fact, Levi speaks a particular language:

> This means that the phrases, "I bear witness for the *Muselmann*" and "the *Muselmann* is the whole witness" are not constative judgments, illocutive acts, or enunciations in Foucault's sense. Rather, they articulate a possibility of speech solely through an impossibility and, in this way, mark the taking place of a language as the event of a subjectivity. (164)

Testimony takes place in the intimacy between the survivor and the *Muselmann*. The figure of the *Muselmann* shows that it is possible to survive the human: man has an unhuman capacity to survive, even after his own humanity is completely destroyed. But the words of the survivor show that it is possible for the *Muselmann* to survive: man has the capacity to live through the inhuman, and to speak again, to bear witness. The survivor bears witness to the *Muselmann* by saying: "this man whose humanity is completely distorted testifies of humanity, this figure whose humanity is completely distorted is truly a man." Agamben concludes that since the human and the inhuman cannot be fully determined by someone else, it is impossible to destroy them completely. The Nazi policy to destroy all potentialities and contingencies through a system of absolute necessities did not succeed. There is always a remainder and witnesses are this remainder. As remnants, they dwell not in historical time, not in eternity, but in messianic time—in the disjunction between history and eternity.[31]

Finally, though Agamben pictures Levi's testimony of Auschwitz as particular and irreplaceable, his testimony points to something being affirmed by literary, religious and philosophical texts. Levi's testimony is particular but not private, it speaks the truth, not primarily a historical truth but a philosophical truth. To put it in terms Agamben does not use himself: in their particularity these words speak the truth about the self, the human, and the world. The self appears as it disappears in the speaking of the

---

31. In his discussion of the remnant as a "theologico–messianic concept" (162), Agamben, refers to the biblical notion of the remnant in Amos, Isaiah and Romans. He concludes: "In the concept of the remnant, the aporia of testimony coincides with the aporia of messianism" (163).

other; the human is in a non-place, in the impossibility to define itself; the world cannot be determined by absolute systems because there will always be remnants.

3.1b Agamben's Analysis and Hauerwas's Account

Stanley Hauerwas is a theologian writing after Auschwitz—and he is fully aware of this. In chapter 1, I suggested that the central question in his work is "how do we live in a world without certainty?"[32] In this chapter, I add that this question includes the question "how do we live in a world after Auschwitz?" On the one hand, Auschwitz is for Hauerwas the well-considered, rational violence against people who are not conceived as loyal citizens because of their ancestry and their convictions. The concentration camps show us the destructive powers of the modernity project. But on the other hand, Hauerwas considers Auschwitz as a part of Christian history. Christians should acknowledge that they are not innocent with regard to the murder of the Jews. In their attempts to control, in their efforts to be relevant, they have contributed to the creation of a culture and society which finally produced Auschwitz.[33]

Hauerwas would perhaps respond to the question: "how do we live in a world after Auschwitz?" with the answer: "through witnessing." But the practice of Christian witness is neither a solution to the crisis of modernity, nor something that would prevent the recurrence of concentration camps. Witnessing is a modest attempt to speak and act faithfully and truthfully, without pretensions to control society, or be relevant to it. Hauerwas emphasizes that Christians can only live truthfully and faithfully after Auschwitz if they learn to speak the truth regarding themselves and the Jews. And the truth is that Christians are guilty of hate and violence against God's chosen people. Bearing witness of this uncomfortable reality is conditional for any further ecclesial testimony. Though Hauerwas considers Auschwitz as a product of both modernity and Christendom, he does not reflect on the specific literature by Auschwitz witnesses, let alone compare their testimonies with his account of Christian witness. But if remembering Auschwitz

---

32. See chapter 1.4.

33. In "Remembering as a Moral Task" Hauerwas argues that one of the reasons why Christians refused to see Jews as God's elected people, was that they misunderstood their own faith as the Constantanian state–religion. The church longed for power and control in order to make Europe a Christian society. For the Constantanian Church the Jews are not God's people, but irrelevant sectarians or recalcitrant disbelievers.

is conditional for truthful and faithful Christian witness, there may be good reasons to wonder what we can learn from Agamben's reflections on Auschwitz testimonies.

However, comparing Agamben's post-structuralist exegesis with Hauerwas's pragmatic account is not that easy.[34] There are some similarities between their conceptions of witnessing and testimony. Both Hauerwas and Agamben emphasize the particularity of their witnesses: what this witness says cannot be replaced by non-testimonial language; what this witness points to is unintelligible without testimony. Like Hauerwas's witnesses, Agamben's witnesses show what is real, they point to the true character of the subject, the human and the world. Yet, Hauerwas and Agamben have divergent understandings of language and meaning and they strongly disagree on *how* witnesses show. For Hauerwas, testimony takes place in a community of witnesses. The truth is shown if witnesses dare to enact their Christian convictions. For Agamben, testimony takes place in the intimacy between the survivor and the *Muselmann*. The truth is shown, when the speechless one makes the speaking one speak, and where the speaking one bears the impossibility of speaking in his own voice.

Nevertheless, with his reading on Auschwitz testimonies, Agamben tells something about the character of language and the nature of man which may not sound completely unfamiliar to Hauerwas. Agamben's reading points to witnesses witnessing in a situation of contingency and crisis. For a Christian theologian such as Hauerwas, Agamben's sketch of the *Muselmann* may—in all its singularity—refer to the situation of man after Fall, man ashamed of being naked, man locked up in himself. Furthermore, Agamben's sketch of the intimacy between the silent witness and the *auctor*, is a strong argument for man's dependence on testimonial acts and testimonial language. Yet, unlike Ricoeur, Agamben does not speak of the conquest of the crisis. His work suggests that this man can only be approached by witnesses who are prepared to bracket off their own subjectivity and to take the position of those who are lost. Since the Fall man can only be approached by testimonies both fragile and authoritative. Therefore Agamben speaks of the witnessing remnant, dwelling in a messianic time.

In fact there's a deep contrast between Agamben's reflections on testimony and Hauerwas's account of witness. Agamben reminds Hauerwas of the witness as *superstes* and as *Muselmann*. Agamben's witnesses are not people living a communal story. The *Muselmann* is silent. He saw what happened but cannot speak. He has no story to tell. The *superstes* speaks. He is

34. In one essay Hauerwas mentions Agamben's understanding of the *superstes*. Yet he does not discuss how Christian witnesses could relate to the witnesses of Auschwitz. See "Disciplined Seeing," 49.

reporting what he has seen, but his words cannot grasp what happened. The *superstes* bears witness of an impossibility to testify. All the stories he knew, all the expertise he acquired, all devotion he once felt, are now obstacles for his testimony. The *superstes* shows—by relinquishing his story, by laying aside his claims to understand what he has seen—that the complete witness is the *Muselmann*.

3.2 Conclusion

By recalling the testimonies of the *superstes* and the *Muselmann*, Agamben implicitly challenges Christians and Christian theologians like Hauerwas. This challenge can be formulated as follows: "Why are Christians actually witnessing? Do they really think that they can and should give their testimony to a world which has heard the testimony of the remnants of Auschwitz?" Agamben's challenge requires an answer. It cannot be brushed away as a skeptical attack, coming from the representatives of the dominant stories of our societies. It is a serious challenge, derived from the testimonies of the victims of these dominant stories. This challenge requires an answer. Yet the answer cannot be given in this chapter but only in the last chapter, after a full theological analysis of Hauerwas's account of Christian witness.

————————————————————————————

CHAPTER 4

Reading Isaiah, Acts, Revelation, and John

STANLEY HAUERWAS HAS A clear-cut view on the Bible. He holds that we can only fully understand Bible texts if we consider for whom these texts were written. Hauerwas argues that we must read the Bible as a collection of books for the church (containing another collection which was and is primarily a book for Israel).[1] As we saw in chapter 1, in one of his more recent essays, Hauerwas relates his thoughts on the character of Christian witness to what Acts says about witnessing.[2] However, neither in this essay nor in other works does he refer to the fascinating prophecies in Isaiah 43 and 44, to the testimonies by Jesus Christ in the gospel of John, or to how the book of Revelation speaks of the faithful disciples holding the testimony of Jesus.

In this chapter I'll argue that, despite this absence, there is Scriptural support for some important aspects of Hauerwas's understanding of witness. Indeed, in some respects all the Bible books I discuss could help to make Hauerwas's somewhat abstract and vague account of Christian witness more tangible and concrete. But as we will see, parts of Hauerwas's

1. Hauerwas's most extensive reflection on the character of Scripture can be found in his *Unleashing the Scriptures*. The primary contention of this book is: "The Bible is not and should not be accessible to merely anyone, but rather it should only be made available to those who have undergone the hard discipline of existing as part of God's people" (9). As we have mentioned earlier, Hauerwas wrote a commentary on the gospel of Matthew more recently in the series "Brazos Theological Commentary. See also "Why The Way."

2. In this article Hauerwas also refers to the gospel of Matthew. However, in this chapter I will restrict myself to those Bible books which, in their descriptions on the relation between God and man, explicitly speak of witnesses bearing testimony. See chapter 2.5 and 2.6.

With the Grain of the Universe are at odds with how these Bible books speak of witnessing. Indeed, there are certain biblical characteristics of the witness and his testimony which do not fit so easily with Hauerwas's account.

As chapter 2 indicated, the most important Bible texts on the witness and his testimony are to be found in Isaiah, the gospel of John, Acts, and Revelation. In this chapter I'll discuss pericopes from these books. The first section is about man as witness to God. It examines how Isaiah speaks about Yahweh's calling of Israel and how Acts and Revelation speak about Christ's disciples as witnesses. The second section is entirely dedicated to the gospel of John. This book requires special attention because, in the gospel of John, Jesus Christ is portrayed as a witnessing agent, bearing testimony about himself. Each Bible book will be discussed in three "sessions." In the first I'll give an interpretative explanation of what each text tells us about the character of God's call and man's witness. In the second, I'll examine this further with the help of insights of the three philosophers discussed in the previous chapter. And in the final session, I'll examine how the understandings of witness in these Bible books relate to Hauerwas's account of Christian witness.

But let me first mention three things. Firstly, during my interpretative explanations I will present my reading of each Bible text. In these subsections I'll briefly refer to what is known about the historical context in which the Bible books were written and the historical events incorporated in it, but only insofar as this background information helps me to interpret the text. In the footnotes of these subsections, I'll try to make clear how my reading relates to the exegesis of authoritative biblical commentaries. For each Bible book I refer to four recent Bible commentaries but I'm responsible for the actual interpretation in the main text.

Secondly, I must mention that in many respects this chapter builds on the work of Paul Ricoeur. Most of the pericopes examined are also discussed by Ricoeur in the third section of his article "The Hermeneutics of Testimony."[3] Ricoeur indicates that although the books of Isaiah, Acts, John and Revelation reveal a new religious dimension of testimony, "the profane sense is not simply abolished but in a certain fashion conserved and even exalted."[4] This insight has been helpful for my own understanding of how these Bible books speak of the witness and his testimony. In the interpretative sections of this chapter I'll explain how Isaiah, Acts, Revelation and John use everyday and legal conceptions of the witness and his testimony

---

3. Ricoeur, "The Hermeneutics," 130–42. For a discussion of this article, see chapter 3.2.

4. Ibid., 131.

to claim: *The God of the Bible is a God who calls men as witnesses to testify of him.* This insight will also prove to be helpful in my analysis of Hauerwas's account of Christian witness.

And lastly, I should point out that in some ways this chapter also relies on Walter Brueggemann's *Theology of the Old Testament*. Brueggemann considers witnessing and testimony as key terms for interpreting the Old Testament.[5] Like Brueggemann I'll read the Bible books as theological documents, texts speaking about Israel's God and his relation to mankind and the world.[6] Moreover, I must admit that I'm fascinated by Brueggemann's suggestion that the Old Testament can best be understood as a collection of testimonies in which Israel bears witness to its God.[7] It's unfortunately beyond the scope of this chapter to discuss if the Hebrew Bible could and should be understood as a collection of testimonies to God, or if the same is true for the New Testament.[8] But it does answer a more modest question: how do particular pericopes in the Bible speak about witnessing and testimony, and how do those texts relate to Hauerwas's account of Christian witness?

1. VOCATION AND TRIBULATION: READING ISAIAH, ACTS AND REVELATION

1.1 Isaiah and the Vocation of Israel

1.1.1 *Witness in Isaiah*[9]

Most Old Testament scholars agree that Isaiah 40–55 is a text written around the end of the sixth century, during Israel's exile in Babylonia, by an

---

5. There are many interesting similarities between Brueggemann's understanding of testimony in *Theology of the Old Testament* and Hauerwas's account of witness in *With the Grain of the Universe*. Hauerwas and Brueggemann use the notions of witness and testimony to describe a similar way of reasoning: witnesses bear testimony in a particular time and place but what they bear witness to concerns all of mankind, regardless of their particular situation. As Brueggemann says, "In appeal to testimony, one must begin at a different place and so end up with a different sort of certitude" (119). Moreover, they both emphasize that the particular testimonies of Scripture can only be understood in relation to a witnessing people. While the first conceives the church as a testimonial community, the latter speaks of the people of Israel as a witnessing people.

6. Furthermore, as in Brueggemann's *Theology of the Old Testament*, the Bible quotations in this chapter will be stichometric.

7. Brueggemann (119–20) has been informed both by Coady's *Testimony* and by Ricoeur's essay on the hermeneutics of testimony.

8. As far as I know there is no New Testament parallel to *Theology of the Old Testament*, i.e. a study of the theology of the New Testament in which witness and testimony are key terms for explaining the second part of the Bible.

9. In this subsection I will refer to commentaries by Baltzer, Berges, Beuken, Blenkinsopp, and Childs.

unknown author or group of authors and editors usually denoted as "Second Isaiah."[10] As we have seen in chapter 2, Isaiah 43 and 44 are unique in the Old Testament for describing Israel as a witness in a lawsuit.[11]

Just before the pericope in which Israel is called as a witness, we read how Israel's situation is lamented: "But this is a people robbed and plundered, all of them are trapped in holes and hidden in prisons; they have become a prey with no one to rescue, a spoil with no one to say, 'Restore!'" (42:22). How did this happen? How is it possible that Israel ends up in such a disastrous situation? Indeed: "Who gave up Jacob to the spoiler, and Israel to the robbers?" (42:24) The bewildering answer is given in the same verse: "Was it not the Lord, against whom we have sinned, in whose ways they would not walk, and whose law they would not obey?" Second Isaiah depicts Israel as a deaf and blind people:[12]

> Listen, you that are deaf;
> and you that are blind, look up and see!
> Who is blind but my servant,
> or deaf like my messenger whom I send?
> Who is blind like my dedicated one,
> or blind like the servant of the Lord?
> He sees many things, but does not observe them;
> his ears are open, but he does not hear. (42:18–20)[13]

10. See Baltzer, Deutero-Jesaja, 57–59; Berges, Jesaja, 28, 43; Beuken, Jesaja, 9; Blenkinsopp, Isaiah, 104; Childs Isaiah, 289–291. Childs does not assign a date to Second Isaiah, Baltzer argues that the text is written in Jerusalem in the fifth century.

11. See chapter 2.4.

12. According to Berges (Jesaja, 261) deafness and blindness is a central theme, not just in Second Isaiah but also in First Isaiah in the text on the vocation of the prophet: 6:10.

13. There is a continuing debate among scholars on the correct interpretation of texts about the עֶבֶד יְחוָה, the Servant of the Lord. The commentators discussed here take various positions in this debate. See the different introductions by Baltzer, Deutero-Jesaja, 44–47; Berges, Jesaja, 60–63; Beuken, Jesaja, 13; and Blenkinsopp, Isaiah, 118–20. Childs, Isaiah, does not discuss the issue of the Servant of the Lord texts in his introduction but in his discussion of the various pericopes. The issues in this debate pertain to the genre, authorship and dating of the texts and the historical and theological relationship to the other parts of Isaiah. One of the most pressing issues concerns the individual and/or group which is designated by this name "Servant of the Lord." Further, there is disagreement on whether 42:18–20 belongs to this textual group or genre. Moreover, while there is agreement that 43:8–13 (which will be discussed below) does *not* belong to this genre, the question remains how this text relates to various texts about the Servant of the Lord. However, with regard to the interpretation of verse 42:19 and verse 43:10 there is at least some consensus. The five commentators (Baltzer, Deutero-Jesaja, 201, 220; Berges, Jesaja, 262, 283–84; Beuken, Jesaja, 151, 174; Blenkinsopp, Isaiah, 104; Childs, Isaiah, 333–36) seem to agree that in these specific verses the term

This is not the only time Israel's situation is lamented.[14] The prophecies of Second Isaiah begin with words of consolation: "Comfort, comfort my people, says your God" (40:1).[15] Second Isaiah proclaims Israel's redemption. Yahweh, Israel's God, will help his people. He makes something new: "a way in the wilderness and rivers in the desert" (43:19). He marches out like a soldier: "he shows himself mighty against his foes" (42:13).

This redemptive work is not only depicted as creative action or military force, it is also described in legal terms. In the first chapter Israel complains: "My way is hidden from the Lord, and my right is disregarded by my God" (40:27). One could say that this complaint is answered in the next chapter in two pericopes (41:1–5, 21–29) in which Second Isaiah describes a lawsuit in which the God of Israel summons all nations and peoples:[16] "Let them come forward, then let them speak; Let us come together for judgment" (41:1). The issue at stake in these lawsuits is the rise of the empire of the Persian king Cyrus and how these new occurrences relate to what Yahweh has promised to Israel.[17] In these lawsuits Yahweh answers the complaints by his people by revealing that he has not forsaken his people, that he is the sovereign Lord of all, the One who cares for them even through the rise of a "goy" king.

In these two lawsuit scenes between the peoples and their gods, Second Isaiah does not conform to the rules of Hebrew legal process.[18] The nations and their gods are summoned to present their case and to show that they predicted the rise of Cyrus. Yet, they do not get the chance to speak and defend themselves. They are immediately silenced through the words of Yahweh who asks questions such as "Who has roused a victor from the east, summoned him to his service?" (41:2). Yet he is not only acting as a representative of a party, but also as a judge giving a verdict. The questions Yahweh asks he also answers: "I, the Lord, am first, and will be with the last" (41:4). The conclusion of these lawsuits is not so much that the gods

---

עֶבֶד does not refer to an individual or a special group within Israel but is a collective identity of the people of Israel. The key for understanding these verses is 41:8 in which Yahweh addresses his people: "But you, Israel, my servant, Jacob, whom I have chosen, the offspring of Abraham, my friend." Here עֶבֶד is used to describe Israel's identity as the servant Jacob, the offspring of Abraham who has been chosen by its Lord.

14. Baltzer remarks: "Die Theologie Dtjes ist eine Theologie der Krise und der Hoffnung" (*Deutero-Jesaja*, 61); Blenkinsopp speaks of "coping with disaster" (*Isaiah*, 104).

15. See Childs, *Isaiah*, 302.

16. Baltzer speaks of "Gerichtsszenen" (*Deutero-Jesaja*, 41, 127, 160–61).

17. See Baltzer, *Deutero-Jesaja*, 128–29; Childs, *Isaiah*, 318.

18. See Childs: "It seems far more likely that the writer has employed traditional legal language, but used it with great freedom to make his own distinctive points" (*Isaiah*, 317). For more on Hebrew process law, see chapter 2.5.

of the nations are wrong, but that they are unable to defend themselves, in fact they are incapable of doing anything at all.[19] These gods are nothing but products of illusion: "No, they are all a delusion; their works are nothing; their images are empty wind" (41:29).

In the lawsuits in chapter 41 Israel plays a passive role: Israel is a spectator at a lawsuit between Yahweh and the people with their gods. In chapter 43 we read again of a lawsuit, but in this scene Israel plays an active role:

> Bring forth the people who are blind, yet have eyes,
> who are deaf, yet have ears!
> Let all the nations gather together,
> and let the peoples assemble.
> Who among them declared this,
> and foretold to us the former things?
> Let them bring their witnesses to justify them,
> and let them hear and say, "It is true."
> You are my witnesses, says the Lord,
> and my servant whom I have chosen,
> so that you may know and believe me
> and understand that I am he.
> Before me no god was formed,
> nor shall there be any after me.
> I, I am the Lord,
> and besides me there is no savior.
> I declared and saved and proclaimed,
> when there was no strange god among you;
> and you are my witnesses, says the Lord.
> I am God, and also henceforth I am He;
> there is no one who can deliver from my hand;
> I work and who can hinder it? (43:8–13)

Just as they were for the lawsuits in chapter 41, all the nations are gathered together and again they are confronted by Yahweh. Yahweh challenges them to bring forth witnesses who could affirm that their gods foretold the things that happened. But then he also speaks to Israel. Yahweh calls Israel as עֵדַי, my witnesses.[20] Israel is summoned to the lawsuit to confirm that Yahweh is the one true God, the Lord who encompasses the past and the future and who is able to foretell the rise of Cyrus.[21]

---

19. See Childs, *Isaiah*, 321–23.

20. According to Beuken (*Jesaja,* 174) "bring forth" in verse 9 is a legal term that can also be found in other lawsuits in the Old Testament.

21. See Berges, *Jesaja,* 282; Blenkinsopp, *Isaiah,* 223; Beuken, *Jesaja,* 173; Childs, *Isaiah* 335. Baltzer (*Deutero-Jesaja,* 219) disagrees and suggests that "this" in verse 9 refers to Scripture.

This seems contradictory.[22] How could a deaf and blind people become witnesses in a lawsuit? But this is precisely what the text suggests. Israel is deafer than the deaf, blinder than the blind, it has been plundered and looted, not capable of seeing the Lord's redemption, not willing to hear his words of deliverance. Nevertheless it is summoned as his witness. Indeed, the words "you are my witnesses" open Israel's ears and eyes. The Lord reminds Israel of his name: "I am He"; the Lord reminds Israel of his deeds: "I saved you when no strange god was among you."[23] By addressing his people as witnesses, the Lord reminds Israel of what it once heard and saw. Through this call, the deaf and blind witness sees, understands and believes. Israel remembers the God who revealed his name to Moses, the God who delivered his forebears from Egypt.[24]

Israel is summoned for its own good. Through its vocation it is healed from its deafness and blindness. Through its vocation it remembers what it is: a people to which Yahweh revealed and proclaimed himself; a people which has been saved by the Lord. But Israel also witnesses for the sake of the nations. It bears witness for all the people who are gathered in the lawsuit, not with words—it remains silent—but simply by being present as a witness.[25] Its silent presence witnesses to the sovereign power of the Lord, and against the false gods of the peoples.[26] Its existence affirms Yahweh's claim that there is no one besides him.[27] Israel is not just the servant of the Lord, it is his witness.[28]

Yahweh's plea in favor of his people ends in words of salvation and blessing (43:16–21), but then suddenly we read of another lawsuit. Now Israel is the accused and Yahweh makes a passionate complaint against his people (43:22–28): "You have not bought me sweet cane with money, or satisfied me with the fat of your sacrifices. But you have burdened me with

22. Baltzer remarks: "Ein blinder oder tauber Zeuge ist ein Widersinn in sich" (*Deutero-Jesaja,* 218).

23. See Baltzer, *Deutero-Jesaja,* 220; Beuken, *Jesaja,* 174; Childs, *Isaiah,* 335.

24. Childs remarks: "Moreover, the function of the witness–bearer is not just directed to the goal of silencing the nations, but in order that that blind Israel may nevertheless know, believe, and understand the reality of God" (*Isaiah,* 335).

25. Baltzer remarks: "Zeuge für Jahwe und sein Wirken zu sein vor der Völkern, ist eine Aufgabe. . . . Zeugenschaft bedeutet weder Unterwerfung noch Bekehrung. Die Herrschaft über die Welt kommt allein Gott zu" (*Deutero-Jesaja,* 221).

26. See Blenkinsopp: "This is one of several indications in Isaiah 40–55 of a kind of mirror–imaging of the Marduk cult, by means of which the author sought to counter the ideology of power articulated through these liturgies" (*Isaiah,* 225).

27. See Childs, *Isaiah,* 335; Baltzer, *Deutero-Jesaja,* 221–23.

28. Baltzer remarks: "der *eine* Knecht ist zu den *viele* Zeugen geworden" (*Deutero-Jesaja,* 220 his emphasis).

your sins; you have wearied me with your iniquities" (43:24). Then Yahweh changes his tone once more and tells his people not to be afraid:[29] "For I will pour water on the thirsty land, and streams on the dry ground; I will pour my spirit upon your descendants, and my blessing on your offspring" (44:3). He promises his people that they will come to speak again and confess that that they belong to the Lord. Through the power of God's spirit they are able to speak:[30] "This one will say, 'I am the Lord's,' another will be called by the name of Jacob, yet another will write on the hand, 'The Lord's,' and adopt the name of Israel." (44:5).[31] And in the final verse of this pericope, the people of Israel are reminded again that they are witnesses of this particular, incomparable God.

> Do not fear, or be afraid;
> have I not told you from of old and declared it?
> You are my witnesses!
> Is there any god besides me?
> There is no other rock; I know not one. (44:8)

While Israel was blind and deaf, now it has seen and heard the works of Yahweh, and through his spirit it is able to bear witness of him.[32]

1.1.2 Isaiah and Agamben's Understanding of Testimony

Second Isaiah's depiction of Israel contrasts with almost all understandings of witnessing discussed in the previous chapters of this study. Israel does not resemble Hauerwas's community of witnesses. It is not a group of authoritative witnesses (Coady) or devoted individuals (Ricoeur). There are, however, some similarities between Second Isaiah's depiction of Israel and Giorgio Agamben's figure of the *Muselmann*. The *Muselmann* is numb, and so is Israel. It is plundered and looted, there is no one to rescue it. Not unlike the *Muselmann* who is subject to his own desubjectification, Israel is completely passive. And while the *Muselmann* is approached by the *superstes*, Yahweh approaches Israel. He addresses Israel by saying: "you are my witnesses."

29. See Childs, *Isaiah*, 341–42; Baltzer, *Deutero-Jesaja*, 243.

30. Baltzer remarks: "Die Gabe des Geistes ist auch das Wunder von Pfingsten, bei dem über Jakob–Israel hinaus das Gottesvolk gewachsen ist" (*Deutero-Jesaja*, 247).

31. According to Blenkinsopp this verse refers to proselytes, non-Jews "who affirm their allegiance to Israel's God" (*Isaiah*, 233). While Baltzer (*Deutero-Jesaja*, 247) and Beuken (*Jesaja*, 199) agree, Berges is not sure about this interpretation (*Jesaja*, 323).

32. Blenkinsopp remarks: "We take this to be a call to re–establish lively contact with their own traditions in this post–disaster situation, including the historical traditions, constructed as they are on the prophetic pattern of prediction and fulfilment" (*Isaiah*, 237).

Though there are similarities between Isaiah and the testimonies from Auschwitz, there is also a huge contrast. In Isaiah 43 and 44 there is contact between the "numb" people and their God. On the one hand this contact involves judgment: Israel is told that its deafness and blindness is caused by its despair. But it also involves deliverance: the one, who saved Israel repeatedly in the past, will save his people in the near future. The witnesses from Auschwitz did not experience deliverance (or judgment) from Israel's God. If they bear witness of him, they bear witness of his absence. This contrast cannot be neglected. In the next chapter we will consider what it means for our reflections on the character of Christian witnessing.

1.1.3 *Isaiah and Hauerwas's Account of Christian Witness*

My reading suggests that Isaiah 43 and 44 support two aspects of Hauerwas's account of witness. Firstly, for Hauerwas Christian witnessing is an answer to God's call and Second Isaiah concurs with this idea of divine calling: Yahweh summons Israel as his witness. In this respect, Second Isaiah's Israelology affirms Hauerwas's ecclesiology. Just as the church is in Hauerwas's work, Israel is portrayed as a people whose untruthfulness and unfaithfulness witness to the faithfulness of the one true God. Simply by being present as a people, Israel bears witness to God's redemption: he alone revealed, saved and proclaimed, when strange gods were among them. And like the witnesses in *With the Grain of the Universe*—who do not remain silent but answer God's call with the help of the Holy Spirit—it is the spirit of Yahweh that enables Israel to proclaim that it belongs to the Lord.

Secondly, in his work Hauerwas describes an acute conflict between Christian witnesses and the people enacting the dominant stories of our times. In our reading of Isaiah 43 and 44, we also find that witnessing involves conflict. The text depicts a conflict between the nations with their gods, and Israel and its God. As in Hauerwas's work, in Isaiah 43 and 44 this conflict is not primarily understood as a dispute between peoples and their religions but as a clash between the one true God and the many false idols. Yahweh's heavy polemic, his silencing of the voice of the other, is necessary to unmask the people's gods as idols. But there is also a contrast. In Isaiah 43 and 44 the conflict is sketched in legal terms. The prophecies portray a lawsuit in which Yahweh brings forth Israel as his witnesses and challenges the nations to also bring their witnesses. As we have seen in the previous chapters, Hauerwas does not reflect on the figure of the witness in the courtroom. And as our examination of Isaiah affirms, for a comprehensive theological understanding of witness, we must take into account the legal connotations of witness.

We have also seen how the prophecies in Second Isaiah describe a radical crisis preceding God's call. Israel cannot see, Israel cannot speak. It is being called as Yahweh's witness at a moment when it is completely deaf and blind. This call, this divine speech act, is not a command awaiting an answer but a summons to which no objections can be made. Yahweh simply states "you are my witnesses." The Lord hauls Israel to the court to be his witness and through this summons he presents himself as the true God. He opens their eyes and ears so that they are reminded who their God is and what kind of people they are. And only after Yahweh has poured out his spirit is Israel able to speak. This idea that man is caught in a testimonial crisis, and that he is saved from this crisis through a divine intervention—through God saying "you are my witness"—cannot be found in Hauerwas's reflections on the character of Christian witness. This text puts into perspective Hauerwas's stress on the importance of the training of the witness. According to Second Isaiah witnessing does not begin with a gradual process of training, but with the intervention of God's calling. Finally, this depiction of Yahweh's vocation evokes another issue. In Isaiah 43 and 44 we learn to know Yahweh as a "rough character" and in some ways his behavior appears to be violent. The nations and their gods are summoned as witnesses but they are immediately silenced through the words of Yahweh. Moreover his summoning of Israel is not a friendly invitation but a powerful command. But if this is how God calls witnesses, then the question arises whether his vocation is by nature a violent act. And if this is true, then what should we think of Hauerwas's suggestion that the witnessing of the people who have been called is pre-eminently a peaceful form of communication? This question will be answered in the next chapter.

1.2 Acts and the Vocation of the Disciples

1.2.1 *Witness in Acts*[33]

In the Gospel of Luke the terms μάρτυς (witness), μαρτυρία (testimony) or μαρτυρέω (to witness/ testify) are scarcely used. Jesus is neither depicted as a witnessing witness, as he is in the book of Revelations, nor is his proclamation described as a testimony, as it is in the fourth gospel. However, just before his arrest, Jesus speaks of the future witnessing of his disciples:

33. In this subsection I will refer to commentaries by Barrett, Pervo, and Zmijewski. I will also refer to an article by Bolt, "Mission and Witness." Finally I will refer to the monograph used by Hauerwas and Pinches in "Witness" Rowe, *World Upside Down.*

> But before all this occurs,
> they will arrest you and persecute you;
> they will hand you over to synagogues and prisons,
> and you will be brought before kings and governors
> because of my name.
> This will give you an opportunity to testify. (21:12–13)

As we will see below, Luke talks of the fulfillment of this prophesy in his second book.[34]

The story of Acts begins where Luke's Gospel ends: with the last teaching of Jesus.[35] Just before his ascension, Jesus instructs his disciples about a new time which is about to commence: a "time between the times"[36] when he will dwell in heaven and his disciples will become his temporary representatives on earth:

> So when they had come together, they asked him,
> "Lord, is this the time when you will restore the kingdom
> to Israel?"
> He replied,
> "It is not for you to know the times or periods
> that the Father has set by his own authority
> But you will receive power
> when the Holy Spirit has come upon you;
> and you will be my witnesses in Jerusalem,
> in all Judea and Samaria,
> and to the ends of the earth."
> When he had said this,
> as they were watching,
> he was lifted up,
> and a cloud took him out of their sight. (1:6–9)

These last words by Jesus Christ are programmatic for the book as a whole. They refer to the words that Yahweh spoke to Israel in Isaiah 43 and 44: "You are my witnesses." Just as the deaf and blind people of Israel are summoned as witnesses, Jesus appoints his unknowing and incompetent disciples to be

---

34. See Zmijewski, *Apostelgeschichte*, 215, 267, 300; Pervo, *Acts*, 593n7.

35. Rowe remarks: "This generative power of the resurrection is in essence the point of Luke's careful literary design: both at the end of the gospel and at the beginning of Acts, the risen Jesus himself is the origin of universal mission. Luke 24:47 is the anticipatory note—or mirror image—of Acts 1:8. (*World Upside Down*, 122)" And in his final chapter he concludes: "The book of Acts has a 'kerygmatic intention.' In just this way, the text itself performs the fulfillment of Jesus's programmatic instruction in Acts 1:8 to carry the witness to him to the end of the earth" (*World Upside Down*, 174).

36. See Zmijewski: "Zwischenzeit" (*Apostelgeschichte*, 28).

his witnesses.[37] Indeed, just as the twelve tribes of Israel in Isaiah are gifted with the Spirit of Yahweh, the twelve disciples in Acts will be gifted with the Spirit of Christ. They will receive the power of the Holy Spirit,[38] and through this gift the silent disciples become speaking apostles who are capable of responding faithfully to the vocation of their Lord. On Pentecost the apostles' journey as Christ's appointed witnesses begins and this journey will lead them to all nations and to the ends of the world.[39]

In the book of Acts the terms μάρτυς, μαρτυρία, and μαρτυρέω (and its derivatives) are often used. Luke describes the apostles as witnesses who give their testimony. This act of witnessing or bearing witness is a verbal act.[40] Luke also speaks about the apostles creating "wonders and signs" (2:43) (and in fact these deeds are quite important since in some way they confirm the apostolic authority[41]) but these wonders and signs are not described as testimony. Still, the verbal act of witnessing is not just synonymous with preaching or proclaiming. The apostles are more than apostles (ἀπόστολοι), more than messengers, they have all the features of legal witnesses. The prophesy in Luke 21 and the reference in Acts 1 to Isaiah 43/44 suggest that Luke conceives of the apostles as witnesses who are testifying in a trial.[42] The proclamation of Christ takes place in a specific space: before public

---

37. Zmijewski remarks: "Die Zwölf *konstituieren* das neue Gottesvolk, die Kirche" (*Apostelgeschichte*, 91). And further: "Lukas übernimmt die schon bei Deuterojesaja (vgl. Jes 43,10.12; 44,8) anzutreffende Vorstellung, wonach '*Israel als Zeuge* vor den Völkern in der Geschichte' [Zmijewski refers to Schneider, *Die Apostelgeschichte*, 229] gilt, und überträgt sie auf die Zwölf. Gerade deshalb aber muß die Vervollständigung vor der Herabkunft des Hl. Geistes geschehen sein, da mit dieser die universale Zeugentätigkeit der Apostel beginnt" (92). See also Pervo, *Acts*, 32n5, Bolt, "Mission and Witness," 196. Strikingly, the edition of the Greek New Testament we have consulted in this study does not mention these references to Isaiah 43 and 44 in the marginal text references: Aland, *Novum Testamentum Graece*, 320.

38. Pervo remarks: "Power is a medium through which the Spirit is active in the life of Jesus and the activity of early missionaries and the church" (*Acts*, 43).

39. Of all interpreters, Rowe emphasizes most that Acts describes a conflict between the Christian way of life and the pagan culture. "But the conflict as a whole and the instantiation of a new culture—for that is what it was—are utterly inconceivable apart from the clash between the exclusivity of the Christian God and the wider mode of pagan religiousness" (*World Upside Down*, 18).

40. See Bolt: "Their testimony was verbal" ("Mission and Witness," 193).

41. See Pervo: "Luke regards miracle as a mode of authorisation" (*Acts*, 42).

42. See Bolt: "Witness is a 'live metaphor' which has "forensic overtones which would be important for the first readers" ("Mission and Witness," 193).

audiences, and—when they are arrested for their public testimonies—before courts of law. The apostles give their testimony to public audiences and legal courts and they are being judged by these audiences and courts.[43]

Many in the audience judge that the apostles' testimony is true. The apostles' testimony creates a new community of baptized people devoting themselves "to the apostles' teaching and fellowship, to the breaking of bread and the prayers" (2:42). This community or ecclesia (ἐκκλησία) (5:11, 9:31, 15:22) is "of one heart and soul" and "everything they owned was held in common" (4:32). But many others refuse to accept the apostolic testimony, especially the religious and political leaders. The apostles are prosecuted by rulers who try to silence their testimony.[44] And despite this persecution, the apostles continue to witness, hoping and expecting that they will be heard, that even the rulers and judges of the earth will accept their testimony.[45] Thus, if the apostles are witnesses, then the earth, from Jerusalem to Rome, is their tribunal, and the people are their judges.[46]

In Peter's speech to Cornelius we read: "He [Jesus] commanded us to preach to the people and to testify that he is the one ordained by God as judge of the living and the dead" (10:42). And in Paul's speech on the Areopagus we find something similar: "He [God] has fixed a day on which he will have the world judged in righteousness by a man whom he has appointed" (17:31). Both of these verses indicate that in Acts the final judgment does not belong to earth's people but to Jesus Christ, the man appointed by God. The testimony of the apostles can only be understood correctly in relation to this idea that the risen Christ is sitting at the right hand and will

---

43. Twice we find the apostles witnessing before a legal court; in their plea before the Sanhedrin Peter and the other apostles call themselves witnesses (5:32); in his plea before Agrippa Paul speaks of himself as "testifying to both small and great" (26:22). However, the legal status of the apostles is not that of the *testis* (see chapter 2.2). They are not neutral thirds giving evidence in a civil case, they are defendants in a trial conducting their own defense and witnessing for their own case. Furthermore, Luke uses μάρτυς, μαρτυρία and its derivates in other situations. In his speeches in Jerusalem Peter presents him and the other apostles as witnesses (2: 32, 40; 3:15). Paul is commanded to testify in Rome like he did in Jerusalem (23:11). Yet, in these non-judicial situations the legal connotation of μάρτυς, and μαρτυρία is still at work. Peter and Paul give their testimony to the audience in order to be judged.

44. Rowe remarks: "Basic then, to Luke's portrayal of the state vis–à–vis the Christian mission is a narratively complex negotiation between the reality of the state's idolatry and blindness—its satanic power—and the necessity that the mission of light not be misunderstood as sedition" (*World Upside Down*, 88).

45. In his plea for Agrippa in Acts 26 Paul tries to convince the king of the truth of his testimony. See also Zmijewski, *Apostelgeschichte*, 849.

46. See Zmijewski, *Apostelgeschichte*, 95. For the relation between testimony and judgement, see chapter 2.2 and 3.2.

come to judge the living and the dead in a final verdict. Luke tells how, in the time between times, this judge has sent his own witnesses to announce the coming day of judgment through their testimony.[47]

The apostles present themselves as witnesses of Jesus Christ.[48] In his second speech in Jerusalem we hear Peter say, "and you killed the Author of life, whom God raised from the dead. To this we are witnesses" (3:15). And in the next chapter we read: "With great power the apostles gave their testimony to the resurrection of the Lord Jesus, and great grace was upon them all" (4:33). The apostles are called by Jesus to bear witness of him and particularly of his resurrection. Yet, as we know from Luke's first book, the apostles did not witness how God raised Jesus from the dead. What they witnessed was how the resurrected Jesus appeared to them. Moreover, only after his self-manifestation, after he ate and drank with them, after he taught them that the Christ would suffer and rise from the dead on the third day (Luke 24:36–50) did they recognize him as the resurrected Lord.[49] As Peter says in his speech to Cornelius,

> We are witnesses to all that he did
> both in Judea and in Jerusalem.
> They put him to death by hanging him on a tree;
> but God raised him on the third day
> and allowed him to appear,
> not to all the people but to us
> who were chosen by God as witnesses,
> and who ate and drank with him
> after he rose from the dead. (10:39–41)

The apostles bear witness of what they saw and heard in Galilee and in Jerusalem. They witness of Jesus Christ, of what he did, of what he taught, of how he died and rose again. However, they are not arbitrary ear and eyewitnesses, they were chosen to meet the risen Lord.[50]

---

47. See Acts 7: 55–56. But as Pervo remarks: "Eschatology . . . , is not a prominent topic in Acts" (*Acts*, 25). See also Zmijewski, *Apostelgeschichte*, 31. Rowe however, reads Acts differently: "Acts is primarily concerned not with outwardly directed apologetic but with the story of God's apocalypse in the mission of the church" (*World Upside Down*, 10).

48. Zmijewski (*Apostelgeschichte*, 92) describes three characteristics of the apostles as witness: 1. they are eyewitnesses, 2. they have been called, 3. they are gifted with the Holy Spirit.

49. See Bolt, "Mission and Witness," 196–97.

50. In the first verses of his gospel, 1:2, Luke speaks of the tradition of "those who from the beginning were eyewitnesses and servants of the word." Luke presents himself as a writer giving an orderly account of all the things which have happened according to those who were there from the beginning. Strikingly, here Luke does not speak of

For Luke the appearance of the risen Lord to the apostles is a singular and unrepeatable event. In the first chapters of Acts, the noun μάρτυς and the verb μαρτυρέω, exclusively apply to those who were chosen to meet the resurrected Lord on earth. While the gift of the Spirit is given to anyone who is baptized in the name of Jesus Christ (Acts 2:38), the ministry of witnessing is exclusively given to the apostles. They are "his witnesses" and what they saw and heard is unique. Yet they are only capable of speaking of what they saw and heard on the Pentecost when they are filled with the Holy Spirit.[51] Once, in one of Peter's speeches, the Spirit itself is described as a witness (Acts 5:32). Peter's speech suggests that since the Spirit has been a witness to the resurrected Lord, he can help the apostles to practice their special task of witnessing.[52]

Luke also describes how after his ascension to heaven Jesus Christ continues to reveal himself. Though Jesus stays in heaven until the last judgment, he shows himself to Stephen—his most faithful disciple—and he speaks to Paul—his most fanatical persecutor.[53] It is Paul who names Stephen μάρτυς. In one of his speeches Paul tells how, while he was in a trance, Jesus spoke to him and Paul answered: "And while the blood of your witness Stephen was shed, I myself was standing by, approving and keeping the coats of those who killed him" (Acts 22:20). Paul calls Stephen a witness not because he was killed for his proclamation but because—like himself—he saw the resurrected Lord. Despite the aggression of his accusers he bears faithful witness of this.[54] But as we read in the original story of the prosecution, his prosecutors literally refuse to hear Stephen. They "covered their ears" (7:57) and stoned him until he died.

μάρτυρ ς but as αὐτόπται which Bolt translates as "first hand witnesses" ("Mission and Witness," 192). According to Bolt the explanation for this, is that this term refers to a broader group of people than the exclusive apostolic witnesses. Nevertheless Luke also suggests that this group who were present from the beginning are not accidental bystanders or neutral thirds but those who were chosen to be what he calls servants of the word. See also Ernst, *Das Evangelium nach Lukas*, 47.

51. See Bolt: "The dominical choice of just this group, despite the availability of others who met the criterion, and their designation as the ones who will be witnesses for every area of the globe (1:8), also suggests an unrepeatable particularity. According to Acts, the witnesses are part of history, and it is impossible for their role to be extended to anyone else" ("Mission and Witness," 211).

52. See Zmijewski, *Apostelgeschichte*, 269.

53. See ibid., 92–94.

54. In the original story of the killing of Stephen we read, 7:55–56, "But filled with the Holy Spirit, he gazed into heaven and saw the glory of God and Jesus standing at the right hand of God. 'Look,' he said, 'I see the heavens opened and the Son of Man standing at the right hand of God'!" According to Zmijewski (*Apostelgeschichte*, 92), Luke has good reasons for denoting Stephen as μάρτυς. Stephen has the typical characteristics

In the same speech Paul suggests that in the same way the original apostles were called, he has been called to become a μάρτυς, a witness for the gentiles (22:15). A few days later Jesus Christ speaks to Paul at night, saying: "Keep up your courage! For just as you have testified for me in Jerusalem, so you must bear witness also in Rome" (23:11).[55] Finally, when Paul is brought before King Agrippa, he gives a riveting speech presenting himself as a genuine witness of Jesus Christ's resurrection:

> To this day I have had help from God,
> and so I stand here,
> testifying to both small and great,
> saying nothing
> but what the prophets and Moses said would take place:
> that the Messiah must suffer,
> and that,
> by being the first to rise from the dead,
> he would proclaim light
> both to our people and to the Gentiles. (26:22–23)

Thus in Acts, Peter and Paul are Christ's most pronounced witnesses. They are not afraid to speak in synagogues and prisons and for kings and governors and they claim that they have the authority to proclaim that Christ is risen from the dead. Often their testimony takes the shape of a high-flown rhetorical speech. But despite this sometimes bold rhetoric, the book of Acts does not hide the fact that the authority of Peter and Paul is completely dependent on Jesus Christ. Without Christ's vocation they are unknowing and incompetent: Peter was mute, Paul was errant. According to Acts, Peter and Paul only became witnesses since Jesus Christ revealed himself to them, called them as his witnesses and gifted them with his Holy Spirit.

---

of a witness: he is filled with the Holy Spirit, he sees the Lord and he bears witness of what he sees. Barrett, makes an interesting remark: "It seems probable that Luke understood Paul to have taken Stephen's place, especially as the leader of a world–wide mission" (*Acts*, II, 1044). Pervo (*Acts*, 566n70) seems to disagree with Zmijewski and suggests that this verse μάρτυς does refer to the martyrdom of Stephen. Rowe (*World Upside Down*, 245n149) accuses Bolt ("Mission and Witness," 192–193) of not seeing the importance of μάρτυς for Stephen.

55. Paul tells that, just after Christ spoke to him, Ananias said to him "For you will be a witness for Him to all men of what you have seen and heard." (Acts 22:15). Strikingly in Acts 9, in the original stories of Paul's conversion, Paul is not described as a witness and in his speech for Agrippa, Paul says it was not Agrippa but *Jesus himself* who appointed him to become his witness (26:16). See also Zmijewski, *Apostelgeschichte*, 785.

1.2.2 Acts and Coady's Analysis of Testimony

If we are reading Acts to learn something about the character of Christian witness, we are immediately confronted with a problem. Since Luke applies the term witness only to the group of original witnesses of the risen Lord (the apostles including Paul and also Stephen), the question arises whether it's possible, from the perspective of Acts, to apply the term witness to those who did not have this special encounter.

In the books of Luke there's no immediate answer to this question. However, some of C. A. J. Coady's insights discussed in the previous chapter may help. Coady's analysis indicates that the reporting of an authoritative testimony by an original witness is a genuine testimonial act.[56] From this point of view the author Luke can be deemed a witness himself, witnessing of the apostles' testimony. Though Luke is not an original witness, he vouches for the authority of the apostles and uses all his rhetorical and literary gifts to pass on what they heard and saw.[57] Luke is a hearsay witness of the apostles' encounter with the risen Lord. And if his testimony is accepted and passed on, a chain or witnesses is created: from the original witnesses to the hearers and readers of Luke's books.

Thus, in some respects, it is possible to say that those people who proclaim the gospel and preach that Jesus is risen from the dead are "his witnesses." Nevertheless, from Luke's point of view there remains a qualitative distinction between the original witnesses who saw and heard the risen Lord and the hearsay witnesses passing on their testimonies.[58] Hearsay witnesses are dependent on the authoritative apostolic testimony. They only know the risen Lord indirectly. Their ministry is not to bear witness of what they saw but to bear witness of what they heard.

1.2.3 Acts and Hauerwas's Account of Christian Witness

As we have seen in chapter 1, in "Witness" Hauerwas and his coauthor Pinches extensively discuss how Acts speaks about witness.[59] The essay fo-

56. See chapter 3.1.

57. See the opening words to Theophilus in Luke 1: 1–4 and Acts 1:1–2.

58. Bolt ("Mission and Witness," 210–214) makes a similar remark.

59. "Witness" 135. For their interpretation of Acts Hauerwas and Pinches are indebted to the analysis by Rowe. That they have chosen this analysis is no coincidence. In fact there is much theological agreement between Hauerwas and Rowe. Like Hauerwas, Rowe is critical of the dominant encyclopedic approach in modern biblical scholarship: "we refract the kerygmatic intention of the book of Acts through the encyclopedic lens" (*World Upside Down*, 176). Moreover, Hauerwas and Rowe agree that there is a mutual

cuses on the stories of Paul and particularly on Acts 22 and 26: the speeches
in which Paul bears witness of his calling as a witness. Hauerwas and Pinches are impressed by the strong rhetoric of these speeches. "Paul witnesses so
as to win people over" (142). A nice example of their reading of Acts is the
discussion of why in the speech in chapter 22 Paul speaks of Ananias calling
him as a witness, whereas in the speech in chapter 26 he speaks about a
vocation by Jesus Christ himself.

> Ananias's role is important in this telling not only because it
> is from him that Paul gets his charge to be a witness, but also
> because he (Ananias) can perform something of a witnessing
> role for Paul's listeners. Paul's encounter on the road is not his to
> interpret; he needs others to place the strange event in a fruitful
> context of meaning. Indeed, Ananias speaks for the church, and
> so for the God who is calling it forth throughout the progression
> of Luke's narrative in Acts. Moreover, it is not by accident that
> Luke's Paul includes about Ananias that he is a "devout man ac-
> cording to the law and well spoken of by all the Jews living [in
> Damascus]" (22:12). In this role Paul clearly hopes his Jewish
> audience will hear Ananias as a kind of second source, a cor-
> roborating witness.
>
> Perhaps this is the reason it is not surprising that Ananias
> is omitted in the subsequent retelling in Chapter 26. Here Paul
> is speaking before the Roman Agrippa who no doubt will be
> entirely unimpressed by the devout follower of the law in Da-
> mascus. This change in the story might seem disingenuous, as if
> Paul is playing to his audience. But of course he is, for he wants
> them to listen. He is, after all, witnessing. (141)

What Hauerwas finds in Acts arguably supports his own understanding of
Christian witness. In the essay one can discern three ways in which Acts
supports Hauerwas's view. Firstly, Hauerwas discusses how Paul and the
other apostles are being called by Jesus Christ to be his witnesses. This reading backs up his conception that theologically, witness must be understood
as a human answer to a divine call. Secondly, in Hauerwas's reading the
testimony given by these witnesses is not an obscure report about a trivial
event but a proclamation of the truth for all the nations: Jesus Christ who
is risen from the dead is Lord of the whole world. This reading underlines
Hauerwas's idea that witnesses have been called to proclaim the ultimate
truth about God, man and the world. Thirdly, he finds that the apostolic

---

relationship between truth and life: "if we are to think along with Acts about the pressing questions that face us today, we must think within the particular way of life it claims
it is necessary to know the truth of its kerygma" (*World Upside Down*, 176).

testimony in Acts causes conflicts between those who believe and those who refuse to. This supports a basic idea in his own view on witness: Christian witnesses and their testimonies are controversial for many audiences. And though Hauerwas does not mention this in his essay, in fact there is a fourth agreement between his account of witness and the book of Acts. As we saw in chapter 1 of this study, *With the Grain of the Universe* speaks of the Holy Spirit helping men to become truthful and faithful witnesses. This understanding of the Spirit is supported by Acts in which the Holy Spirit is the divine power through which the apostles are able to answer Christ's vocation.

Yet in my view there's also an omission in this essay. What is not being discussed is the difference between Hauerwas's account of witness and the way the book of Acts speaks about witnesses and their vocation. Firstly, the essay does not reflect on how the vocation stories in Acts refer to Isaiah 43 and 44.[60] Like in Isaiah, in Acts there is a testimonial crisis, prior to the call of the witness. Though the disciples were taught and trained by Jesus when they were with him on the road from Galilee to Jerusalem, they were completely shattered when their Rabbi died on a cross; they were mute and numb until Jesus revealed himself to them; they were unknowing and incompetent until he called them as his witnesses. Moreover, after his experience on the road from Jerusalem to Damascus, Paul is numb and blind. He can only see and speak again after Ananias tells him that he has been called by Jesus to become his witness. What Hauerwas and Pinches do not consider in their discussion of Acts is the complete incompetence and passiveness of the men who are being called. This conclusion confirms the observation in the subsection on Isaiah. The description in Isaiah and Acts of vocation as a divine intervention, through which man is saved from a testimonial crisis, puts into perspective Hauerwas's strong emphasis on the necessity of training and exercise. In Acts the story of the witnesses begins with the vocation of Jesus Christ, and only after this intervention, after they are invested with the ministry of witness, does Acts tell how the Holy Spirit teaches the apostles to answer their vocation and become truthful and faithful witnesses of Jesus Christ.

Secondly, Hauerwas and Pinches describe Paul as a model for Christian witness, an example all other Christians could follow in their attempts to be faithful to Jesus's vocation to be his witnesses. Yet what they fail to see is that in Acts Jesus Christ exclusively calls the apostles.[61] As we have seen

60. In his discussion of Acts 1, Rowe (*World Upside Down*, 120–23) also fails to mention the references to Isaiah 43 and 44.

61. Rowe writes: "Such a witnessing role, however, is not limited to the apostles and Paul." Then he remarks that in 22.20 Paul calls Stephen "your μάρτυς" (*World Upside Down*, 121). However, what he fails to mention is that except for the apostles and Paul,

above, for Luke the genuine witnesses are the apostles, the men to whom the risen Lord revealed himself and who were called to be his witnesses. There is an ecclesia in Acts, a new community created through the apostolic testimony, but these people are not described as witnessing witnesses. In Acts the ecclesia is a hearing community, whose existence is dependent on the apostolic testimony. Thus, we must say there is a tension between Hauerwas's work and the book of Acts. In Acts witnessing is a ministry exclusively given to the apostles. But for Hauerwas the ecclesia is more than a group of hearsay witnesses repeating the apostles' testimony. He claims that all Christians are invested with the ministry of witness. The conclusion of this subsection is that this claim is not supported by Acts but, as will become clear below, it is not completely without Scriptural support.

1.3 Revelation and the Tribulation of the Faithful

1.3.1 *Witness in Revelation*[62]

The scholarly consensus is that Revelations is written in the late first century for Christian communities in Asia Minor by a Christian prophet named John.[63] Just as Second Isaiah gives a prophetic reading of Israel's exile, the author of Revelations uses Scriptural language, prophetic images and apocalyptical themes to interpret the situation of the oppressed Christians in Asia Minor.[64] Typical for Revelation—and unusual for all Old Testament prophetic and apocalyptic literature—is the equation of prophecy and testimony: "the testimony of Jesus is the spirit of prophecy" (19:10).[65]

In some ways the author of the Apocalypse is an eyewitness. He introduces himself as Christ's "servant John, who testified to the word of God

---

Stephen is the *only* person who is called μάρτυς. Along with Zmijewski (*Apostelgeschichte*, 92), I think that in Acts the title of witness only applies to those disciples who personally *saw* the resurrected Lord. In other words: in Luke's view Jesus Christ has chosen to reveal himself to an exclusive group of men, and these men are invested with the ministry of witness.

62. In this subsection I will refer to commentaries by Beale, Giesen, Satake, and Witherington.

63. See Beale, *Revelation*, 4–27; Giesen, *Offenbarung*, 36–40; Satake, *Offenbarung*, 32–51; Witherington, *Revelation*, 3–5.

64. See Beale "Commentators now generally acknowledge that John has utilized the three genres of apocalyptic, prophecy, and epistle in composing the book" (*Revelation*, 37). See Giesen, *Offenbarung*, 24–34; Satake, *Offenbarung*, 72; Witherington, *Revelation*, 32–40.

65. See chapter 2.5 and 2.6.

and to the testimony of Jesus Christ, even to all that he saw" (1:2). Like the apostles in Acts, the author of Revelation is called to bear witness of a particular event, of something which was revealed to him alone. However, his experience is not the physical experience of eating and drinking with the resurrected Lord. John saw things while he was "in the spirit on the Lord's day" (1:10).[66] He received a vision from Jesus about "what must soon take place" (1:1) and in his writing he bears witness of what he saw.

Just as how many of the Old Testament prophets suffer for their prophecy, this New Testament witness suffers for his testimony. He is an exile who is banished to Patmos "because of the word of God and the testimony of Jesus" (1:9). Like the author of Acts, the author of the Apocalypse is faced with the persecution of Christ's disciples. He is writing to his peers who also must persevere in a situation of actual or imminent oppression. But John and Luke interpret this oppression differently.[67] The book of Acts presupposes a certain amount of trust in "the powers that be": the apostles are being prosecuted, but communication with their prosecutors is not impossible. They witness, hoping that their testimony will convince their judges. In the book of Revelation there is no communication between prosecuted and prosecutors. The prophetic claim of the author is that the time will come, and has already begun whereby governors, kings and emperors will try to silence all those who hold the testimony of Jesus.[68]

In the letter to the church in Pergamum—one of the seven letters written by Jesus for churches in Asia Minor incorporated in Revelation—we read,

66. Beale remarks: "He has been entrusted with testifying to the revelation of the heavenly Jesus because he has been faithful in witnessing to the revelation of the earthly Jesus" (*Revelation*, 203).

67. Witherington remarks: "His outlook seems far more inward looking and protective than, for instance, the approach of Luke in Luke–Acts, not least because he sees the Roman Emperor and his minions as demonic in character and action, unlike Luke" (*Revelation*, 27).

68. The scholarly consensus is that Revelation is written during the reign of the Roman emperor Domitian. However there is a debate concerning whether there was actually oppression of Christians during the reign of Domitian. While Giesen (*Offenbarung*, 29) and Satake (*Offenbarung*, 58) argue that under Domitian there was no systematic oppression of Christians, Witherington remarks: "We cannot say that we have no evidence of a systematic persecution of Christians by Roman officials in this period" (*Revelation*, 8). Beale takes what he calls a "middle position": "But John may foresee not only that persecution will intensify in the future but also that it is already in the process of slowly intensifying to some degree" (*Revelation*, 29).

I know where you are living,
where Satan's throne is.
Yet you are holding fast to my name,
and you did not deny your faith in me
even in the days of Antipas
my witness, my faithful one,
who was killed among you,
where Satan lives. (2:13)

According to John, Pergamum is ruled by Satan himself.[69] Where Satan rules, any communication is impossible, testimonies are not accepted, witnesses are killed. Antipas is killed by the rulers of his city for his refusal to renounce the testimony of Jesus. He had to be silenced since he was witnessing to the word of God. But the seven letters are more than an encouragement to persevere, they warn the people in the churches of Asia Minor against fickle compromisers, people who see no problem in joining the cults of the emperor or pagan deities.[70] According to John the coming time would be a time of testing. The tribulation will separate the faithful from the unfaithful. And while the unfaithful will compromise their testimony under imminent or actual persecution, the faithful "hold the testimony of Jesus" (12.17).[71]

In Revelation, you do not have to have seen Christ in order to qualify as a witness, as is the case in Acts. The term μάρτυς applies not to an exclusive group of apostles but to all the people who are suffering for their testimony of Jesus: those such as Antipas, the two witnesses sent by Jesus to prophesy (11:3), and the witnesses of Jesus whose blood is drunk by the whore (17:6). But witnessing and martyrdom are not equated—this occurs in the decades after the Apocalypse was written.[72] In Revelation someone

69. Beale remarks that in the late first century Pergamum was "the capital of the whole area for the cult of the emperor" and also "a centre of pagan cults of various deities" (*Revelation*, 246).

70. See Witherington "Revelation thus could be an attempt to interject some cognitive dissonance into a situation where some have become far too comfortable with the compromises they have been making to fit into their Greco–Roman communities" (*Revelation*, 27).

71. Three times we find in Revelation the typical phrase "to hold testimony" (ἔχω τὴν μαρτυρίαν, 6:9; 12:17; 19:10). The faithful are brothers and sisters who have received a testimony from Jesus Christ and who are holding it in a situation of serious tribulation. They know they might be prosecuted for proclaiming the testimony openly or even for holding it covertly. See Giesen: "Die Wendung: 'das sie hatten', ist im Sinn der Ausdauer in der Bedrängnis mit 'das sie festhielten' zu übersetzen" (*Offenbarung*, 183).

72. See chapter 2.7.

does not have to be oppressed in order to be a witness. It is the other way round: people become martyrs for being μάρτυς.[73] After "they have finished their testimony" the two witnesses are overcome and killed by a beast (11:7).

Often Revelation speaks of the faithful proclaiming or holding of the "testimony of Jesus." Jesus is both the object and subject of this testimony (the objective *and* subjective genitive). The phrase "testimony of Jesus" refers to the testimony *about* Jesus, the narrative of his life, death, resurrection, ascension and return. But it also refers to the testimony *by* Jesus, to the words he originally spoke to his disciples.[74] Moreover, Revelation is unique in the New Testament for applying the term μάρτυς to Jesus. In the opening sentences of his writing, John greets his readers with peace and grace from "Jesus Christ, the faithful witness, the firstborn of the dead, and the ruler of the kings of the earth" (1:5). And in the letter to the church of Laodicea Jesus speaks of himself as "Amen, the faithful and true witness, the origin of God's creation" (3:14): titles which refer to Isaiah 43 and 44. Just as Israel has been a witness to God's redemption in the past and will be a witness to God's future deliverance, Jesus is a witness to his own resurrection as the new creation of God.[75]

Here we come to the heart of Revelation's understanding of witness and testimony. Those who are called to remain faithful in the coming tribulations, those who are called to hold testimony despite repression, should know that there is someone like them: Jesus Christ.[76] Though Christ is *unlike* them—he is the one who loves, they the beloved; he gives his blood, they receive it; he is the king, they are his bond servants—he is also *like* them—he is a faithful witness, they keep his words and his testimony; he is the one condemned to die for his witnessing, they will suffer and die with him; he is the firstborn of the dead, the beginning of God's creation, and they will rise with him. This union in death and in life with the Amen, the faithful and true witness, will be their only true comfort. If they persevere in this union, they will be the same as Antipas, true and faithful witnesses of Christ.

73. See Giessen: " 'Zeugnis' meint in der Offb ebensowenig das Martyrium wie das Verb 'bezeugen' . . . . Das Martyrium kann allerdings Folge des Wortzeugnis sein" (59). Witherington (*Revelation*, 8) and Beale (*Revelation*, 190) agree. See also chapter 2.7.

74. See for instance 1:9, 6:9, 20:4. See also Beale: "Therefore, both in 1:1 and 2 and in the similar genitive phrases throughout the book, it is perhaps best to see an intentional ambiguity and therefore a 'general' genitive which includes both subjective and objective aspects" (*Revelation*, 184).

75. See Beale, *Revelation*, 300–301.

76. See Satake: "Während Gott im Himmel auf dem Thron sitzt und sich in die Probleme, die die Gemeinden beschäftigen, nicht einmischt, steht der himmlische Jesus unmittelbar an ihrer Seite und zeigt sich bereit, ihnen behilflich zu sein" (*Offenbarung*, 103).

Moreover, Revelation suggests that what will happen to the faithful corresponds to what has happened to Christ.[77] In chapter 12 John speaks about a vision of a war in heaven: a war between Michael and his angels and the dragon and his angels. After the dragon, Satan, is defeated, he is thrown down from heaven to earth together with his angels. When John sees this, he hears a voice, saying: "the accuser of our comrades has been thrown down, who accuses them day and night before our God" (12:11). The voice continues:

> But they have conquered him
> by the blood of the Lamb
> and by the word of their testimony,
> for they did not cling to life even in the face of death. (12:11)

This is a remarkable verse. Satan is conquered and can no longer make false accusations against the brethren and he is defeated not only through the atoning blood of the Lamb but *also* through the words of the faithful. Those who do not love their lives and are prepared to die have contributed to his defeat. This characteristic of the witness and his testimony is typical of Revelation. Through witnessing, the faithful struggle alongside Christ. Indeed, there is strength in their testimonies: their words of truth are powerful weapons against Satan and his deception.[78]

Finally, in chapter 20, John writes about a vision of a new era of a thousand years:

> Then I saw thrones,
> and those seated on them
> were given authority to judge.
> I also saw the souls of those

---

77. See Beale on verse 1:6: "Christ's death and resurrection (v 5) established a two-fold office, not only for himself (cf. also vv. 13–18) but also for believers. . . . They not only have been made part of his kingdom and his subjects, but they have also been constituted kings together with him and share his priestly office by virtue of their identification with his death and resurrection" (*Revelation*, 192). And one page further Beale continues "Believers spiritually fulfil the same offices in this age by following his model, especially by being faithful witnesses by mediating Christ's priestly and royal authority to the world . . . . The remainder of the book will explain exactly how they do this in the midst of suffering brought on by life in a pagan society" (*Revelation*, 192).

78. Beale remarks, "How have they 'overcome' the devil? Through Christ's death they have been declared not guilty of the accusations launched against them. Therefore, they are exempt from the ultimate punishment. Satan's accusations are unable to unleash the infliction of the 'second death.' And just as Satan's and the world's guilty verdict on Christ was overturned through Christ's resurrection, so Christ's followers have their verdict reserved in the same manner through their identification with Christ's resurrection" (*Revelation*, 664).

> who had been beheaded for their testimony to Jesus
> and for the word of God.
> They had not worshiped the beast or its image
> and had not received its mark on their foreheads or their hands.
> They came to life
> and reigned with Christ a thousand years. (20:4)

Just as Christ is raised from the dead and lifted up to sit on his throne to reign over the world, those who were killed for the testimony of Jesus are raised from the dead to sit on their thrones and reign with Christ. This sovereignty and judgment is given to them, to the people who were condemned by the judges of the earth, to the faithful who were put to death by the rulers of the world.[79] And finally in the new Jerusalem all the bond servants shall be united around the throne to serve the Lamb and to reign with him "forever and ever" (22:5).[80]

1.3.2 Revelation and Ricoeur's Analysis of Testimony

The relation between witnessing and suffering in Revelation could be further explained with the help of Ricoeur's semantics of testimony. According to Ricoeur, rulers tend to loathe those who claim to have a just cause and subsequently respond to their testimony with violent persecution. But Ricoeur also stresses that the suffering of a witness cannot be presented as an argument for the truth of his testimony. Martyrdom refers to an ultimate test, a limit situation. The author of Revelation seems to follow this rule. In Revelation, martyrdom is not an argument but a consequence of bearing testimony to the truth. Indeed, the faithfulness of Jesus's disciples is being tested during the persecution. Those who pass the test show they are loyal to the truth. The testimony of Jesus is kept by these Christ-like witnesses who are prepared to suffer and die for their testimony.

Furthermore, Ricoeur's semantics helps us to understand the difference between the witnesses in Acts and those in Revelation. If Acts emphasizes what Ricoeur calls the "referential pole" of testimony—witnessing as reporting on what is seen—Revelation emphasizes the "confessional

---

79. While Witherington (*Revelation*, 249) argues that this text applies only to the martyrs, Beale (*Revelation*, 999–1000), Giesen (*Offenbarung*, 433–34), and Satake (*Offenbarung*, 385–386) argue that it applies to all faithful Christians who have died "in the Lord."

80. Commentators (Beale, *Revelation*, 1115; Giesen, *Offenbarung*, 476; Satake, *Offenbarung*, 418) agree that *this final verse* applies to all faithful Christians. Witherington (*Revelation*, 272) even suggest that it also applies to many people from all the nations.

pole"—witnessing as proclaiming what is believed, and suffering for it.[81] Yet, both books do not neglect what's emphasized in the other. In Acts, Stephen is a witness because he has seen the resurrected Lord. He is, however, also killed for his confession that Jesus Christ was raised from the dead. In Revelation, John of Patmos suffered for his confession of Jesus Christ. He does, however, also present himself as an eyewitness, bearing witness of what he has seen.

Though faithful Christians in Asia Minor are not original witnesses of a physical encounter with Jesus Christ, they are more than carriers of a message which is not theirs: the "testimony of Jesus" has become "their testimony." Their ministry is to remain faithful to this testimony. In the times of tribulation they cannot witness openly to their bond with Jesus Christ but they hold his story, and hide his words secretly. Yet, if they are arrested and brought to court they will not renounce their Lord but will show openly what they were holding and hiding: the testimony of Jesus.

1.3.3 Revelation and Hauerwas's Account of Christian Witness

As my reading of Revelation already indicates, I will argue that it supports Hauerwas's account of Christian witness more than all of the other Bible books discussed. Unlike Acts, Revelation suggests that all Christians are called to bear witnesses of the testimony of Jesus. The spirit of prophecy is in every disciple and it is their ministry to be faithful and truthful to the testimony of Jesus. The churches in Asia Minor are being encouraged to collectively hold the testimony of Jesus and to become what Hauerwas would call a community of witnesses.

For Hauerwas, witnessing means showing what the world is like. Likewise, John of Patmos bears witness to a particular vision of the world he lives in. His testimony is an instruction about the times that will come: he offered to train Christians to read their contemporary situation with the help of the Scriptures. Moreover, just as Stanley Hauerwas could be described as a witnessing theologian, John of Patmos considers himself a witness bearing testimony through his writing. In the same way as Hauerwas warns his fellow Christians against the cults of patriotism and greed, John teaches the communities of Asia Minor that they should not compromise and join the cults of the emperor. And just as Hauerwas's work exposes the subtle oppression of liberal society, John foresees physical violence against faithful Christians by the Roman Empire and local leaders. Further, Hauerwas describes an age of imminent or actual oppression in which the faith of Christians is being

81. Ricoeur, "The Hermeneutics," 136.

tested, as does John. They both incite Christians to be faithful to the truth
that is Jesus Christ and to become his true witnesses even if the ultimate
consequence of witnessing is martyrdom. Thus, for Hauerwas and for John,
truthful and faithful witnesses live in conflict with the powers that be, with
society and even with some of their fellow Christians.

Indeed, Hauerwas's understanding of this conflict as a struggle between
the triune God and the devilish powers of violence and death is supported
by the Apocalypse which considers conflicts between humans as a reflection of the spiritual conflict between God and Satan. See for instance the
remarkable pericope in chapter 12 where John says that the "accuser of the
brethren" will be thrown down not only through the blood of the Lamb but
also through the words of the faithful. This fascinating prophecy is a strong
argument for some crucial claims in *With the Grain of the Universe*. The
truthful words of witnesses are not without effect but help in the struggle for
truth and for the salvation of the world. Their witness is a peaceful weapon
against Satan and his false accusations.

Nevertheless, there are some obvious contrasts between Hauerwas's
understanding of witness and witness in Revelation. Firstly, while in Hauerwas's account witness is abstracted from its judicial sense, in Revelation
it is not. As in Isaiah and Acts this legal sense of witness is indeed very
much present. Secondly, the notion of witnessing through life is absent in
Revelation. Unlike in Hauerwas's work, in Revelation witnessing is a verbal
act: not the *lives* of the faithful, but their *words* help to dethrone Satan. But
we must not forget that while the concept of *testimonium vitae* is absent in
Revelation (this is a rather recent invention, as we saw in chapter 2 of this
study) the idea that the lives of faithful Christians refer to their Lord is not.
After all, Revelation does propose that every Christian is called to become
a witness and live a Christ-like life, something also advocated by Hauerwas.

1.4 Evaluation: Scriptural Support and Critique

1.4.1 *Conflicts, Judicial Metaphors and the Testimony of Life*

The interpretive explanations in this section indicate that there is a significant overlap between the three discussed Bible books. Second Isaiah, Acts,
and Revelation speak of a conflict taking place between true beliefs and false
convictions. In the discussed pericopes, legal terms, judicial metaphors, and
stories about lawsuits are being used to describe the features of this conflict.
The three Bible books agree that this must not be conceived as a quarrel
between Israel and their neighbors or between the disciples and the Jewish

and pagan unbelievers. Israel and the disciples are involved in a struggle which is not primarily theirs. The actual conflict takes place between the nations and their idols and the one true God, between the skeptical unbelievers and the risen Lord, between Satan and the Lamb. Israel and the disciples are called to be present during this dispute as witnesses. Thus, for Second Isaiah, Acts, and Revelation, witnessing is not spontaneous human action, it's a human answer to a divine call. Man is called to serve God by bearing witness to him. For Second Isaiah, Israel's ministry is to be present at the lawsuit and, through Yahweh's spirit, Israel speaks out that it belongs to its Lord. In Acts the apostolic ministry is to proclaim the risen Lord, and through the Holy Spirit they can be faithful to this ministry. In Revelation the ministry of every Christian is to hold the testimony of Jesus Christ.

The comparisons between the three Bible books and Hauerwas's account of Christian witness have indicated that Isaiah, Acts and Revelation support some vital aspects of Hauerwas's account of witness. The discussed Bible books affirm Hauerwas's idea that God calls people as his witnesses and that, because of the assistance of the Holy Spirit, Christians could serve God by bearing witness in the ongoing battle between truth and lies, faithfulness and sin. Yet the comparisons with Hauerwas also indicate that while these Bible books creatively apply legal terms, judicial metaphors and stories about lawsuits to narrate how people are called as witnesses, Hauerwas's understanding of witness in *With the Grain of the Universe* remains abstract.

Finally, the comparisons have shown that there is no evidence of explicit Scriptural support for one of the most central claims of *With the Grain of the Universe:* that Christians bear witness not only through what they say, but also through what they do and how they live. In the discussed Bible books, witnessing does not refer to a way of living. It is the verbal act of speaking the truth. Yet we could say that there is implicit support for Hauerwas's claims. After all, we have seen that in all the discussed Bible books the life of the witness is significant. In Isaiah, Yahweh's vocation is the beginning of the transformation of Israel's life from sinfulness to faithfulness and truthfulness. In Acts, the calling of the apostles radically changes their lives and by being faithful to their vocation they are brought before kings and governors. In Revelation, John of Patmos encourages his fellow Christians to remain faithful to the testimony of Jesus, and to live a Christ-like life. Thus, Isaiah, Acts and Revelation agree that the witness's vocation to speak the truth has drastic consequences for the life of the witness. Trustworthy witnesses are those who do what they say and say what they do.

1.4.2 *The Ministry of Witnessing*

Though there is significant overlap between Second Isaiah, Acts and Revelation, it's becoming evident these books have different understandings of what witnessing involves. While some differences arise from the divergent contexts in which these texts were written,[82] others stem from differing understandings of the ministry of witness, of what it means to be called as a witness. On one side there is Revelation, which depicts Jesus Christ as the ultimate witness, and Christians as the people being called to bear witness with him. The union with Christ in death and life is the only true comfort to these faithful witnesses. Their testimony even helps to silence Satan's false accusations. But then, on the other hand, there's Acts in which Jesus is not witnessing but calling the exclusive group of apostles as his witnesses. Their task is to bear witness of what they saw and heard in Galilee and Jerusalem. Through the power of the Holy Spirit they are capable of proclaiming to both the public and to courts of law that Christ is risen from the dead. And Second Isaiah offers a third understanding of the character of witness. His prophecies speak of a distinction between God's action and man's passiveness. Israel is deaf and blind and completely dependent on God's redemptive deeds. It is God who summons his people and brings them to court to be present as his witness. Only after God's interference is Israel able to speak out that it is God's beloved people.

As we've seen above, one of these alternative understandings of the ministry of witness fits best with Hauerwas's account in *With the Grain of the Universe*. Indeed, somewhat surprisingly, the strongest Scriptural support for his understanding of Christian witness is not offered by Acts, the book which Hauerwas himself discusses in his essay, but by Revelation. Both in Hauerwas's work and in Revelation the ministry of witness is to remain faithful in a world without certainty.

For a full theological understanding, however, alternative interpretations of the ministry of witness should not be ignored. We have indicated above that both Second Isaiah and Acts put into perspective Hauerwas's idea that witnessing is dependent on training. Though the idea of training is not absent in Isaiah and Acts, Israel and the disciples experience a crisis and what they have learned cannot release them from their despair. They are

82. See for instance the contrasting views on the witness's suffering. According to Second Isaiah, Israel's despair is the result of its unfaithfulness—Israel sinned against its Lord—whereas the disciples' tribulation in Acts and Revelation is the result of their faithfulness—they are prosecuted for witnessing Jesus Christ. But whereas Luke believes that it might be possible that the prosecutors will be convinced by the apostolic testimony, John of Patmos has found that his prosecutors have no ear for the testimony of Jesus.

incompetent and unknowing because their God handed them over to the plunderers and because their master died on the cross. Yet they are called, not because they are different from other people but simply because they have been chosen as God's people and as Jesus's disciples and because God wants them to become witnesses of his truth and faithfulness: "You are my witnesses!" This call is neither the narrative of a storyteller, nor the moral imperative command of a trainer, it is a summons by a ruler setting out a lawsuit, a summons against which no objections can be made. As we shall see below, in the gospel of John we can find a similar understanding of the ministry of witness.

2. CIRCULARITY AND BELIEF: READING THE GOSPEL OF JOHN

As it was in the previous section, this section's discussion of the gospel of John is in three parts: an interpretive exposition, a further explanation with the help of philosophical insights and a comparison with Hauerwas's account of witness. Again the background information in the interpretive exposition is derived from commentaries but the interpretation is my own.

2.1 Witness in the Gospel of John[83]

The fourth gospel was written in the decades after the fall of Jerusalem in 70 AD by an unknown author (or authors) traditionally called John.[84] Many commentators think that the community in which the gospel was written had had a traumatic experience: because of their confession and proclamation of Jesus as the Christ, they were shut out from the synagogue.[85] Thus,

---

83. In this subsection I will refer to commentaries by Neyrey, Theobald, Thyen, and Wengst.

84. See Neyrey, *John,* 2–4; Theobald, *Johannes,* 81–92; Thyen, *Johannesevangelium,* 3; Wengst, *Johannesevangelium,* 21n2.

85. After the fall of Jerusalem and the collapse of the temple, Jewish life altered dramatically. The various groups and sects with their different interpretations of the Tenakh and of their Jewish identity disappear. Judaism survives as rabbinic Judaism. Many commentators argue that the fourth gospel's portrayal of the conflict between Jesus and "the Jews" reflects the conflict between rabbinic Judaism and Jewish Christians. With their claims that Jesus is the coming messiah these Christians must have challenged rabbinic Judaism. To the rabbis' ears these Christian claims sounded dangerous, reminding them of the false prophecies of the rebellious Zealots. Phrases like "for the Jews had agreed already that if anyone confessed that He was Christ, he would be put out of the synagogue." (John 9:22) suggest that these Christians were expelled by the

the author of the fourth gospel stresses that Jesus's words and acts have been controversial from their very beginning. In the same way as the Old Testament prophets were repudiated by the people of Israel, Jesus was repudiated: the majority of the people of Israel and its leaders refused to believe him. But what's new in the fourth gospel is that this prophet is described as a witnessing (μαρτυρεω) agent, a man giving testimony (μαρτυρία).[86] Indeed, this portrayal of Jesus is unique in the New Testament.

The Gospel of John consists of a prologue (1:1–18), two parts (1:19–12:50 and 13–20), and a later addition or epilogue (chapter 21).[87] The first part tells about Jesus's manifestation as the Christ and contains almost all the references to witnessing and testimony. They are to be found in the pericopes about John the Baptist's announcements of Jesus Christ and in two pericopes about the dispute between Jesus and his audience. In the second part of the gospel—the story of the passion and resurrection—the verb μαρτυρέω and the noun μαρτυρία are scarcely used.

The first reference to witnessing can already be found in the seventh verse of the prologue. The gospel speaks of a man sent by God, a man called John, who came "to bear witness of the Light, that all through Him might believe" (1:7).[88] Just after the prologue, John the Baptist speaks. He explains that he is not witnessing of himself, he is witnessing of the one who will come after him but who was before him. After seeing a dove descending from heaven upon Jesus, John declares that this is him: "And I have seen and testified that this is the Son of God" (1:34).[89] In chapter 3, John the

---

leaders of rabbinic Judaism. While Wengst (*Johannesevangelium*, 21–26) argues that this conflict is an inner Jewish conflict, Theobald (*Johannes*, 46–47) argues that there is a discontinuity between Johannine community and the Synagogue. Thyen (*Johannesevangelium*, 3) is more sceptical about what we can know of the community in which the fourth gospel was written, Neyrey (*John*, 1–27) does not takes sides in this debate.

86. While Jesus is described as a witnessing agent and as man giving testimony he is *not* denoted as μάρτυς. The same is true for other terms. In 5:30 we can find that Jesus is described as a judging agent, a man giving judgements but not as judge. In my reading, the fourth gospel depicts Jesus as an agent in action, Static nouns such as "judge" or "witness" are unsuitable to describe Jesus.

87. According to Thyen (*Johannesevangelium*, 4–5), chapters 10 and 11 belong to the second part. While according to Wengst (*Johannesevangelium*, 33–34) chapter 21 is a later addition, Theyen and Theobald (*Johannes*, 27–29) hold that it is an original epilogue. Neyrey (*John*, 225, 332–333) does not take sides.

88. In this section, I will use the New King James version instead of the New Revised Standard translation, since in some crucial verses the former gives a more literal translation of the Greek. See for instance 8:14. While the NKJ translates literally "Even if I bear witness of Myself, My witness is true" the NRS interprets "Even if I testify on my own behalf, my testimony is valid."

89. See Theobald: "Was der Prolog in V. 7f. metaphorisch sagt—Johannes sollte

Baptist again explains his relation to the Son of God: "he who is of the earth is earthly and speaks of the earth. He who comes from heaven is above all. And what he has seen and heard, that he testifies; and no one receives his testimony. He who has received his testimony has certified that God is true" (3:31–33). In John's announcements there is a clear distinction between testimonies from earth and testimonies from heaven. People such as John the Baptist come from the earth and report from what they have seen and heard on the earth. But according to John there is one person coming from heaven and witnessing of what he has seen and heard in heaven: *he* is God's beloved Son, *he* speaks words from heaven. But it seems no one receives his words, that this testimony from heaven is too strange, too new to be understood. Yet, there are some who do understand and accept this testimony and their response affirms "that God is true" (3:33).[90]

In the fourth gospel this act of receiving testimony is portrayed as an act of believing (πιστεύω). The gospel is full of stories of people coming to believe, stories of people endorsing Jesus's testimony of himself. See, for instance, the confession of Martha in chapter 11: "Yes, Lord, I believe that You are the Christ, the Son of God, who is to come into the world" (11:27). Moreover, this group of believers is not restricted to a small group of disciples. The gospel tells us repeatedly that "many believed in His name" (2:23).[91] Nevertheless, the author of the fourth gospel also emphasizes that the majority did not accept Jesus's testimony. These people who refuse to accept his words are consequently called "the Jews" and "the Pharisees." The gospel describes heated disputes between Jesus and the Jews and the Pharisees. In two of these disputes the issue at stake is the authority of Jesus's testimony. We will now briefly discuss these disputes.

The first dispute takes place during Jesus's second visit to Jerusalem. Jesus heals a man on the Sabbath and defends this deed by claiming that God, his Father, gave him the authority to heal on this special day. The Jews are offended by this. They conspire to persecute and kill Jesus "because he not only broke the Sabbath, but also said that God was his Father, making himself equal with God" (5:18). Jesus gives an extensive answer. He speaks

---

'Zeugnis vom Licht ablegen' –, das wird jetzt narrativ entfaltet. Hieß es in V. 8a: 'jener war *nicht* das Licht,' so entspricht dem die erste Szene V. 19–28, wenn sie Johannes auf der Fragen der Jerusalemer Gesandten dreimal (!) antworten lässt 'Ich bin es *nicht!*' (V.20f.)" (*Johannes*, 152).

90. Theobald remarks: "Dieselbe paradoxe Redeweise bietet auch der Prolog (1,11f.). Hier dient sie dazu den Glauben als ein unmögliche Möglichkeit erscheinen zu lassen: Menschlich gesehen völlig unerwartet, ist die Annahme des himmlischen Zeugnisses Jesu eine dem Menschen allein von Gott geschenkte Möglichkeit, kurz, Gnade" (*Johannes*, 292).

91. See 7:31; 8:30; 10:42; 11:45.

about the close relationship between the Father and the Son. The Son does nothing purely from Himself. Whatever the Father does, these things the Son also does. The Father has given the Son "to have life in Himself" (5:26), so that his Son can give eternal life to those who hear and believe his words. Moreover, the Father has given the Son "authority to execute judgment" (5:27) over disobedience. Then, Jesus comes to speak about his testimony:

> I can of Myself do nothing.
> As I hear, I judge;
> and My judgment is righteous,
> because I do not seek My own will
> but the will of the Father who sent Me.
> If I bear witness of Myself,
> My witness is not true.
> There is another who bears witness of Me,
> and I know that the witness which He witnesses of Me is true.
> You have sent to John,
> and he has borne witness to the truth.
> Yet I do not receive testimony from man,
> but I say these things that you may be saved.
> He was the burning and shining lamp,
> and you were willing for a time to rejoice in his light.
> But I have a greater witness than John's;
> for the works which the Father has given Me to finish—
> the very works that I do—
> bear witness of Me,
> that the Father has sent Me.
> And the Father Himself,
> who sent Me,
> has testified of Me.
> You have neither heard His voice at any time,
> nor seen His form.
> But you do not have His word abiding in you,
> because whom He sent,
> Him you do not believe.
> You search the Scriptures,
> for in them you think you have eternal life;
> and these are they which testify of Me.
> But you are not willing to come to Me that you may have life.
> (5:30–40)

At first sight Jesus's argument seems obvious: in the same way as his judgment is just because he is not seeking his own will but the will of the Father, his testimony is true because he is not witnessing of himself, but the Father is witnessing of him.[92] His testimony is confirmed, not by the testimony of John the Baptist, but by that of the Father authorizing and enabling him to do what he does (healing a cripple on the Sabbath) and to say what he says ("God is my Father"). But a closer look reveals a tension in this argument. Jesus suggests that only he is able to confirm the confirmation of the Father: "I know that the testimony which he bears of me is true." This statement is puzzling for two reasons. Firstly, though Jesus denies he is witnessing of himself, in fact he *is*. He makes a statement about himself and claims that he is the only one who has the authority and competence to say what he says, for no one but he knows what he knows. Secondly, Jesus's argument is circular.[93] He claims he can do nothing on his own, that his audience should believe him because his testimony is confirmed by the testimony of the Father. Yet, he adds that he is the only one who is capable of knowing that the confirming testimony of the Father is true.[94]

For an accurate understanding, it is crucial to be aware that this speech is part of a healing story. The story begins with Jesus giving new life to a man who has been a cripple for 38 years. Jesus's act of healing is a testimonial act. This "work" should have spoken for itself. It bears witness to Jesus, it shows that he has been sent by the Father to give eternal life to mankind. But the Jews refuse to accept this testimonial act. On the contrary, Jesus's gift of life is responded to with a conspiracy to kill him. But in his reaction to the Jews, Jesus does nothing to resolve the conflict. He repeats his controversial claim: he speaks of an intimate relationship between God and his Son, suggesting that he is this Son working together with the Father to give life and execute judgment. In the dispute with the Jews, Jesus's testimony of himself

92. While in court the judge and witness are different roles played by different people in this pericope and in chapter 8 Jesus plays both the role of the judge and the role of the witness (though the gospel does not use the nouns "judge" and "witness" as we have above). As a witness he comes to the earth to make himself known to mankind but as a judge he is authorized to judge those who do not wish to receive testimony. Neyrey argues that the dispute with the Jews has the features of a trial. But indeed a strange trial in which "the accused becomes the accuser and the judges are judged" (*John*, 115).

93. Here I follow the reading of Wengst: "Das, was legitimiert, ist identisch mit dem, was legitimiert werden soll. Es liegt hier ein geschlossener Kreis vor. Er könnte nur um den Pries aufgebrochen werden, dass an die Stelle des Zeugnisses Gottes ein menschliches Zeugnis träte. Ob Gott präsent ist, kann nicht objektiv demonstriert werden; das muss sich schon in der Verkündigung dieses Zeugnisses selbst erweisen. Und es erweist sich, indem durch sie Gemeinde entsteht und lebt. Die Legitimation Jesu liegt in der Selbstevidenz der Verkündigung" (*Johannesevangelium*, 207). The other commentators do not mention this circularity.

94. See Thyen: "Überall in unserem Evangelium . . . tritt Jesus ständig als Zeuge 'in eigener Sache' auf. Und doch steht all das unter der ständige Prämisse, daß er nichts von sich selbst her tut noch überhaupt tun kann" (*Johannesevangelium*, 319–320).

is a provocation. It reminds us how in Isaiah 43 and 44 Yahweh addresses the nations and their Gods. Jesus does not try to convince his unwilling audience with open and lucid reasoning but instead gives a circular and contradictory argument.

During his third visit to Jerusalem, Jesus gives another extensive speech about his ministry of witnessing. This speech is the conclusion of a story that begins with the scribes and Pharisees bringing an adulterous woman to Jesus to test him. Jesus passes the test and unmasks the hypocrisy of the people. When the woman is gone he says: "I am the light of the world; he who follows Me shall not walk in the darkness, but shall have the light of life" (8:12). But the Pharisees react to Jesus: "You are bearing witness of Yourself; Your witness is not true" (8:13). Jesus answers them, saying,

> Even if I bear witness of Myself,
> My witness is true,
> for I know where I came from and where I am going;
> but you do not know where I come from and where I am going.
> You judge according to the flesh;
> I judge no one.
> And yet if I do judge,
> My judgment is true;
> for I am not alone,
> but I am with the Father who sent Me.
> It is also written in your law that the testimony of
> two men is true.
> I am One who bears witness of Myself,
> and the Father who sent Me bears witness of Me. (8:14–18)

In contrast to chapter 5, in chapter 8 Jesus acknowledges openly that he is bearing witness of himself. Just as he says that he is not one to judge, but even if he judges, his judgment is true, he is also not one to witness of himself, but even if he is to witness, his testimony is true. Indeed, Jesus cannot but witness of himself since no one else knows where he comes from and where he will go. Though Jesus admits that he is witnessing of himself, he claims that his testimony complies with the rules of Hebrew law. According to Jesus he is not a single witness with an unconfirmed testimony, there is a second witness, the Father, validating the testimony that Jesus gives of himself. The answer of the Pharisees is predictable. They ask him where this second witness is: "Where is Your Father?" and Jesus answers: "You know neither Me, nor My Father; if you knew Me, you would know My Father also" (8:19). As it was in chapter 5, this answer is circular.[95] Jesus does not

---

95. Neyrey reads this scene as "the trial that never ends" (*John*, 152) in which Jesus

prove that there is a second witness to confirm his testimony. He simply claims that if the Jews would know him, they would know the second witness, the Father.[96] In other words: the acceptance of the second witness is only possible for those who have already accepted the testimony of the first.

Jesus's testimonies in chapters 5 and 8 are provocative. In his disputes, Jesus is not trying to convince the Jews.[97] He is never searching for common insights or shared views but only emphasizes the contrast between himself and the Jews: he is the one who knows and they are people unwilling to accept his testimony.[98] Jesus preaches as an Old Testament prophet who is not concerned if his arguments are contradictory or circular, whose only concern is proclaiming the truth. Jesus claims that he has a special relationship with the God of Israel: God is *his* Father, he is *his* Son. Moreover he claims that the Father cannot be known but through his only Son since no one but he "has seen the Father" (6:46). Since nobody has seen what he has seen, since nobody has heard what he has heard, nobody can say what he says. His testimony is incomparable but true.[99]

Many in Israel reject Jesus's testimony exactly for this uniqueness. In fact, the fourth gospel suggests there is an "agreement about disagreement" between those who accept and those who reject Jesus's testimony. They agree that Jesus presents himself as a single witness and that there is no completely independent second witness available to confirm his testimony.

"acts more and more as judge; his speech contains serious accusations against his judges" (*John*, 154).

96. According to Wengst in the beginning of the dispute between Jesus and the Jews there is still some basic agreement about who God is. "Es geht nicht um einen bisher unbekannten Gott, sondern um den in Israel bekannten Gott." But in John 8:19 something changes: "Aufgrund der Voraussetzung, dass der Vater sich im Sohn zeigt, dass der Gott Israels in Jesus präsent ist, wird geschlossen, dass den Vater überhaupt nicht kennt, wer ihn nicht im Sohn erkennt" (*Johannesevangelium*, 317). Jesus's claim that he is the Son of God becomes so excluding that it excludes the idea that the Jews could have any knowledge from God. Wengst concludes that while the Jewish writer of the fourth gospel may have had good reasons to make this exclusive claim towards the majority of the Jewish people, we have good reasons *not* to make this claim anymore. Theobald (*Johannes*, 572–575) disagrees with Wengst's explanation, and argues that that it makes no sense to presuppose a basis agreement between Jesus and the Jews.

97. Wengst remarks about chapter 8 "Das Kapitel demonstriert eindrücklich die Unmöglichkeit eines Dialogs, wenn ein exklusiver Anspruch erhoben wird und die Diskussion allein darum geführt werden soll" (*Johannesevangelium*, 311).

98. To be sure, the Johannine Jesus is not always that provocative. He also he teaches as a patient teacher. See the conversation with Nicodemus (3:1–21) and the Samaritan woman (4:1–42).

99. See Thyen "Die 'Wahrheit' auch seines Zeugnisses für such *selbst* begründet Jesus also mit seinem *Wissen* um sein Woher und sein Wohin" (*Johannesevangelium*, 424).

There are others bearing witness of Jesus, for example, the testimony of John the Baptist, but they speak earthly words. For some, Jesus's acts are testimonial works—a man can walk after 38 years of paralysis, a woman is rescued from being stoned to death—but others reject these acts as sinful provocations. And even the references to the authoritative testimonies of Scripture cannot settle the dispute since there is serious disagreement on the interpretation of these Scriptural testimonies.[100]

In chapter 5 and chapter 8 we already find that the Jews want to kill Jesus for his provocative testimonies (5:18; 8:40). And by the end of the first part of the gospel the counsel of high priests and Pharisees has devised a plan to kill Jesus (11:53). However, in the second part, the passion story, there are no extensive testimonies in which Jesus bears witness of himself. Jesus's speeches to his disciples are *not* described as testimonies: they are not public claims about Christ's mission in the world but private instructions to the twelve disciples about Christ's return to heaven and the coming Spirit. Moreover, Jesus "lifting up," his suffering, dying and resurrection are *not* described as testimony. The gospel makes a clear distinction between Jesus's proclamation of himself as the Christ through witnessing words and testimonial works, and Jesus's salvific acts of suffering, dying and rising from the dead. Testimony is not salvation, it is the proclamation of salvation.

Yet, in one of his teachings Jesus promises the twelve disciples that when he goes, he will send the Spirit and the Spirit will witness of him.[101] This testimony of the Spirit could be seen as an instruction for the disciples which enables them to give their own testimony.

> But when the Helper comes,
> whom I shall send to you from the Father,
> the Spirit of truth who proceeds from the Father,
> He will testify of Me.
> And you also will bear witness,
> because you have been with Me from the beginning. (15:26-27)

Though this speech to the disciples takes place before Jesus's resurrection, this pericope reminds us of Luke 24 and Acts 1. Just as in Luke-Acts, in the fourth gospel Jesus foretells his disciples that they will bear witness of him. Jesus calls them as his witnesses since they were with him from the beginning, but it is the Spirit of truth who will instruct them on how to speak the right words.[102]

---

100. See Theobald *Johannes*, 419, Wengst *Johannesevangelium*, 209.

101. In 14:26 and 16:13 Jesus also speaks about the coming Spirit, but only in 15: 26, 27 we read that the coming Spirit will bear witness to Christ.

102. Thyen holds that the author of the fourth gospel knew the other gospels. In

There is but one pericope in the second part of the gospel where Jesus refers to his journey on earth, his mission to bear witness of himself. During his examination by Pilate, Jesus says: "For this cause I was born, and for this cause I have come into the world, that I should bear witness to the truth. Everyone who is of the truth hears My voice" (18:37). Unlike the Jews in chapters 5 and 8, Pilate is not being provoked by Jesus's testimony. Pilate is confused.[103] He answers: "What is truth?" (18:38). The Roman governor cannot understand this man. For him it remains completely incomprehensible why this Jew is not defending himself against the accusations of the leaders of his people. He cannot understand why this man is prepared to die for his testimony to the truth, he does not see that this man is the embodiment of the truth.[104] But though Pilate finds no guilt in Jesus, he yields to the wishes of the Jewish leaders and hands him over to be crucified.

In the last verses of chapter 20 the author finally addresses his readers: "but these are written that you may believe that Jesus is the Christ, the Son of God, and that believing you may have life in His name" (20:31).[105] It seems that these verses reveal the ultimate purpose of the fourth gospel. This gospel is meant to be an instrument of the Spirit of truth, an instrument which instills belief in the minds and hearts of its hearers. And even the polemical testimonies of chapters 5 and 8 serve this goal. They may provoke and confuse the hearers of the gospel but provocation and confusion are not the intentions of these testimonies. The ultimate intention is to instill belief by urging the hearer to ask: "where do I stand?" On the side of Pilate who is confused and not prepared to get involved, on the side of the Pharisees who proudly refuse to accept this testimony, or on the side of Martha and all those other women and men who believe that Jesus is the Christ, the Son of God?[106]

---

his interpretation of this verse he suggests that the author "plays" with the synoptic logic in Luke 12.11 and 21:21. According to Thyen we must understand Jesus's words as an imperative call: "Ja ihr seid es vielmehr, die da als Zeugen auftreten müssen und werden" (*Johannesevangelium*, 654).

103. See Wengst, *Johannesevangelium*, 226–28.

104. See Thyen, *Johannesevangelium*, 721.

105. See Wengst, *Johannesevangelium*, 206, 307; Thyen *Johannesevangelium*, 775.

106. The interpretation of the conclusive remark in John 21:24, "This is the disciple who testifies of these things, and wrote these things; and we know that his testimony is true," is highly disputed. According to Wengst (*Johannesevangelium*, 325–27) this verse must be understood as a remark by the later editor about the author of the fourth gospel. Thyen (*Johannesevangelium*, 793–796) disagrees and reads the verse as the conclusion of an original epilogue. Again, Neyrey (*John*, 332–33) does not take sides. The second part of Theobald's commentary on John has not been published yet.

2.2 The Gospel of John and the Approaches of Coady, Ricoeur and Agamben

Some of the insights of the philosophers discussed in the previous chapter help to explain further the "logic" of testimony in the gospel of John. In his testimonies, Jesus presents himself as a genuine eyewitness. Nobody has seen what he has, and he has come to bear witness of what he has seen. Like the eyewitnesses in Coady's work, Jesus claims that he has the relevant competence, authority, and credentials "to state truly that *p*."[107] But of course with regard to Jesus, the statement "that *p*" is unique: it is the claim that he comes from heaven and he knows the Father and the Father has sent him to give eternal life to mankind.

Jesus is more than an ordinary eyewitness. Some aspects of Agamben's analysis help to explain what this "more" involves. The Son behaves like an *auctor*, the witness whose testimony "presupposes something—a fact, a thing or a word—that pre-exists him and whose reality and force must be validated or certified."[108] In the gospel of John the ultimate testimony belongs to the Father. Yet the Father does not speak for himself. He only speaks through the testimonies of the Son. The Son is subjected to the Father but becomes the subject to bear witness of the Father's testimony. And he is able to bear witness of and for the Father because of the relationship between them. The Son bears witness to this intimate relationship. He witnesses to the ultimate love by the Father for his Son *and* for the world. Since this ultimate testimony of the Father is communicated in the testimonies by the Son, those who refuse to believe the testimonies of the Son have no access to the testimony of the Father. But those who believe the Son, hear in his words the ultimate, loving testimony of the Father. Thus, although from one perspective the testimonies of the Son seem to validate and certify the testimonies of the Father, from another perspective they need authorization by the ultimate testimony of the Father.

Finally, we have seen that Jesus proclaims himself not only through his words but also through his works. Ricoeur's semantics explains how verbal testimonies are related to testimonial acts.[109] There is a mutual relationship between these testimonies: while Jesus's words explain the true meaning of his work, his works confirm that his words are true. Furthermore, from Ricoeur's perspective, Jesus is the paradigmatic example of a keeper of

107. Coady, *Testimony*, 43.

108. Agamben, *Remnants*, 150.

109. See for Ricoeur's interpretation of testimony in the gospel of John: "The Hermeneutics," 139–142.

truthfulness and faithfulness. Jesus is an "I," an individual swearing a personal oath, saying: "Believe me, I have the authority and integrity to speak the truth, I vouch personally for what I say." Jesus is not prepared to alter his testimony to avoid conflict with his audience. This faithfulness to the truth arouses aggression: the Pharisees seek to kill Jesus because he is claiming to tell a truth they do not accept.

2.3 The Gospel of John and Hauerwas's Account of Christian Witness

Both in the gospel of John and in Hauerwas's work, provocation is an important rhetorical instrument. In the discussed gospel pericopes, Jesus is provoking the leaders of his own people: the Jews and the Pharisees. The verb "to witness" and the noun "testimony" are typically used to legitimize Jesus's provocation. The author suggests that Jesus is permitted to provoke his hearers because he has come to witness the truth. Hauerwas uses the instrument of provocation in his radical critique of liberal society and the way Christianity relates to it. From his perspective, the theologian's task is to tell the truth. But since Christians and non-Christians are deceived by false stories about themselves, the world and God, theologians need such provocation to jolt them from their misconceptions and attract their attention to a true story. Perhaps we could even say that in the fourth gospel and in Hauerwas's work provocations serve a similar goal. The ultimate intention of this rhetoric is to provoke belief in the minds and hearts of the readers.

Moreover, Hauerwas and the author of the fourth gospel seem to agree that the character of Christian life itself is controversial. For them the obligation to be faithful to Christ cannot but cause conflicts between those who accept and those who do not accept Christ's testimony. In his work, Hauerwas suggests that one consequence of witnessing could be painful exclusion—and as we know in this respect, the Mennonites are an example for all other Christians. The fourth gospel supports this idea. Exclusion is the potential fate of anyone who witnesses that Jesus is the Christ.

Finally, both Hauerwas and the author of the fourth gospel agree that for those who refuse to accept their testimony, their reasoning looks circular. In *With the Grain of the Universe* Hauerwas admits that for some readers his own argument appears to be "hopelessly circular" (231): testimonial speech may refer to testimonial lives but these testimonial lives presuppose testimonial speech. The argument in the gospel of John also appears circular: the author refers to the authoritative testimony of Jesus Christ, but this claim that Jesus's testimony is authoritative fully depends on the testimony of the gospel writer. Indeed, as we have seen in the interpretative expositions, Jesus's own testimony is circular too: the testimony of the Son is confirmed by the testimony of the Father. However, that the Father confirms the testimony of the Son can only be known through the testimony of the Son.

Despite these resemblances there are also significant contrasts between Hauerwas's account of witness and the way the gospel of John speaks about witnessing and testimony. As we have seen in the gospel of John, Jesus bears witness through his words *and* his works. In fact the gospel portrays Jesus's life as a testimonial life: through sharing his life the Son bears witness, he shows that he has been sent by the Father to save mankind. In some way, this understanding of Jesus's testimonial life resembles Hauerwas's understanding of the Christian life as one of witnessing. Hauerwas and the gospel agree that a complete testimony is more than a speech act: testimony includes deeds and lives.

However, Hauerwas's conception of *Christians* living testimonial lives is not supported by the gospel of John. In the gospel there is only one person who bears witness through his words, his deeds and his life: Jesus Christ. Others—such as John the Baptist and the disciples—do not bear witness through their deeds or lives but only by their words. The author of the fourth gospel seems to have a good reason for making this strict distinction between Christ's testimonies and other testimonies. He wants to stress that only Christ's testimony is full and complete. Jesus proclaims himself as the Christ and his work confirms this claim: his acts show he is who he claims to be. Indeed, since Jesus proclaims himself, his life is the embodiment of his statements. In this respect Jesus Christ's testimony about himself contrasts with all the other testimonies about him. These testimonies are not complete but can best be conceived as verbal signposts pointing at Christ. Though John the Baptist lives the life of an Old Testament prophet his testimony is a verbal statement: "I am not, but he is." And in the same way as John points away from himself, so do the disciples. The testimony of the disciples looks like a verbal signpost. Through speaking of what they saw and heard the disciples point back to Jesus Christ. And the same is true for the testimony from the Spirit: it is a verbal instruction to the disciples. The Spirit of truth does not speak on his own initiative but only of what he heard from Christ.

The contrasts between *With the Grain of the Universe* and the fourth gospel are obvious. For Hauerwas, the church's witness is more than a signpost pointing back to Jesus, more than a human echo of Jesus Christ's completed testimony. The Holy Spirit witnesses to the Father and the Son by making a truthful and faithful ecclesial community out of proud and sinful individuals. Indeed, thanks to the Holy Spirit, Christians can bear witness through their speech *and* acts. Hauerwas may have good theological reasons to differ from the author of the fourth gospel, but we cannot deny that his understanding of the ministry of witness is not supported by the gospel of John.

2.4 Evaluation: Scriptural Support and Critique

I wish to make three concluding remarks. Firstly, the current section supports some of the outcomes of the previous section. In the fourth gospel, the disciples are called to bear witness to Jesus as the Christ and will be gifted with the Holy Spirit, while Jesus's own testimony causes conflicts with those who refuse to accept it. Thus, we can conclude that Isaiah, Acts, Revelation *and* the gospel of John support Hauerwas's reflections on witness as the human answer to the divine call, and as speaking the truth in a situation of conflict. In the next chapter I will further examine how we must think of witness in relation to notions of vocation, Spirit and truth.

Secondly, we have found more resemblances between Hauerwas's understanding of witness and the gospel of John. In John, witnessing is a provocative act. The author describes how the testimonies of Jesus give rise to a conflict between him and his audience. Yet the intention of these texts is to instill belief in the hearts and minds of the readers and in Hauerwas's work we see a similar rhetorical strategy. Moreover, in Hauerwas's work and in the gospel of John a similar "circular" way of reasoning can be recognized. In the next chapter, in the section on witness and truth, I will further examine the provocative and circular character of witness.

Finally, in the gospel of John, we find no support for Hauerwas's idea that Christians are called to bear witnesses through their lives. While in John, Jesus bears testimony through his words and works, John the Baptist and the disciples bear witness only through their words. The ministry of John the Baptist and the disciples consists of the proclamation that Jesus is the Christ—as does that of the apostles in Acts. In the next chapter, I will examine whether it's possible to integrate these different views on the ministry of witnessing.

CHAPTER 5

Vocation, Spirit, and Truth in Christian Life

THIS CHAPTER OFFERS A final analysis of Hauerwas's account of Christian witness in *With the Grain of the Universe*. After the conceptual analyses in chapters 2 and 3 and the biblical analysis in chapter 4, here I'll evaluate Hauerwas's understanding of witness through a systematic theological analysis. I'm aware Hauerwas dislikes the noun "system."[1] Though I call my analysis in this chapter "systematic," it's not my intention to impose a system on Hauerwas's ethics and theology. I'll only try to order his thoughts on Christian witness in such a way that it's possible to see whether and to what extent he gives an adequate theological reflection on Christian witness. I only speak of a "systematic theological analysis" because this best describes what I'm doing here.

The central question of this chapter is: "If it's true that Christians must be conceived as witnesses, are Hauerwas's reflections on Christian witness adequate?" To answer this question we need to do more than merely examine the implicit order in Hauerwas's reflections on witnessing. What we need is a touchstone to test these reflections—a criterion, acceptable not just for Hauerwas and those who sympathize with his theology, but also for at least some of his critics. One option is to develop such a criterion with the help of texts of authoritative theological authors. Such a touchstone could be used to test whether and to what extent Hauerwas meets the criteria derived from these texts.[2] Another option is to develop a touchstone with the help of Scripture. The benefit of this second option is that almost all Christian theologians agree that in one way or another Scripture forms the basis of theol-

1. See the Introduction of this study.

2. For such an analysis of *With the Grain of the* Universe, Healy, "Karl Barth." Healy uses Barth as a "touchstone" to test Hauerwas and his account of witness.

ogy. The problem is, of course, hermeneutical: the Bible can be interpreted in many ways and theologians disagree on how these interpretations relate to systematic theology.

In this chapter, I opt for the second alternative. Though I'm aware of the divergent approaches to Scripture in Christian theology, I'll turn to the Bible to develop some criteria for analyzing theological reflections on Christian witness. To find these criteria, I restrict myself to the texts that were discussed in the previous chapter because these are the only Bible texts that explicitly speak of man as witness to God. With the help of the previous chapter's biblical explorations, I'll formulate three rules of discourse.[3] The first rule is about the witness's vocation, the second is about the assistance of the Holy Spirit and the third is about the relationship between witnessing and truth.[4] I'll try to formulate these rules in such a way that they are not just suitable for analyzing Hauerwas's account but also for other reflections on Christian witness. Yet, I realize that in the actual interaction between the Bible texts and the work of other theologians, other themes may be more important and the rules may need to be reformulated.

This chapter consists of four sections. Each of the first three sections discusses a separate rule of discourse. These sections have a similar structure. First I show how a basic theological rule can be derived from the biblical explorations in chapter 4, then I go on to examine whether (and if so, how) Hauerwas conforms to this rule. I'll also take up several issues discussed in the previous chapter: some, however, require a more profound examination than others. In the fourth section I'll try to answer three major questions that have been posed in the previous chapters.

3. The idea of rules of discourse stems from George Lindbeck, *The Nature of Doctrine*. According to Lindbeck, doctrines are "communally authoritative rules of discourse, attitude and action" (18). Lindbeck suggests that while the official dogmas of the church explain some rules of discourse, other rules are not explained, for instance, because for most Christians they are self-evident. In *God and Creation* Kathryn Tanner (31–32) speak in a similar way of "rules of discourse" for speaking adequately about the relationship between God and world. The first rule is to "avoid both a simple univocal attribution of predicates to God and world and a simple contrast of divine and non-divine predicates." The second rule is to "avoid in talk about God's creative agency all suggestions of limitation in scope or manner" (47). Tanner shows how these rules can be discerned in pre–modern Christian language (including theology) and criticizes modern theology for having forgotten them. My suggestion in this chapter is that, with regard to witness, we can discern rules of discourse in the ecclesial practice of reading and explaining Scripture.

4. Hovey (*Bearing True Witness*, 3) discerns three "stadia" of witnessing: 1. seeing, 2. coming forward, and 3. Testifying. In his book he orders the reflections on the character of Christians according to these stadia. Though there is nothing against it, I think the great benefit of the way this chapter is ordered is that it follows the implicit order of how crucial Bible texts such as Isaiah 43 and 44 and Acts 1 speak about witnessing.

I will occasionally interrupt my argumentation by telling a short story about the lives of people who, in my view, could be conceived as faithful witnesses. I should say in advance that I do not want to suggest that the stories I tell are representative of all forms of Christian witness. These examples are indeed the products of my own biases and I realize they are also somewhat slanted in other ways, for instance, because all the witnesses I summon are white and male. Nevertheless, these stories are more than illustrations. In fact, I consider the telling of them as a vital aspect of the analysis of this chapter. If Hauerwas's reflections on Christian witness are adequate, then it must be possible to identify concrete witnesses, women and men, who speak truthfully and live faithfully.

1. VOCATION

In this section I will discuss the first basic theological rule:

> In our reflection on the character of Christian witness we must take into account that we can only speak about the human act of witnessing to God in a meaningful way if we consider how this action is preceded by God's act of calling people as his witnesses and that God calls these witnesses to make himself known to the world.

1.1 The First Rule

As Christian theologians we must refrain from identifying Christians or the church with Israel or with the apostles. Isaiah's prophecies remind us that it's not the church but the people of Israel who are the first witnesses to God and his acts of deliverance. Neither can we identify Christians with the apostles, because, as we have seen in our discussion of Acts, Luke makes a clear distinction between the apostles and other Christians, suggesting that the task of witnessing is primarily given not to all the people who believe in Jesus Christ, but only to the small group of apostles. Moreover, in the gospel of John all statements that Jesus is the Christ are dependent on the ultimate testimony by Jesus Christ himself.

In the book of Revelation, however, we do not find these distinctions between witnesses. Although the Apocalypse does not explicitly speak about the vocation of witnesses, it seems to suggest that all Christians have been called to bear witness and to be witnesses. The author of Revelation addresses Christians as a people who must remain truthful and faithful in the coming time of tribulation. Indeed, he promises them that if they succeed, they will become witnesses who resemble Christ, the true and faithful witness. But while our reading of Revelation may suggest there are good reasons for speaking of all Christians as a people who have been called as witnesses, for a better understanding of what this vocation implies, we must leap backwards again from Revelation to Acts 1 and Isaiah 43 and 44. Though Christians can be identified neither with Israel nor with the apostles, the prophecies about Israel's vocation and the stories about the calling of the apostles are crucial for a complete theological understanding of the character of Christian witness.

There are two features of these texts which are particularly important for a theological understanding of vocation. First, the calling of Israel and the apostles is a *constitutive* call. Vocation is not an event in which divine and human agents work together. On the contrary: the analyses of Isaiah 43 and 44 indicate that while man remains completely passive—Israel is deaf and blind—God acts by calling numb and despairing human beings to be his witnesses. Moreover, Jesus's calling of the apostles in Acts 1 should be understood along with Isaiah 43 and 44. Like Israel in Isaiah, the disciples in Acts are unknowing and incompetent. Their calling is not an invitation, but a summons to be present as witnesses. In the same way as a court gives a person the legal status of a witness, the calling "you are my witnesses" appoints Israel and the apostles as witnesses to their Lord. This constitutive call is independent of the one who is addressed: how Israel and the apostles react is of no importance; they are and will remain witnesses of their Lord.

Second, vocation can also be understood as a command. Israel and the apostles are called with a specific aim: to make the Lord known to all people. The people of Israel are not passive witnesses to Yahweh and his mighty deeds, through the spirit of Yahweh they are able to speak and confess that they belong to their Lord. And the call of the apostles is more than a constitutive summons: just as how a witness summoned by a court is obliged to abide by the court's rules, Jesus's vocation does not only appoint the disciples as his witnesses but also orders them to be *led* by his vocation and to bear witness of his resurrection. Since they are endowed with the ministry of witness, the apostles must act in accordance with it.

Finally, the books of Acts and Revelation help us to understand the context of this witnessing. Jesus's order pertains to the "time between times." According to Luke, in the period between his ascension and his second coming the disciples are Jesus's temporary representatives. Until he comes to judge the living and the dead they have the order to proclaim the good news of Jesus's resurrection, and they must bear witness in Jerusalem and to the ends of the earth. Indeed, though they know that Jesus sits at the right hand of God and will come to judge the world, in the time between times the earth is their court, and the people of the earth are their judges. In Revelation this "time between times" is described in more dramatic terms as a period of imminent or actual tribulation in which Christians are obliged to hold the testimony of Jesus.

All this leads us to the first basic rule for theological reflection on the character of Christian witness: one must not speak of witness as something invented by Christians in their attempts to live faithfully to their convictions but as something given by God in his attempt to call unfaithful men to be his faithful people. And while Revelation shows that there are good reasons to speak of Christians and of the church as a people called by Jesus Christ, Isaiah and Acts indicate that this call must primarily be understood as a constitutive call. This means that in theological reflections on the church as a witness, one must not forget how the existence of this witness is completely dependent on the call of the Lord and that the church remains his witness even if it misunderstands the Lord, even if it forsakes its calling, and even if it openly renounces its vocation. Thus, firstly, the vocation by Jesus Christ tells the church what it *is*—his witness—but secondly, through this vocation the church learns what it *ought to do*—it must act in correspondence with its calling, and bear witness of him.

In my view, the notion of "ministry" could help us to understand how these two aspects of the vocation of the witness—the *is* and the *ought*—are related to each other. When Jesus Christ calls women and men to be the church, he invests them with the ministry of the witness. This particular group of people *is* his witness since it received this ministry. But now they hold the ministry of the witness, they *ought* to do what a witness does—to act in accordance to their call as witnesses. In the time between times the church is appointed as Jesus's own minister to hold and proclaim the testimony to the Son, to his Father and to the Spirit, for all the people of the earth.

1.2 Hauerwas and the First Theological Rule

In *With the Grain of the Universe*, the theme of divine vocation is not extensively discussed. In fact there are only a few sentences which hint towards the idea that it is God who calls Christians as his witnesses.[5] What I'll argue, however, is that in fact all Hauerwas's reflections on the character of Christian witness presuppose a notion of divine calling. According to my reading of the Gifford Lectures, Hauerwas's reflections conform to the rule that we can only speak of the human action of bearing testimony to God in relation to God's action of calling people as his witnesses.

5. See for instance: "the calling to be God's witness" (202) or "the witness to which Christians are called" (207).

I must admit, however, that *With the Grain of the Universe* can be read in another way.[6] Some readers may get the impression, especially from the last Gifford lecture, that Hauerwas suggests that human witnessing is not necessarily preceded by a separate divine call. See for instance the following phrase:

> Witnesses are no evidence; rather they are people whose lives embody a totality of beliefs and, accordingly, make claims about "how the world is arranged." (214)[7]

This sentence could be understood as if it were completely self-evident that Christians embody their beliefs, that it's not surprising that Christians are witnesses. In this reading, Christian life is conceived as a practice in which Christians produce their own group identity. The idea that witnessing is dependent on a divine calling remains just an idea: a possible but insignificant addition to an already complete depiction of Christian life. Yet in my view, this alternative reading is problematic and must be considered as an inadequate interpretation of Hauerwas's account of witness. Without the conception of a divine vocation preceding and independent of human testimony, Hauerwas's reflections on the church as witness can be reduced to just another insignificant self-justification of the Christian self-perception in which the divine spirit and human agents are natural partners working together in shaping Christian identity.

To put it more strongly: without the notion of a divine vocation, Hauerwas's work degenerates into a twenty-first-century reinvention of all those nineteenth-century theologies in which pneumatology and anthropology are mingled until there is nothing left but pious rambling about the Christian spirit. Since this alternative reading would make Hauerwas a defender of everything he opposes in theology—the unbiblical and unholy reduction of God's deeds to man's activities—this is indeed a misreading.

What this alternative reading neglects is that for Hauerwas the true character of the church never matches its self-perception. In fact this is consistent in all of his work. Hauerwas does not wish to confirm the self-perception of Christians and Christian communities, but undermines it by showing that much of this self-perception is deceptive. He reminds his readers that the true purpose of the church and the Christian life can only be known if we learn to listen to how this purpose is revealed in the stories of Israel and Jesus Christ.[8] If this holds true, then the small number of remarks in

---

6. In this chapter references to *With the Grain of the Universe* appear in the text.

7. Hauerwas cites Marshall, *Trinity and Truth*, 182.

8. As he puts it in *Community of Character*: "we are possessors of the happy news that God has called people together to live faithful to the reality that he is the Lord of this world" (149).

With the Grain of the Universe about God's calling should not be understood as trivialities, but as significant references to one of Hauerwas's most basic theological presuppositions: God calls Christians as his witnesses.[9]

Without this vocation, without the event of a mighty God calling an incompetent people, there would be no communities of witnesses. In fact, all Hauerwas's reflections on the character of Christian witness must be understood as explorations on how Christians could be faithful to this vocation. Yet what *With the Grain of the Universe* lacks, especially in the last and conclusive lecture, is an effort to prevent the above-mentioned misreading. In other words: Hauerwas refrains from reminding his readers that his reflections on the necessity of witness presuppose the basic theological rule that man's witness is preceded by God's calling. [10]

For a complete understanding of how Hauerwas conforms to the first basic theological rule, we have to discuss three more issues. The first issue concerns the object of God's calling. Who is actually being called? Until now we have spoken somewhat indeterminately about God calling "Christians" but this is not specific enough. Though *With the Grain of the Universe* mostly speaks of "Christians" as "witnesses," its basic idea is that all Christian witnesses form one community of witnesses. In this respect Hauerwas completely agrees with Barth, who

> did not think that Christians could be witnesses as individuals. The individual Christian is always in the church. . . . According to Barth, then, individuals as witnesses are part of the larger witness of the church, and the church, as this witness, must be visible. (198–99)

Secondly, we have discerned two features of divine vocation: vocation as a constitutive summons and as a command. Though this detailed reflection on the character of vocation is absent in the Gifford Lectures, the idea of distinguishing between the two features of the church's calling can be discerned in Hauerwas's other work. Hauerwas has always stressed the relationship between *is* and *ought*: only if we know who we are can we know what we should do.[11] If we relate these ethical insights to his account of witness, we can maintain that the divine calling which is presupposed in *With the Grain of the Universe* must be understood as (1) a constitutive

---

9. That this is the right way to read Hauerwas is affirmed by a recent essay "Disciplined Seeing" and particularly the remarks (137–46) about how Luke narrates the vocation of Paul.

10. Healy (*Hauerwas*, 117) makes a similar point.

11. See chapter 1.5.2.

summons through which the church knows what it *is*—his witness—and (2) a command through which it knows what it *ought* to do—bear witness to the Father, the Son, and the Holy Spirit.

The third issue is the teleological character of vocation. In the Bible, witnesses are called with a goal in mind: God calls them to make himself known to all people. In *With the Grain of the Universe*, this idea can be discerned in the lectures on Barth. For Hauerwas, Barth's theology is an affirmation of his own view that God is known in the world thanks to the ministry of Christianity. God wants to make himself known to man and he uses the church as a participant in his self-revelation. In the time between times, witnesses must proclaim his name and his lordship. In the final lecture, an important addition is made: there is a good reason why God calls Christians *as witnesses*. Hauerwas argues that the particular knowledge about the one true God is seriously compromised when inadequately communicated, for example, by the force of knock-down arguments or physical violence. The stories and convictions about God can only be properly communicated non-violently and witnessing is, *par excellence*, a non-violent way of communication since it does not enforce or dictate the truth but instead shows it by telling stories and living lives.

THE TESTIMONY OF FEDDE SCHURER

My first witness is the Frisian poet and pacifist Fedde Schurer (1898–1968). I summon this first witness in particular to explain that the contrast between creating a quasi-Christian group identity and living in obedience to Christ's vocation, can be discerned in the concrete life of the church. First I'll tell a little bit about Schurer's background, then I'll give a theological analysis of his life.

a. The Life of a Frisian Poet and Pacifist

Fedde Schurer lived his entire life in the Netherlands but his mother tongue was Frisian, a language spoken in northern parts of the Netherlands.[12] As a popular poet, local journalist and politician, Schurer was one the most prominent advocates of "the Frisian movement." For Schurer, Frisian was not a regional dialect

12. For a complete biography on Schurer, see Liemburg, *Fedde Schurer*.

of some backward farmers, but a rich and beautiful language. He wrote religious poems, translated work from Heinrich Heine in Frisian, and during the war he published protest songs against the German oppressor. Perhaps his most important contribution to Frisian culture is his rhymed version of the complete Psalter. Thanks to Schurer, Frisians could sing the psalms not in the language of Dutch governors but in that of their everyday life. Schurer was also involved in politics and in the late 1950s, he was elected in the national parliament for the Social Democratic party.[13]

Two conflicts are significant for Schurer's life. The first takes place in the 1930s in Lemmer, a small provincial town in Friesland. Schurer worked as a schoolteacher at a primary school that was closely related to the orthodox Reformed church Schurer and his wife belonged to. Shocked by the horrors of World War I, Schurer became more and more attracted to pacifism. In his town he began to promote the Christian peace movement openly. Seriously troubled by the behavior of their young teacher, the school administration exhorted Schurer to retract his non-violent convictions because a good Christian schoolteacher could not be a pacifist. But Schurer refused. Realizing that this conflict offered an opportunity to promote Christian pacifism, he openly challenged the school administration. Schurer writes:

> I will never accept that a Christian is obliged to obey the government if this government demands its citizens . . . to use slaughter machines, to poison women and children, and to do all sorts of activities in which the devil and all his angels rejoice themselves.[14]

In the end, Schurer was dismissed. Not only did he lose his job, he and his wife were also expelled from their church. Yet his plan to promote pacifism succeeded. The national press wrote about the conflict and many prominent Christians openly supported Schurer and his non-violent convictions. After the conflict, the Schurers left Friesland and moved to Amsterdam. Fedde became

---

13. As a member of parliament, Schurer criticized the cold war politics of the Dutch government and his own socialist party. Ibid., 333–49.

14. My translation. In Dutch: "Nooit zal ik toegeven, dat een Christen verplicht is de overheid te gehoorzamen als die overheid vraagt van haar onderdanen . . . slachtmachines te bedienen, vrouwen en kinderen te vergiftigen en al zulke werkzaamheden te verrichten waarover zich de duivel en al zijn engelen verblijden" ibid., 108.

a schoolteacher at a public school and together with other "dis-senters," the Schurers formed a small reformed church which united with the mainline Dutch Reformed Church in 1946.

The second conflict takes place in the 1950s. The Schurers have returned from Amsterdam to Friesland and Fedde works as a reporter for a regional journal. In a 1952 article, he fiercely protests against a local judge who does not allow people to speak Frisian in court. Schurer is charged for insulting the court and is found guilty. After the session, Schurer walks out of the court-house and is welcomed by a large group of people. Spontane-ously they take their hero onto their shoulders and march into the streets. The local police, however, feel intimidated and charge against the crowd, injuring many. Again the national press writes about Schurer.[15] Finally the public indignation about Schurer's trial and the violent police response lead to a change in the poli-tics of the Dutch Government. Frisians win the right to speak their language in the courtroom and to receive a Frisian educa-tion in primary school.

In a poem about the Lord's Anointed in Isaiah 61 written in 1966 Schurer reflects on his own life.[16]

In spyltúch bin ik yn Gods hân	I am a pleasant instrument in God's hand
ik sjong fan fred' en ljocht	I sing of peace and light
en de deemoedigen yn 't lân	And to the humble in the land
bring ik in bliid berjocht.	I bring joyful tidings.
De bûgden ûnder soarch en smert	Those who succumb under the weight of worry and pain
sil romt' en rykdom ha	Shall receive opportunity and riches
ik sjong de brutsenen fan hert	I sing to the broken-hearted
wer freugd' en útsjoch ta.	A song of joy and perspective

15. See ibid., 254–96.

16. Schurers friend Jan Buskes quotes this poem in an essay on Schurer. According to Buskes this poem can be understood autobiographically. See Buskes, *Vier vrienden* 121–22.

Ik spylje alle finz'nen foar	I play for the prisoners
it âlde frijheidsliet	The old freedom song
ik spylje foar de tichthûsdoar	I play by the prison gate
salang't dy iepen giet.	Until it finally opens.
Ik sjong foar elke earme siel	I sing for each poor soul
dy't yn it leed ferslacht	Who is submerged in his sorrow
fan d' alderearste sinnestriel	About the very first sun ray
en 't wiken fan de nacht.	And the receding of the night.
Ik sjong, ik sjong foar rap en rút	I sing I sing for every poor soul
yn dizze goud'ne moarn:	On this golden morn
o minsken, strûp jim fodden út	O people, shed all your rags
en lûk de feestklean oan.	And put on your feast apparel .
Ik sjong it wurd oer berch en dún	I sing the word over mountain and dune
fan libben en behâld -	About life and preservation
en moarn, dan romje wy it pún	And tomorrow, then we will clean up the debris
en bouw' in nije wrâld.	And build a new world.[380]

b. Analysis

In my view, Fedde Schurer is a witness. I read his life as a faithful answer to Christ's call in Acts 1. Schurer grew up in a church which became more and more obsessed with its pure reformed identity—claiming that their Neo-Calvinistic ideas were the unquestionable truth. Through the conflict about his pacifism, he discovered that the God of the Bible was different and called him away from the safe haven of his own denomination. While Schurer is disappointed by the behavior of his fellow believers, he does not lose his faith in the church. He becomes a member of a denomination which is less obsessed with its group identity and, through this, he obtains a better ear for God's vocation. Furthermore, the very idea that the Christian life is qualified by God's vocation and not by man's worries about religious, cultural, and racial purity, prevented Schurer from mixing Frisian culture and

17. Schurer, *De gitaer*, 133. Translation John de Boer and Akke van der Kooi.

Christian faith into a religion-legitimized separatist ideology. Though he was one of the most prominent propagators of Frisian language and culture, Schurer knew that the deepest truth about his life was Jesus Christ in which there is *neither Frisian nor Dutch.*

Schurer intuitively knew what Hauerwas's work suggests. While many Christians, and particularly Christian leaders, are busy trying to determine what characterizes them as a group and what distinguishes them from others, he discovered that in fact the question of identity has already been answered by Jesus Christ's vocation. Whether they realize it or not, Christians are a people invested with the ministry of witness. In other words: there *is* such a thing as a true Christian identity but this true identity is a *given* identity. It cannot be distorted or attacked by attempts to create an artificial group identity. This true identity is safe in Christ. He is a true and truthful witness. He wants them to become like him.

As it is for Hauerwas, for Schurer this awareness that the true Christian identity is a given identity is the theological basis of his prophetic witness of peace. Though they live in different times and places, they are both confronted with the fact that the peacefulness that Christ demands from his people is different from the way many of their fellow Christians believe and is also different from how they live. They bear witness against the beliefs and behaviors of their sisters and brothers. To be sure, the content of their critiques is rather different. Schurer accuses the Dutch Neo-Calvinists of having a narrow-minded view on how Christians must live. He argues that while they use biblical norms for creating a Christian counterculture, at the same time they support an unbiblical politics of capitalism, militarism and colonialism. Hauerwas accuses American mainstream Christians of being superficial. He argues that they are only interested in individual redemption and have no views about how Christian life could make a difference to the late modern society. But Schurer and Hauerwas agree in their critiques that Christians feel too much at home in their society. They protest again this Constantinianism, suggesting that their fellows are deaf to Jesus's vocation to become his witnesses, his peacemakers.

Schurer's life affirms one of Hauerwas most famous one-liners: *"Christianity: it's not a religion: it's an adventure."*[18] Schurer's life *is* adventurous. Through this conviction that he has been called to be a peacemaker, Schurer breaks free from the parochial subculture of Neo-Calvinism. He discovers that faithfulness to the gospel is quite different from living a narrow-minded life. Because of his peacemaking activities he makes all kinds of alliances with all kinds of people: Roman Catholics, liberals and particularly socialists. But in this adventure Schurer remains faithful, not just to Friesland but to the peaceable kingdom.

2. HOLY SPIRIT

This section discusses the second basic theological rule:

> *Our reflections on the character of Christian witness are only accurate if we take into account that man cannot answer God's call to be his faithful and truthful witnesses without the help of the Holy Spirit.*

2.1 The Second Rule

If one thing is consistent in all the explorations of the various Bible books, it's that without God's help, man is incapable of becoming a faithful and truthful witness. Whereas the ninth commandment claims that in Israel, man must not bear false testimony against his neighbor, the prophecies of Second Isaiah suggest that Israel's natural tendency is to deceive God and itself. However, the divine vocation as it is depicted by Second Isaiah not only reveals Israel's unfaithfulness, it's also the beginning of a renewed relationship between Israel and God. Yahweh sends his spirit and through this power Israel is able to speak truthfully and faithfully again.

In the previous chapter we found that both Acts and John make a clear distinction between the deeds of Jesus Christ, the master who calls his apostles, and the deeds of the Holy Spirit, the divine power that helps the disciples to answer their master's call. In the gospel of John the work of the Holy Spirit can only begin after the work of Jesus Christ is completed: "If I do not go away, the Helper will not come to you; but if I depart, I will send Him to you"(John 16:7 NKJ). Jesus Christ promises them that the Spirit will

---

18. See the title of an essay by Hauerwas "Christianity: It's Not a Religion: It's an Adventure."

come, and bear witness of him. Indeed, through the Spirit's witnessing the disciples are instructed to give their own testimony. Acts 1 recounts how Jesus orders his disciples to wait until the Holy Spirit comes: "You will receive power when the Holy Spirit has come upon you; and you will be my witnesses in Jerusalem, in all Judea and Samaria, and to the ends of the earth" (Acts 1:8). And when the Spirit comes at Pentecost, the disciples are able to obey their calling and bear witness of Jesus Christ as having risen from the dead. Pentecost can be understood as the starting point of the transformation of the disciples into men capable of answering their master's call. When the story continues, it turns out that the transformation by the Holy Spirit is successful: through their witnessing in situations of imminent and actual oppression, Peter and Paul show that, thanks to the help of the Holy Spirit, they have become truthful and faithful witnesses of Jesus Christ.

Though in Revelation, there are no such references to the Holy Spirit, the Apocalypse does refer to a similar transformation of the witness. John of Patmos not only warns the churches of Asia Minor not to compromise, he also believes and predicts that in the coming time of oppression many Christians will be transformed into truthful witnesses capable of holding the testimony of Jesus and living faithfully to him.

On the basis of these biblical insights, we can establish the second basic theological rule, one which pertains to the pneumatological dimension of Christian faith: in our reflections on the character of Christian testimony or the witnessing church we must explain how the Holy Spirit helps individuals and communities to answer Jesus Christ's vocation and shapes them as faithful and truthful witnesses.

2.2 Hauerwas and the Second Rule

It can easily be established that Hauerwas complies with this second rule. In the Gifford Lectures we find many references to the work of the Holy Spirit. In the sixth lecture Hauerwas criticizes Barth for not saying clearly enough that: "through the work of the Holy Spirit, we are made part of God's care of the world through the church" (145). And in the last lecture, Hauerwas remarks that:

> Christians behave in this way because they understand themselves to have become characters in the story that God continues to enact through the ongoing work of the Holy Spirit. (212)

In this section I'll argue that Hauerwas conforms to the second rule and that his reflections on the character of Christian witness in *With the Grain of the Universe* and his other work must be understood as explorations of how the Holy Spirit helps the church to answer truthfully and faithfully to its vocation.

For Hauerwas, the Holy Spirit completes God's work in Jesus Christ by creating communities of women and men who believe that they have been called together as witnesses. Through the work of the Holy Spirit, these women and men find that the divine call, against which no objection can be made, has liberated them from their blindness and deafness, from their confusion and incompetence, and has transformed them into a ministering people: speaking, acting, and living as dedicated witnesses of God. The fruit of the work of the Holy Spirit is the existence of concrete and visible communities of witnesses.

The Holy Spirit does not create these communities all at once, but through a gradual process of training. For Hauerwas, witnessing truthfully and faithfully is a communal skill which can only be learned gradually through practicing. In this process, Christians are encouraged to give up their old lives and loyalties and start new lives communally with each other and with their Lord Jesus Christ. In one way this training is a moral exercise in which Christians are taught to give up vices such as mendacity and falseness and to acquire the virtues of truthfulness and faithfulness. And in another it is an intellectual exercise in which Christians learn to understand that they are—like Israel—a character in God's story of creation, reconciliation and redemption and that their role is to make known to the world that Jesus is the Son of God. In fact, Hauerwas suggests that living the communal life is itself a moral *and* intellectual exercise taught by the Holy Spirit. Through practicing the communal life, the church is capable of giving a worthy answer to Jesus's call and of acquiring the features of a faithful and truthful witness of the triune God.

Hauerwas sometimes tends to overemphasize the significance of exercising.[19] But this emphasis is relaxed during his thoughts on the created world as a contingent world.[20] In a contingent world we do not know for sure what to say and do. We speak and act without knowing if we do right or wrong. If this is true, then good training is rather different from drilled discipline. As Hauerwas puts it,

> Christians believe that God has given us life-forming practices
> that enable us to live without seeking false comforts in a world
> of contingency we do not and cannot control.[21]

19. See chapter 3.2.1b.1.
20. See chapter 1.4.1.
21. "Connections," 80.

This view is supported by our reading of Isaiah and Acts. Through the spirit of Yahweh, Israel is gifted with a speech which enables it to distinguish between seeking false comfort in the images of idols and trusting Yahweh. Through the Spirit of Christ, the disciples remain truthful and faithful in a world they do not and cannot control.

At the same time, Hauerwas stresses that no man is immune to failure, that truthful and faithful witnesses make serious and tragic mistakes. Indeed, one of the most important aspects of the Holy Spirit's training is that Christians learn and re-learn that they are sinners: "the sins of the faithful testify to the One who makes it possible for us to know and confess our sins."[22] Christians are encouraged by the Holy Spirit to interpret their own lives with the help of the biblical narratives about man's sin and God's forgiveness. Through this training, they are taught not to deceive themselves, or each other, but to confess how they sin, individually and as a community. This moral and intellectual insight is the crucial starting point of all faithful and truthful witnessing.

Peacefulness is one of the characteristics of the communal witness by the church. Through the help of the Holy Spirit, the church could become "a witness to the peace that is an alternative to the death that grips the life of the world" (230). Christian communities bear witness to this peace, for instance, by solving conflicts by encouraging forgiveness and reconciliation. This communal testimony to peace as an alternative to the dominance of the powers that rule our world may be answered with mockery, repression and physical violence. Throughout his work, Hauerwas tries to explain how the Holy Spirit helps Christians to resist the temptation to react with counter-violence and shows them ways to remain faithful to their testimony of peace. And he points to the lives of women and men who did remain faithful and truthful even under the threat of torture and death. Thus martyrdom is "the most determinative display of what being a witness entails" (212).

As we know, Hauerwas has been accused of tribalism or "social sectarianism."[23] According to his critics, he is propagating a church which isolates itself from the rest of society, "a tribe of witnesses" so to say. While it is true that Hauerwas uses "tribalistic" rhetoric now and then and urges Christians to be more loyal to the Christian faith, the previous section has indicated that for Hauerwas the essence of the church does not coincide with the identity of this or that particular Christian group. The church is qualified by its vocation to be a witnessing community. In this section we have seen that the Holy Spirit guides the church to answer this vocation, not

22. "Hooks," 92.
23. See chapter 1.5.5.

by isolating this community from the rest of society but by training them to be present as a community of peace. Therefore, I reason that if we take into account Hauerwas's complete oeuvre, the accusation of tribalism is unfair.

An important aspect in Hauerwas's account is the notion of "life." On the one hand, he conceives the communal life of the church as an exercise for acquiring the characteristics of a faithful and truthful witness. But he also conceives this communal life of the church itself as a testimony. Without such an ecclesial life there is no answer to Jesus's call—indeed, the ecclesial life *is* the answer to Jesus's call. In some ways the examinations of the previous chapters affirm that he is correct: we cannot speak of testimony and witnessing without referring to witnesses and to the lives they live. Paul Ricoeur indicates that testimony always refers to a subject, a witnessing agent, a human being of flesh and blood.[24] Without this reference to living witnesses implicitly or explicitly swearing an oath of honesty and integrity, testimony ceases to be testimony and becomes a mechanical repetition of information. Moreover, Acts and Revelation agree that testimony is a statement which can only be uttered by living witnesses—real women and men who are invested with the ministry of the witness and gifted with the Holy Spirit. As the book of Revelation stresses, Christian witnesses are not only called to speak truthfully, i.e. to proclaim frankly and honestly that Jesus is the Christ, they are also called to live and die in faithfulness to this testimony.

Hauerwas, however, goes further than Ricoeur. For him, faithful and truthful witnesses bear witness not just by holding and proclaiming the testimony that Jesus is the Christ but first and foremost by a specific way of living which is in itself a testimony that Jesus is the Christ. The work of the Holy Spirit is not restricted to the encouragement of verbal acts of proclaiming the gospel. The Spirit encourages the church to bear witness through all of its practices, through the many facets of communal life. This communal testimony does not only include well-defined ecclesial practices such as liturgy, diaconate, and catechesis, but also the social interaction within the community: the institutional organization and the daily life of every individual community member. Thanks to the help of the Holy Spirit, this complex reality of communal living can become the church's truthful and faithful answer to Christ's vocation: "You are my witnesses." Nevertheless, the question remains: does Hauerwas in some ways overemphasize the importance of the testimonial life? I will answer this question below in Section 4.

We will now discuss two other shortcomings in Hauerwas's account. Firstly, due to his focus on witnessing as a communal way of living, Hauerwas seems to have no eye for the individuality of witnesses. Ricoeur's

24. See chapter 3.2.

analysis of testimony, meanwhile, indicates that we cannot neglect the witness as an individual. Faithful and truthful witnesses are those individuals who distinguish themselves from others by remaining faithful to their oath and speaking the truth, even if their audience does not like what they have to say. Moreover, this individual witness, witnessing against the common norms of its community, is a well-known figure in the Bible and in Christian tradition. Consider the prophets who prophesied against Israel—though the Old Testament does not call them witnesses—and of Jesus's prophetic testimony in the gospel of John. Arguably, Hauerwas *himself* often acts as "a prophetic individual," who is witnessing against the common sense of his Christian community.[25] In fact there is no valid reason in Hauerwas's theology for not allowing the idea that the Holy Spirit guides the individual in its testimony for and against its community.

Secondly, Hauerwas ignores the witness's inner life. Ricoeur's analysis of testimony indicates that we cannot speak of faithfulness and truthfulness without mentioning this.[26] Truthfulness indicates that the witness is full of truth. Faithfulness refers to an innermost drive. Together faithfulness and truthfulness refer to a witness's passion, a devotion to telling the truth which is immune to repression. Despite his hesitation to speak of the inner disposition of the witness, I'm of the view that Hauerwas cannot deny the importance of the inner life and must admit that the Holy Spirit also works in it. Indeed, along with Paul and Calvin we could say that the Holy Spirit bears witness *in* our souls.[27] The inner testimony of the Spirit could be conceived not just as the impulse of our innermost experiences but also as the inner criterion for our passions and devotions.[28]

Finally, in his Gifford lectures on Barth, Hauerwas makes a fascinating observation:

> "Witness" is one of Barth's ways of displaying what it means for us to participate in the life of the Trinity. (195n)

I think that this observation also applies to Hauerwas. Like Barth, he maintains that by stimulating the church to give a truthful and faithful answer to God's call, the Holy Spirit involves the church in the life of the Trinity.

> Just as the Son witnesses to the Father, so the Spirit makes us witnesses to the Son so that the world may know the Father. (207)

25. See chapter 2.1b.3. Healy (*Hauerwas*, 67) makes a similar point.

26. See chapter 2.1b.3.

27. See chapter 1.5 and 1.7.

28. Healy (*Hauerwas*, 95–96) makes a similar point.

The Holy Spirit trains the church to participate in the self-revelation of the triune God, and through this training it resembles Jesus Christ more and more, who lived and died as a true and faithful witness. This is how Hauerwas conforms to the second basic theological rule.

THE TESTIMONY OF THE MONKS OF TIBHIRINE

My second witness is a film. In my view *Of Gods and Men,* directed by the French filmmaker Xavier Beauvois, portrays what a witnessing community guided by the Holy Spirit could look like. In particular it helps us to understand how communities can strive for holiness without isolating themselves from the world they live in. I'll first give a short synopsis of the film before analyzing it theologically.

a. Of Gods and Men

The community of Notre-Dame de l'Atlas is a Trappist monastery in Tibhirine, Algeria. In 1996, seven of the nine brothers from this monastery were kidnapped, during the Algerian Civil War. Two months later their heads are discovered—their bodies are never found. It's not sure if they were killed by the Armed Islamic Group or by the Algerian army.[29]

Of Gods and Men gives an impressive picture of the life of the brothers before their assassination. We see them celebrating mass, working the land, saying their prayers, and eating their meals. But the community of monks is also connected with their neighbors in the local village. They give free medical care to the villagers, they are present at the circumcision celebration and they sell honey at the local market. There is mutual respect and friendship between the Christian monks and Muslim villagers.

Then the monks and the villagers are startled by the murder of foreigners and locals by Islamic fundamentalists. A civil war breaks out between the government and rebel groups. When the troubles come to the village, the monks refuse to take sides. They do not want armed protection by the Algerian army and give medical care not only to army soldiers but also to rebels. The monks are deeply worried about the violence. They know they are in serious danger because they are distrusted by both the

29. See John Kiser, *The Monks of Tibhirine.*

authorities and the rebels. Some of the brothers want to leave, but others argue that the villagers need them, that it is their duty to stay in the Atlas Mountains.

As the movie unfolds, we see how they continue to pray, how they confess their fears to each other, how they discuss staying with the villagers or leaving them. Finally they make the unanimous decision to stay, whatever happens. As it's almost Easter, the discipline and sobriety of daily life in the monastery is interrupted by a spontaneous party. The monks eat together and drink wine, while Tchaikovsky's "Black Swan" plays loudly in the background. Then, at night, the monastery is attacked. Two monks hide themselves, but the others are kidnapped. A final shot shows the monks and their kidnappers walking away in the snow, somewhere high in Atlas Mountains. The film concludes with a reading of the testament of Christian, the prior of the monastery. After the monks were killed, this document was found in the monastery.[30]

Testament of Dom Christian de Chergé
(opened on Pentecost Sunday, May 26, 1996)

Facing a GOODBYE . . .

If it should happen one day—and it could be today—that I become a victim of the terrorism which now seems ready to engulf all the foreigners living in Algeria, I would like my community, my Church and my family to remember that my life was GIVEN to God and to this country. I ask them to accept the fact that the One Master of all life was not a stranger to this brutal departure. I would ask them to pray for me: for how could I be found worthy of such an offering? I ask them to associate this death with so many other equally violent ones which are forgotten through indifference or anonymity. My life has no more value than any other. Nor any less value. In any case, it has not the innocence of childhood. I have lived long enough to know that I am an accomplice in the evil which seems to prevail so terribly in the world, even in the evil which might blindly strike me down. I should like, when the time comes, to have a moment of spiritual clarity which would allow me to beg forgiveness of God and of my fellow human beings, and at the same time

---

30. Chergé, "Testament."

forgive with all my heart the one who would strike me down. I could not desire such a death. It seems to me important to state this. I do not see, in fact, how I could rejoice if the people I love were indiscriminately accused of my murder. It would be too high a price to pay for what will perhaps be called, the "grace of martyrdom" to owe it to an Algerian, whoever he might be, especially if he says he is acting in fidelity to what he believes to be Islam. I am aware of the scorn which can be heaped on the Algerians indiscriminately. I am also aware of the caricatures of Islam which a certain Islamism fosters. It is too easy to soothe one's conscience by identifying this religious way with the fundamentalist ideology of its extremists. For me, Algeria and Islam are something different: it is a body and a soul. I have proclaimed this often enough, I think, in the light of what I have received from it. I so often find there that true strand of the Gospel which I learned at my mother's knee, my very first Church, precisely in Algeria, and already inspired with respect for Muslim believers. Obviously, my death will appear to confirm those who hastily judged me naive or idealistic: "Let him tell us now what he thinks of his ideals!" But these persons should know that finally my most avid curiosity will be set free. This is what I shall be able to do, God willing: immerse my gaze in that of the Father to contemplate with him His children of Islam just as He sees them, all shining with the glory of Christ, the fruit of His Passion, filled with the Gift of the Spirit whose secret joy will always be to establish communion and restore the likeness, playing with the differences. For this life lost, totally mine and totally theirs, I thank God, who seems to have willed it entirely for the sake of that JOY in everything and in spite of everything. In this THANK YOU, which is said for everything in my life from now on, I certainly include you, friends of yesterday and today, and you, my friends of this place, along with my mother and father, my sisters and brothers and their families. You are the hundredfold granted as was promised! And also you, my last-minute friend, who will not have known what you were doing: Yes, I want this THANK YOU and this GOODBYE to be a "GOD-BLESS" for you, too, because in God's face I see yours. May we meet again as happy thieves in Paradise, if it pleases God, the Father of us both.

AMEN! INCHALLAH!

Algiers, 1st December 1993
Tibhirine, 1st January 1994
Christian +

b. Analysis

In my view *Of Gods and Men* is a film about witnesses. It pictures
the life of the monks as a *testimonium vitae*. Through their liturgy
and daily work, they witness to the love of the God they serve.
Through their friendship with the villagers they show a way for
Christians and Muslims to live peacefully together. Indeed, the
brothers are so dedicated to their vocation to be peacemakers in
the Atlas Mountains that they discover that, despite their fears
and doubts, leaving Algeria is no option for them. As faithful witnesses to Christ, they stay. And like their master in the garden of
Gethsemane, they are fully aware of the consequences.

All the major themes in Hauerwas's work are present in
this film. It is about community—but not in a nostalgic way. The
monks are pictured as men of flesh and bones who have their
conflict but manage to live a communal life. The film is about
exercise and training—but not in a common way. These monks
are trained by the rules of their Trappist order and by rhythms of
their daily celebrations. The film is about mission—but not in a
manipulating way. The monks do not use rhetorical techniques
to convert their Muslim neighbors, they simply become friends.
The film is about peacefulness—but not in a naive way. The
monks show a way to remain peaceful in an extremely violent
environment. The film is about martyrdom—but not in a glorify-
ing way. The monks simply accept that martyrdom is the ultimate
consequence of their way of living.

This film is also about God and his hidden presence in the
life of these monks. It indeed perfectly illustrates Hauerwas's
understanding of how the Holy Spirit works in our lives. This
understanding of the work by the Holy Spirit is rather different
from how Christians usually understand it. Nowadays, because
of the growing influence of Pentecostalism many people see
the Holy Spirit as a power creating ecstatic experiences in their
souls. For Hauerwas the Spirit works in our reality, not through

spectacular actions, but by binding himself to communal life. The near presence of the Holy Spirit can be discerned, not in the emotions of the religious subject but in the practices of a disciplined community.

In my view this film shows us how the Holy Spirit guides a Christian community through their disciplined life. There is no arrogance in the way the monks treat each other and their Muslim neighbors. In his testament, Dom Christian speaks about how he too is an accomplice in evil. The monks know that the basis of a holy life is the confession of sin. For them the road to perfection begins with a sense of being imperfect, of being completely dependent of God's forgiving grace. It is the Holy Spirit who has raised this awareness in the soul of the monks. It is the Holy Spirit who guides them step by step to a life of holiness. By the end of the film the monks seem to have lost all their fears and doubts. Feeling the presence of the Spirit of Christ near, they know what to do.

Finally, I propose that the film itself can be conceived as a testimony. Just as the book of Revelation, it is a testimony of real people staying faithful in times of tribulation. Surprisingly, in secular France, *Of Gods and Men* was a hit, drawing in large audiences. It appeared that both the critics and the public were deeply impressed by how this film portrays the discipline, friendliness, and unconditional peacefulness of the monks of Notre-Dame de l'Atlas.

3. TRUTH

This section discusses the third basic theological rule:

> In our reflection on the character of Christian witness we must take into account that we can only grasp the witness as witness if we describe how, in a world of mendacity and treacherousness, witnesses make known the one true God, and vouch for the truth of their testimony—without the false pretension that they have control over the One of whom they bear testimony.

3.1 The Third Rule

In the explorations of the previous chapter we found that all the discussed Bible books apply a forensic analogy to the notions of witness, witnessing and testimony. It seems that these analogies are especially helpful for showing what Israel and the disciples know about God, and how they communicate what they know. Thus, like witnesses in court, Israel and the disciples:

a. know of something special and bear testimony to this;

b. find themselves involved in a conflict about the truth of their testimonies; and

c. must vouch for the truth of their testimony.

These three aspects need some further explanation.

a. Firstly Israel and the apostles are in the service of God's self-revelation. God wants to make himself known to the world and he chooses witnesses who must show the world who he is. In Second Isaiah, Israel's silent presence witnesses to the sovereign power of the Lord, and that there is no one beside him. In John, the disciples are foretold that they will bear testimony of Jesus's testimony of himself. In Acts the apostles bear witness to Jesus Christ who has truly risen from the dead. In Revelation, Christians are encouraged to hold the testimony of Jesus Christ, who is the true and faithful witness.

b. Secondly all these witnesses bear witness in a situation of conflict. The four discussed Bible books refer to a struggle between truth and lies. In one way God *is involved* in this conflict: as the Lord of Israel who settles a trial against the nations and their idols, and as Jesus Christ who provokes his audience with his testimony about himself as the way, the truth and the life. But in another way God *involves* his witnesses in this conflict. While in Second Isaiah, Israel's silent testimony affirms God's case, in the New Testament, the Holy Spirit transforms the disciples into witnesses of the controversial news that their Lord Jesus Christ has risen from the dead. Moreover, the biblical authors do not attempt to withhold this contentious news, but use provocative language to expose the contrasts between the dominant narratives and beliefs and the testimony to God.

c. Thirdly, in the same way as legal witnesses, Israel and the disciples vouch for the truth of their testimony. Through its presence at the trial, Israel vouches for the Lord's faithfulness. By presenting themselves as witnesses, the disciples in the New Testament swear: what we say about Jesus Christ is true. The reason why these witnesses vouch for the truth is not so much that they have "strong convictions" that something is the case, rather they found that in some way they have become participants in the self-revelation of the one true God.

With the help of these three forensic and biblical aspects of witnessing, three more detailed formulations of the third rule can be given.

a. A theologically adequate account of Christian witnessing must explain what Christian witnesses know and how they communicate what they know. On the one hand, we must consider that Christians are a people who have been called to play a role in God's self-revelation. They know of something special, they have a story to tell about the God who reveals himself in Israel and in the life, death, and resurrection of Jesus Christ and it is their vocation to make this story known to mankind. But we must also realize that Christians are no more than witnesses giving testimony—what makes them unique is not *that* they communicate or *how* they communicate, but *what* they communicate.

b. A theologically adequate account of Christian witnessing must explain how Christians relate to the ongoing conflicts between truth and lies. On one side we must consider that they cannot remain detached from this conflict as neutral bystanders: they are called by their Lord as his witnesses, they must bear witness in favor of his case—and perhaps they are even obliged to use the instrument of provocation. Yet we must also realize that Christians are mere witnesses—this conflict is not *their* conflict but *God's* conflict.

c. A theologically adequate account of Christian witnessing must explain why and how Christians can vouch for the truth of God. In one respect, we must consider Christians as a people who have the authority to claim that their testimony is true. In another respect, we must realize that this people cannot claim to control or possess the truth. They can only claim that they are possessed and controlled *by* the truth—the truth of God's self-revelation.

3.2 Hauerwas and the Third Rule

This section discusses the three formulations of the third rule in succession. First, I will analyze how Hauerwas's witnesses communicate their testimonies, then I'll examine how they become involved in a conflict about this testimony, and finally I'll discuss how they can vouch for the truth of their testimony.

3.2.1 *Truthful Communication*

For Hauerwas, the church has been called to instruct mankind about what kind of world we live in and what kind of creatures we are. As he puts it in one of the few sentences in the last Gifford lecture that explicitly refers to the Christian's vocation:

> Witness, at least the witness to which Christians are called, is, after all, about God and God's relation to all that is. (207)

With the Grain of the Universe describes how Christians could answer positively to this call. If they let themselves be guided by the Holy Spirit, they will become a community that reflects in every aspect of their communal life that the true God is the triune God, that this world is God's fallen creation which will be restored, and that men are sinners who have been saved by the cross. Of course, Hauerwas does not forget how Christians often ignore their vocation and how Christian communities are losing their way because of their own mendacity and self-deception. But he also wants his readers to not close their eyes to the fact that there are individual Christians and Christian communities who try to live truthfully and faithfully and who succeed in doing this in many parts of their lives. These lives are the lives of faithful and truthful witnesses, individuals and communities who have been taken in the service of God's revelation.

In fact there are three reasons why the church must bear witness. Firstly, the church bears testimony for the sake of non-Christians. With the help of the Holy Spirit, Christian witnesses show that they are a people liberated from their despair by the triune God, and that all men are invited to take part in their community of faith. Secondly, the church is called to bear testimony for its own sake. The Holy Spirit motivates Christians to bear witness, since in this process of constant witnessing they will acquire a deeper and better understanding of the true character of God, man and the world. But Hauerwas also suggests that, ultimately, Christians bear witness for God. Through the guidance of the Holy Spirit, they take part in the life of the Trinity by obeying Jesus Christ's call.

It's clear that, for Hauerwas, witnesses are people who have received a narrative, and that these people have the vocation to communicate this story and the related beliefs to each other and to others. Just as a witness in a court is, Christian witnesses are called to make known what they know. But what makes Hauerwas's argument so interesting *and* complicated is that Christian witnesses communicate in a different way to legal witnesses. For Hauerwas, the most appropriate way to make this narrative known is not so much asserting, but showing. Christian witnesses bear witnesses by enacting the story of the Bible in their individual and communal lives.

The notion of *testimonium vitae* or "testimony of life" has not always been part of the Christian vocabulary but has only recently been adopted by Christian theology.[31] There is a parallel between the way Hauerwas (and other theologians) apply this notion in their work and the way Luke applies the term μάρτυς in his writings. For Luke, the message that Jesus is risen from the dead is an exclusive message. But when he tells his readers about the apostles proclaiming this message to the whole world, he uses common Greek terms for witnessing and testimony. Of course he has good reasons for adopting the notion of witnessing in our terms: witnessing is a form of communication which does not belie what is being communicated. However, Luke does not suggest that witnessing by itself is an exclusive communication skill. What makes the apostles unique is their *vocation*, not their communication.

In a similar way, Hauerwas has good reasons to speak of the church as a witness witnessing through life. It helps him to describe how Christians communicate their stories and beliefs. Witnessing through life is a way of communication which fits well with that which is communicated: the Gospel, i.e. the good news that Jesus is the Christ. Witnesses show this narrative in their lives and this showing

> cannot be coercive because the story that shapes the witness is a story of a God who would have us love freely. The gospel—the good news that was and is Jesus—is wonderful because there is no greater surprise.[32]

But while Hauerwas argues that this story of a God who loves us freely cannot be understood apart from the people who have found that they have a role within it, he does not suggest that witnessing is an exclusive communication skill in itself. What makes Christians unique is their *vocation*, not their communication.

---

31. See chapter 2.8.
32. "Hooks," 90.

Now it's clear that Hauerwas conforms to the first formulation of the third theological rule. He speaks of witnesses as people who know of something special and bear witness to this without making the unjustified suggestion that they are more than just witnesses.

3.2.2 A People in Conflict

Throughout his work, Hauerwas portrays a conflict between narratives, a struggle between the dominant stories of our time and the stories of Israel and Jesus Christ. He speaks of Christians as agents involved in this struggle. Christians are a people in conflict. This is primarily an *internal* conflict: Christians are in conflict with *themselves*. When they read Scripture, they are constantly challenged to give up their false views and unfaithful behavior. Yet thanks to the work of the Holy Spirit, Christians are persuaded by the good news of the Bible: they enact the gospel in their lives and learn to live as faithful and truthful witnesses. As soon as this happens, the conflict between narratives also becomes an *external* conflict as a contrast emerges between the lives of these witnesses and the lives of other people.

Hauerwas criticizes contemporary Western Christianity for its tendency to veil this conflict and to adapt Christian faith to the norms of dominant ideologies such as liberalism or capitalism. If Christians live in faithfulness to the good news of the Bible, the conflicts with these ideologies are unavoidable. Moreover, the vocation to bear witness implies that Christians must face these conflicts peacefully—by protesting prophetically against these ideologies and by living a life which is an alternative to these dominant narratives. *With the Grain of the Universe* mentions the example of John Paul ii and John Howard Yoder. They both

> represent a recovery of the Christological center of the church's life and witness. That center, moreover, requires and entails that the church be a witness to the peace that is an alternative to the death that grips the life of the world. (230)

Despite the radical nature of this statement, Hauerwas does not explain how witnesses are related to non-Christians and how these two groups of people interact. This raises a problem. *With the Grain of the Universe* can be understood as if it supports the idea that, while Christian witnesses are a people gifted with the unique skill of witnessing truthfully and faithfully, all non-Christians are deluded by various false ideologies. In this reading, the conflict under discussion is conceived as a clash between the dominant culture and a Christian counter-culture. If this interpretation is correct, then

Hauerwas's account does not adhere to the second formulation of the third rule: that one must speak of the conflict in such a way that it remains clear that it is not a Christian conflict but *God's* conflict.

But what this interpretation forgets is the situation in which Christians and non-Christians find themselves. According to Hauerwas, we live in a world "without certainty," in a context in which it is not self-evident what we must think and do. It's in this confusion that Christians are called to become witnesses to the good news that Jesus is the Christ. Just as legal witnesses are not attorneys, the Christians in *With the Grain of the Universe* are not the initiators of the conflict in which they find themselves. It is God who, in his self-revelation, initiates the conflict by unmasking dominant stories as idolatrous ideologies. Christians are nothing more than witnesses called to testify in favor of God's case. Therefore, Hauerwas's work cannot be reduced to a plea for a Christian counterculture. In my view, it must be read as a theological and ethical reflection on how Jesus Christ calls Christians as his witnesses and on how the Holy Spirit helps them to answer this call. From this perspective it's clear that Hauerwas conforms to the second formulation of the third rule.

The relationship between Christians and non-Christians requires some further explanation. I've argued before that there's nothing in Hauerwas's account of witness which goes against the idea that non-Christians can also be conceived as witnesses living a particular way and having a specific view.[33] To supplement this we could suggest that, especially for those Christians who have learned to understand themselves as witnesses witnessing to a particular view and a specific way, non-Christians also appear as witnesses. Though non-religious people and members of other religions do not feel addressed by Jesus Christ's call to become *his witnesses*, they can be considered as people who through their lives bear witness to a specific view of man as existing in a world with or without God. After all, like Christians, non-Christians are creatures of God acting within a fallen creation, they are gifted with language, speaking after Babel.

This is most clear with respect to people from other religions. For Christians, Buddhists, Hindus, Jews, Muslims and others are not only committed to a collection of narratives, they also appear as witnesses to a specific way of living and a specific set of convictions. The same is true for individuals and groups who are committed to non-religious worldviews. And in fact even the great many people in the secularized West who live their "own story," free from what they consider as "imposed convictions," could still be

33. See chapter 3.2.1b.2.

regarded as witnesses. From the perspective of Christian witnesses, these people are witnessing to a belief that we create our own stories and to a conviction that we need to be liberated from non-authentic convictions.

Thus, Christian witnesses find themselves in a "multi-testimonial society."[34] On the one hand they will often find that non-Christians do good and speak the truth. The witness of the church is affirmed by a witness outside the church. And if this happens, they have reason to praise God whose Spirit is like the wind that blows wherever it pleases, to inspire whoever he wants. Hauerwas himself acknowledges explicitly that the Church's witness is affirmed by the witness of those such as the Radical Democrat Romans Coles.[35] But Christians will also discover that in some respects— or in many—their testimony conflicts with other testimonies. The gravest controversy is not between those who live in accordance with various non-dominant stories, but between Christians and those who represent the dominant stories in our society.

Yet, the reason Christians get involved in this conflict is not that they are a discordant people who believe that those who do not belong to their group are wicked or reprehensible. Like the witnesses in the book of Revelation, the witnesses in Hauerwas's work simply believe that they can only serve one Lord and that they should not compromise in being faithful to him. Yet, the more they live faithfully to him, the more their lives reveal the contrast between the way of their Lord and the dominant movements in Western society. That is why Christian life could be described as a "counterculture." One thing is clear, however: Christians should not pretend they are capable of giving temporary or conclusive judgments on those who are living according to the dominant stories of our times. They are witnesses, not judges. The seat of the judge must remain empty, until their Lord comes to judge all people, Christians and non-Christians.

Finally, this idea that Christians are witnesses witnessing in and for a multi-testimonial society also could help us to interpret the provocative rhetoric in Hauerwas's work. Hauerwas does not pretend that as a theologian he's allowed to sit on the judge's chair and give verdicts on certain phenomena in society. He's a witnessing scholar, a theologian who's found, in the struggle between the dominant stories of our time and the stories of Israel and Jesus Christ, that he cannot remain a bystander, that he must answer to his call and bear witness of the stories of Israel and Jesus Christ. He has, however, also found that many of his fellow scholars and Christians do not see the gravity of what's at stake in this testimony. This is why Hauerwas,

34. See chapter 3.2.1b.2.
35. See chapter 1.4.2.

like the authors of Isaiah, John, Acts and Revelation, uses provocation as an instrument to reveal the actual conflict between the dominant narratives and beliefs of our time and the testimony to the one true God.

3.2.3 Vouching for the Truth

Witnesses are not just mere communicators of stories and beliefs. In a certain way, they also show that what they communicate is true. *With the Grain of the Universe* claims that if the church is faithful to its vocation and dares to live in line with biblical stories and Christian beliefs, it will gain the authority to make clear implicitly through its actions, and claim explicitly through its words, that these stories and beliefs are true. But, as we know, the argumentation for this claim remains somewhat opaque. Hauerwas does not fully explain why the notion of witnessing and the figure of the witness are indispensable for a theological reflection on truth. Therefore, before I discuss the third formulation of the third basic theological rule, I will give an overview of Hauerwas's understanding of the expertise of the witness and his conception of truth.

In the courtroom, everyone agrees that witnesses and testimonies play an important role in the process of truth finding.[36] The witness's testimony is used as evidence for claims that something did or did not occur. Witnesses vouch for the truth of their testimonies: they swear that they are willing to tell the truth and they are capable of giving an authoritative statement about what they saw or heard. The apostles in the book of Acts resemble these legal eyewitnesses. For Luke, the fact that the apostles were eyewitnesses is a necessary condition for their authority. The apostles are able to vouch for their testimony that Jesus has risen from the dead because they have seen Jesus as the resurrected Lord. One could say that contemporary Christians are "hearsay witnesses" of the original eyewitness testimony by the apostles and that the authority of these Christian witnesses is primarily derived from the testimony of the apostles. Yet Hauerwas does *not* make this suggestion. The witnesses of whom he speaks are different from hearsay witnesses.

Hauerwas's witnesses are like another kind of courtroom witness: the expert. The expert witness testifies on the basis of what he knows, he gives his vision based on scientific knowledge. His authority does not stem from observation but from scientific expertise acquired through practicing a specific scientific subject. Because of their scientific expertise, they can vouch for the truth of their testimony. If the witnesses in Acts are eyewitnesses, the witnesses in Hauerwas's work are expert witnesses. The authority of faithful

36. See chapter 3.1.

and truthful witnesses does not stem from a particular observation but from a specific expertise. With the help of the Holy Spirit these witnesses have tested biblical stories and Christian beliefs in their lives and found that they show a way to live truthfully in a world without certainty. They can testify that these stories and beliefs pass the test. Moreover, by giving this testimony, they vouch personally for the truth of Christian faith: they can guarantee their audience that these stories and beliefs help them to live truthfully and faithfully without seeking untrustworthy comfort in a world we do not and cannot control.

According to Peter Ochs, Hauerwas's is a pragmatic account of the truth. Truth does not apply to our "immediate intuitions of the world," but only to the "temporally extended relationship that we have with the world."[37] This means that we cannot acquire immediate "true" knowledge of ourselves, God and the world. The views that we have in mind, are mediated by the many stories that have been told to us during our upbringing, at primary schools and in universities, in books and films, by our closest relatives and anonymous souls on the internet. Moreover, for Hauerwas there is no universal criterion for testing the "truth" of these various views. Though science delivers plenty of useful data, this data does not speak for itself and cannot be a criterion for evaluating these views—and if scientists do make claims about the character of God, man or the world, these are philosophical and/or theological claims that must be evaluated as such.[38] In the past, philosophers have argued that "reason alone" is a neutral criterion that could be universally applied to test the adequacy of man's vision, but in our late modern time many philosophers have come to realize that we can only criticize delusive beliefs by telling alternative stories which offer other, better perspectives on man living in a world with or without God. The same goes for all the major religions and their theologians—they tell stories which offer perspectives but they cannot claim to have a universal criterion at their disposal to evaluate the veracity of other perspectives.

This awareness of not having immediate knowledge or a universal criterion at our disposal is not the tragic end but the happy beginning of all philosophical and theological reflections on truth. Hauerwas uses truth as a predicate of a particular vision. The word "truth" mostly refers to the intellectual *and* moral quality of a perspective. A true interpretation of reality is one which makes sense in a double way: firstly it offers a reliable understanding of ourselves and others, of the situation we live in and the intellectual problems we have to deal with, and secondly it shows a steady

37. Ochs, "On Hauerwas' *With the Grain of the Universe*," 78. See chapter 1.3.

38. Ibid., 84.

way to live a virtuous life. So, when Hauerwas speaks of the truth of a vision, truth does not refer to an absolute quality, but to a relative quality. We cannot judge from a universalistic standpoint that one view is absolutely valid for all people at all places and all times, but we can argue that as far as we know, as far as we can see, this view is the best.

This understanding of truth offers a good argument for Christians to counter two universalistic misinterpretations of Christianity: the foundationalist approach which tries to demonstrate that Christianity is a system of universal truths, and the liberal approach which reduces Christianity to a source of universal religious experiences. According to Hauerwas, Christians can and should relearn that for them, truth can be found neither in universal systems nor in universal experiences, but in "the story of God's dealing with them in Israel and Jesus."[39] Jesus Christ's testimony of himself as "the way, and the truth, and the life" (John 14:6 NKJ) is the best argument against universalistic misinterpretations. If Jesus Christ is the truth, then truth cannot be found in systems or experiences, but it must be found in this specific person and in the stories of his life, death and resurrection.

Thus, the writings of the Old and New Testament offer a specific view on the character of God, ourselves and the world. Moreover, Hauerwas claims that the biblical view is superior to other views. This claim of superiority is be made in two rather different discourses: a "cultural linguistic" discourse and a revelational theological discourse. In cultural linguistic terms, he argues that the biblical vision is superior because of its extraordinary intellectual and moral quality. But there is another, deeper way of speaking of truth. He uses "revelational theological" terms and speaks of truth as an attribute of God which manifests itself in God's self-revelation. Indeed, what is unique is that in the writings of Israel, God reveals himself as the one true God; and that in the gospel and letters of the New Testament, God makes himself known as Father, Son and Holy Spirit.

This double view on truth can also be discerned in Hauerwas's account of witness. His claim that Christians witness to the truth of Christian stories and beliefs can be understood "cultural-linguistically" and "revelational-theologically." In the terms of the first discourse we can say that Christian witnesses vouch with their lives for the special character of the Christian view: as far as they can see, this outlook offers the best viewpoint available. But the only reason that Christians vouch for the superiority of this view is that they believe that it does not originate from their own insights but

---

39. *Community of Character*, 150.

from God's revelation. For Christians, their authority as witnesses is completely dependent on the authority of the one they bear witness to. Thus, the cultural linguistic truth-claim is relative to the revelational theological truth-claim.

In the terms of the revelational theological discourse, we could say that Christians are capable of vouching for the truth because they are taken in service of God's self-revelation. Christian witnesses are people who have been called as ministers of the triune God. It is their duty to make this God known to the world—and through the power of the Holy Spirit they are able to obey their calling. Thus, if Christians vouch for the truth of Christian convictions, they also vouch for the truth of God's self-revelation, the truth that Jesus Christ is the way, the truth and the life. Now we can see how Hauerwas also conforms to the third formulation of the third rule. He speaks of Christian witnesses as people who have the authority to claim that their testimonies are true, without making the false suggestion that they control or possess the truth.

As we know, Hauerwas has been accused of fideism or "intellectual sectarianism."[40] According to his critics, he suggests that faith is primary and reason only secondary. This section indicates that this accusation is incorrect. Hauerwas does not make a false contrast between faith and reason, suggesting faith is superior. Yet he and his criticizers disagree on how theologians should use reason. According to Hauerwas there is no good justification to apply reason for building foundations on which Christian faith can rest. Yet, he holds that there are good justifications to use reason to explain how Christian faith makes sense. And in his explanation he refers to the necessity of witness.

Hauerwas concludes his Gifford Lectures by claiming that the very existence of concrete ecclesial communities, living the biblical stories and practicing the virtues of truthfulness and faithfulness, is an argument for the truth of Christian faith: not "knock-down evidence" but indeed a serious indication. This *testimonium vitae*, this practice which is neither self-referential nor self-justifying, indicates that the triune God, to whom these practices refer, is not an illusion. He wants his readers to see that, even from a cultural-linguistic perspective, these lives cannot be reduced to human initiative but must be ascribed to the agency of God's Holy Spirit.

> The burden of my argument in this last lecture, and the over-arching ambition of all of my lectures, is to show that Christian practice and theology are neither self-referential nor self-justifying. Christian practices and beliefs cannot be self-justifying

40. See chapter 1.5.5.

> because Christians, as Barth insists, must be witnesses to the
> God who is the Father, Son and Holy Spirit. (207)

But he admits that some of his readers may contend that his argumentation is "hopelessly circular" (231). Christian witnesses claim to have authority since they are called to be witnesses to God's self-revelation, but this claim that they have been called is not confirmed by an independent third witness but only by the Bible and by other Christian witnesses in past and present. In fact, a similar objection can be given to the argument in the gospel of John, which also appears to have circular argumentation.[41] But I maintain that this perceived circularity in the gospel of John *and* in Hauerwas's writings is not the circularity of a closed circle but that of a spiral. Like the author of the fourth gospel, Hauerwas tries to move his readers from the position of the disinterested third person to that of a witness who's addressed by the words of Jesus Christ "you are my witnesses." But like the author of the fourth gospel, the author of *With the Grain of the Universe* knows that only the Holy Spirit is capable of transforming skeptics into believers.

I will not tell another story of witnessing here as I think those of Fedde Schurer and the Monks of Tibhirine are sufficient for this section. By telling these stories I hope I've explained that it's possible to identify witnesses in a world without certainties. That these stories can be told and analyzed with the help of Hauerwas's account of witness in some way proves that his account is not just a theory about witness but that the lived Christian life forms a central part of his understanding of witness. Moreover: I think the life testimonies of Schurer and the Monks in many ways show the truth of Christian faith.

4. THREE FURTHER QUESTIONS

Now that we've argued that Hauerwas substantially conforms to our three rules of discourse, there are some issues which require further examination. They are not new but emerge from the analyses in the previous chapters. Each issue is connected with one of the three themes. The first is about the relation between vocation and violence, the second the relation between the Holy Spirit's training and the crisis of testimony, and the third the relation between witnessing as showing and witnessing as referring. I've reformulated these issues into questions which will be answered successively in the three parts of this section.

41. See chapter 4.2.

4.1 Vocation and Violence

The first question is:

> *How does the idea of vocation which we've found in Isaiah and*
> *Hauerwas relate to the force to which the legal witness is subjected?*

In chapter 2 we discussed how in ancient and modern process law witnesses cannot refuse to testify in court. They are forced to swear the oath and to speak the truth under the threat of detention.[42] It could be argued that in the vocation story in Isaiah 43 and 44 Israel and the nations are treated in a similar way. Is Yahweh not violently silencing the testimony of the nations? Is he not forcing Israel to testify in court?[43] These suspicious questions could also be applied to our display of Hauerwas's account of witness. Does the notion of divine calling not unwittingly but unavoidably evoke the idea of a God who is enforcing men to become his people? Does the forced vocation of God's people not imply a violent rejection of those who do not belong to the church?

In my view, this suspicion follows from a misreading of Isaiah and Hauerwas. It is true that in the lawsuits in Second Isaiah Israel is subjected to God's will. Indeed the God who calls Israel to be his witness gave Israel away to "the robbers" (42:24). But this divine will must not be understood as the disinterested force of a supreme being but as the passionate concern of a covenant partner. Israel was trapped in its blindness and deafness and can only be saved through a powerful intervention. Yahweh intervenes for Israel's sake, to deliver his people from despair. Israel is subjected to Yahweh's will and through its subjection becomes a subject again. But what about the nations also present at this lawsuit? It seems they cannot defend themselves. It seems they are immediately silenced by Yahweh's plea. If we read more carefully it turns out that the actual conflict is not between Israel and the other nations, but between Yahweh and the gods of the nations. In the lawsuit, Yahweh unmasks these gods as idols. This act is necessary, not just for the sake of Israel but also for the sake of the nations. Only when they realize their gods are a delusion can they start to believe in the one true God.

---

42. See chapter 2.2.

43. In this subsection I restrict myself to a discussion of the problem of violence in the vocation of Israel in Isaiah 43 and 44. I do realize that in the Bible, there are texts in which God does behave violently against other nations (Ps 139:19–22) or his own people (Jer 20:3–6). Hauerwas is fully aware of this problem. "The text of the Bible in and of itself does not require pacifism. Rather, only a church that is nonviolent is capable of rightly reading, for example, Romans 13,4." *Dispatches from the Front*, 118.

Though sometimes it might seem that Yahweh's passionate concern for the well-being of his own people is possible only at the expense of other peoples, in the long term all nations shall profit from his preference for Israel.

This chapter has indicated that Hauerwas's account of witness presupposes the idea of a mighty God calling an incompetent people. This does not mean that Christians are *imposed* to be witnesses. Vocation can best be understood as an act in which God *invests* his people with the ministry of witnessing. Investing is a powerful act in which the minister is subjected to the will of his master. Yet it is not a violent act but an act of trust. The master promises the minister that this ministry of witnessing is not an impossible duty or an unreachable ideal but a task which can be fulfilled. The master trusts that the minister can and shall act in accordance with his calling. Like Israel, Christians will find that by fulfilling the ministry of witnessing, they become more and more what they truly are, a people created for peace. In Hauerwas's view, the conflicts between the politics of the peaceable kingdom and a politics of the world are irresolvable. This conflict is necessary, not just for the sake of Christians but for the sake of all mankind. For without it, the world would not know that their gods are a delusion, that the one true God is the triune God. Ultimately, the world shall profit from God's care for the church.

Thus the answer to our first question is that, theologically, vocation does *not* necessarily presuppose coercion and violence, and that there is no such relation, neither in Isaiah nor in Hauerwas.

4.2 Training and Crisis

The second question is:

> How does Hauerwas's description of training guided by the Holy Spirit relate to the crisis of testimony experienced by survivors of catastrophes?

In chapter 3 we suggested that Agamben's reflections on witnessing and testimony challenge Christians and Christian theologians such as Stanley Hauerwas. This challenge was formulated as follows: why are Christians actually witnessing? Do they really think they can and should give their testimony to a world which has heard the testimonies of the horrors of the concentration camps?

From Hauerwas's perspective a true and honest response must begin by feeling the gravity of the challenge. If the Holy Spirit is to train Christians to become a truthful and faithful people, then he also teaches them not to hide but to face the survivor and hear his testimony. And in some ways the virtues of truthfulness and faithfulness are very much required here. In this confrontation, truthfulness means facing the survivor's testimony, without the false suggestion that this testimony is a "conceptual difficulty" or a "moral problem" that could be solved by indifferent theoretical reflection or knee-jerk ethical action. In this confrontation, faithfulness means hearing the survivor's testimony, even if one's existence as a Christian witness is painfully challenged. Indeed, if they are truthful and faithful, Christians will not only feel astounded by the horrors of which these survivors speak, but they will also feel ashamed because of the guilt of many individual Christians and the church. As the first letter of Peter suggests, the judgment of the Spirit does begin not with others but "with the household of God" (1 Pet. 4:17).

Nevertheless, I think Hauerwas would add that in this confrontation, Christians cannot deny who they are. They might be completely confused, not knowing what to say and do, but confusion is not their ultimate response. Though they are deeply shocked and prefer to forget their calling, they cannot extricate themselves from it. Also in confrontation with the Auschwitz testimonies by the sons and daughters of Israel, Christians are reminded of Jesus of Nazareth who is a son of Israel. Even in the face of complete despair, the Holy Spirit teaches them to hope. Also when facing the witnesses to the horror of these catastrophes, Christians cannot deny are they are witnesses of deliverance.[44]

Thus the answer to our second question is that Hauerwas's understanding of training could help to formulate a response which does not deny the gravity of the challenge.

4.3 Showing and Referring to what is True

The third question is:

> How does Hauerwas's understanding of witnessing, as "showing what is true" relate to the understanding of witnessing as "referring to what is true."

In chapter 3 we suggested that because of the dominance of the concept of witnessing through life, it seems that in Hauerwas's work, specifically worded testimonies are no more than aspects of the communal *testimonium*

---

44. The insight that while Christians must admit that their faith is seriously challenged by the testimonies from the survivors of Auschwitz they cannot deny that for them Jesus truly is messiah, stems from the German theologian Friedrich–Wilhelm Marquardt. Marquardt dedicated his life and theology to the rediscovery of the Jewish roots of Christianity. For an English translation, see *Theological Audacities*.

vitae. This was affirmed in chapter 4 where we argued that Hauerwas does not see what Acts and John suggest, namely that there is another way of witnessing. In my reading of the New Testament there are two ways of witnessing: witnessing as showing and witnessing as referring.[45] Moreover, I argue that witnessing as referring cannot be replaced by witnessing as showing. Witnessing is a specific speech act which produces a testimony of words. These words give information, they form a description, and they tell a story. In Acts, testimony has the shape of a proclamation saying that Jesus truly revealed himself as the risen Lord. In John, human testimonies refer to Jesus and his testimony of himself.

A full theological account of Christian witness must take into account the entire scope of biblical views on the ministry of the witness. I think that it's possible to integrate these different Scriptural understandings into a single theological discourse about the ministry of Christian witnessing. Such a discourse must begin with Jesus Christ who, according to the gospel of John, is the ultimate witness: the One whose testimonial words are confirmed by his testimonial deeds and vice versa. And if we take into account Acts and John and Revelation, we must say that Jesus Christ, who witnessed of himself, called his disciples to bear witness of him—through referring (Acts and John) and through showing (Revelation). But though there is one vocation of Jesus Christ, and one ministry with which Christians are invested, this one vocation "you are my witnesses" is answered in two different ways.

On the one hand, Christ's vocation is answered through acts of faithfulness. With Revelation we can say that every Christian is called to hold the testimony of Jesus. From this perspective, Jesus's vocation is answered by those Christians who do not fail Jesus Christ, but remain faithful during temptations, repressions and other tests. Indeed, Revelation suggests that every Christian is called in a similar way, and in this respect there is no difference between the apostles and the other witnesses. Since this call is

---

45. Healy criticizes Hauerwas in a similar way in "Karl Barth." He stresses that that there are significant differences between the understanding of witness in Barth's *Church Dogmatics* and in *With the Grain of the Universe*. For Barth, witness is "not, or not in the first instance, a particular kind of life. It is as it points away from itself to the 'divine nevertheless' amid the confusions of history—the church's history as well as the world's—that the church is truly a 'sign and witness' (CD 3/3, 199), not, or not in the first instance, as it embodies a particular configuration of practices" (296–97). I think Healy is right. In my own terms: while for Hauerwas the dominant model of witnessing is "showing," for Barth it is "referring." But I would like to add to Healy that, as it does in the New Testament, in theology these two models could complement each other. The one ministry of witness is carried out in two different ways. There are no valid reasons for saying that either "referring" or "showing" should be the dominant model of witness.

answered for the most part obediently, a certain "hierarchy" appears: be-tween the faithful, those named by Hauerwas as "the elite of the Church called the saints"[46] and the not so faithful or unfaithful. Moreover, Revela-tion suggests that those who remain faithful during the tribulations begin to resemble Christ, the true and faithful witness. Consider, for instance, how Jesus speaks of Antipas in Revelation: "my witness, my faithful one" (2:13). The witnesses in Revelation do not point away from themselves, like the witnesses in the gospel of John. Their testimony is a lived image. What Hau-erwas shows in *With the Grain of the Universe* is what it means to be such a witness, shaping one's life as a representation of Jesus Christ.

But Christ's vocation is also answered by referring testimonies. In the fourth Gospel John the Baptist is the human witness *par excellence*. He presents himself as an authority, as someone whose testimony is trustwor-thy. But he points away from himself. His testimony is: "not me but him." John's words and gestures point away from the witnessing subject to the one he bears witness to. Indeed, the gospel wants us to become signpost witnesses ourselves, people whose words and gestures refer to Christ. The gospel wants us to belief that it's not our lives that matter, but only the life of the one we bear witness to.

Acts suggest that we must distinguish between the original witnesses of the resurrected Lord and the others. Here we see a different "hierarchy" than in Revelation. Jesus Christ did not reveal himself to all men, but to a particular group of people who were chosen to meet him and he admon-ished them to bear witness of what they saw. Their apostolic testimony is unlike all other testimonies by other Christians. In some ways we could say that all Christians are called to bear witness. But they are called to become hearsay witnesses. It is their vocation to point back to the original apostolic testimony of Christ's resurrection. This calling has been answered firstly by the authors of the New Testament writing their books, secondly by the early church fixing the canon, and thirdly by preachers preaching the gospel in all different contexts. Finally, it also can and will be answered by all sorts of Christians, recounting the apostolic testimony in their own words.

Thus the answer to our third question is that the way the New Testa-ment speaks of witness is richer than Hauerwas's account. In this respect his understanding of witness is one-sided. But we have suggested that it's pos-sible to integrate these different Scriptural understandings into a theological discourse about the ministry of witness in which showing *and* referring are described as truthful and faithful ways of answering Jesus Christ's vocation.

---

46. *Unleashing the Scriptures*, 8.

THE TESTIMONY OF BONO

My third witness is Bono, the lead singer of the Irish rock band U2. I summon this witness to show that the notion of witnessing as referring can be discerned not just in the New Testament but also in the everyday Christian life. The testimony of Bono helps us to see that though the lived life of many Christians is different from that of Fedde Schurer and the Monks of Tibhirine, in some way they can be conceived as genuine witnesses. First I'll discuss some interviews with Bono, then I'll give a theological analysis of his life.

a. A Thought that Changed the World

In the early 1980s, when U2 became popular in the alternative rock scene, Bono and two other members of the band joined a Christian community called the "Shalom Fellowship." They were enthralled by the community's Bible study programs and their ideals about living without property. When the community leader questioned the lifestyle of the band members, suggesting that a true Christian could not play in a rock band, they seriously thought of quitting the band.[47] Finally, they left the Shalom Fellowship, believing that playing in a rock band was not against God's will but a way to serve God. Because of this experience but also because of his worries about the conflict between Protestants and Roman Catholics in Northern Ireland, Bono became skeptical about institutionalized religion.

> I often wonder if religion is the enemy of God. It's almost like religion is what happens when the Spirit has left the building.[48]

But there is something which attracts Bono to the Christian faith.

> The most powerful idea that's entered the world in the last few thousand years—the idea of grace—is the reason I would like to be a Christian. God has some really weird kids. Though, as I said to [U2 guitarist] The Edge one day, I sometimes feel more like a fan, rather than actually

47. Assayas, *Bono on Bono*, 123, 166.
48. DeCurtis, "Bono," 4.

in the band. I can't live up to it. But the reason I would
like to is the idea of grace. It's really powerful.[49]

But though Bono is reserved in speaking of himself as a Christian, he is not reserved in using Christian language. In his interviews he speaks freely about God and Jesus, about what he found in the Bible and about his prayers. His lyrics are full of Bible quotations and references to Christian beliefs. Bono sings about radical devotion, about a lifelong search for God, about weakness and hypocrisy and about complete submission to love.[50] Indeed, not only are his lyrics Christian, but for Bono music itself has a spiritual meaning.

> I love hymns and gospel music, but the idea of turning your music into a tool for evangelism is missing the point. Music is the language of the spirit anyway. Its first function is praise to creation.[51]

From the early 1980s onwards, Bono has been engaged in social and political activism. He believes that as a Christian he cannot be indifferent to social injustice.

> To me, faith in Jesus Christ that is not aligned to social justice—not aligned with the poor—is nothing.[52]

Since the band played at Live Aid in 1985, U2 has become a propagator for peace, justice and an honest distribution of wealth. The band supported campaigns for organizations such as Greenpeace and Amnesty International. Moreover, Bono's engagement does not stop when the camera is off. In the 1980s, for instance, he and his wife went incognito to Ethiopia and El Salvador. In the last two decades, Bono has become a sort of unofficial diplomat for the poor in the world. He uses his fame to call attention to social problems, such as HIV/AIDS and third world debt.[53]

In *Bono on Bono*, a series of interviews with the French journalist Michka Assayas, we learn to know Bono as a character with many contradictions. He's an ambassador of the poor but

---

49. Ibid., 4–5.

50. See respectively "Gloria," "I Still Haven't Found What I'm Looking For," "Acrobat," and "Moment Of Surrender."

51. DeCurtis, "Bono," 5.

52. Stockman, *Walk On*, 44.

53. For a very critical analysis of Bono's social work, see Browne, *The Frontman*.

also one of the most rich and mighty men in the music industry. He admires the value of simple friendship, but he also loves to play the role of the charismatic rock star. He speaks openly about his own virtues and vices, but this openness can also be conceived as a subtle strategy to win sympathy from his public. But in the interviews we also learn that Bono knows of something which exceeds his colorful character:

> It's clear to me that Karma is at the very heart of the Universe. I am absolutely sure of it. And yet, along comes this idea called Grace to upend that 'as you reap, so will you sow' stuff. Grace defies reason and logic. Love interrupts, if you like, the consequences of your actions, which in my case is very good news indeed, because I've done a lot of stupid stuff. . . . I'm holding out that Jesus took my sins onto the cross, because I know who I am, and I know I don't have to depend on my own religiosity.[54]

In a song, called *Grace* from the same period Bono sings about grace as a thought that changed the world. Grace takes the blame, covers the shame. Grace travels outside of karma. Grace finds goodness in everything and discovers beauty within ugliness. [55]

b. Analysis

I think Bono is a witness. Not because of his great charisma or his efforts for social justice. He is a witness, but a rather different one from Fedde Schurer and the Monks of Tibhirine. Bono knows he is no saint. He openly admits he cannot live the life he knows the gospel requires from him. I think Bono is a witness because he fits the basic definition: he knows of something special and he speaks about this. And indeed, what he knows is very special. He knows about the heart of the gospel: grace.

I summon Bono as my last witness to remind Hauerwas and his readers (including myself) that Christian witnessing can take a shape that does not fit so easily with our theological conceptions. As a rock star Bono is used to standing in the spotlight but when he sings about grace he is not asking attention for himself or for the glamorous life he lives. He is pointing away from

---

54. Assayas, *Bono on Bono*, 204.

55. U2, "Grace." Because of copyright rules I cannot cite the full text here.

himself, to something that changed the world. In this way, Bono's testimony affirms the conclusion of the last section. If the monks of Tibhirine exemplify witnessing as showing, Bono exemplifies witnessing as referring. He is a signpost witness. Just as John the Baptist, Bono's testimony is "not me but him."

Like the apostles in Acts, Bono simply cannot remain silent about what he reads in the Bible and what he finds in his life. He cannot but speak and sing about grace interrupting the consequences of our actions. And resembling a genuine nonfoundationalist and postliberal theologian, he realizes that this "thought that changed the world" is not a general religious idea but a reality accomplished by Jesus on the cross. And what makes his testimony authoritative is precisely his confession: "I've done a lot of stupid stuff." Bono knows what it means to receive God's grace undeservedly.

Thus, in reading the New Testament attentively, we can discern testimonial practices that we otherwise would have missed. After all, the vast majority of ordinary Christians are more like Bono than Fedde Schurer or the Monks of Tibhirine. They have a lot to confess, but they bear witness to the way grace finds beauty in ugly things. [56]

5. RÉSUMÉ AND CONCLUSION

Before concluding this chapter, I will give a résumé of the other chapters of this book.

Chapter 1 introduced the theologian Stanley Hauerwas and his account of witness. *With the Grain of the Universe* is unique in Hauerwas's oeuvre for its comprehensive reflection on the character of Christian witness. In his final Gifford lecture, Hauerwas argues that we cannot understand the true character of all that is without the life of witnessing witnesses. Yet Hauerwas does *not* fully explain why he relies on the notion of "witness" and what make it so crucial for his arguments. He realizes that such explanations often tend to overshadow the actual argument, while not taking into consideration the particularity of Christian life and how it witnesses to God. Nevertheless, in the following chapters we have tried to explain and evaluate Hauerwas's understanding of witness.

We started in chapter 2 with an examination of *terms*. By setting out the different meanings of the words "witness" and "testimony" Hauerwas's

56. Healy (*Hauerwas*, 97–98) makes a similar point.

position has been conceptualized. The outcome was ambiguous. Hauerwas has intuition for the "logic" of witnessing. Yet, since he does not fully explain why Christian life could best be described as a testimonial practice and to what extent this testimonial practice resembles the practice of witnessing outside the Christian community, his account of Christian witness remains in some ways unclear. Moreover, he pays little attention to the Old and New Testament texts which refer to God calling men as his witnesses.

Chapter 3 was an examination of *descriptions*. It turned out that the lack of clarity in Hauerwas's account could be resolved with the help of philosophical reflections on testimony. Through Coady's analyses we learned that the witnesses in Hauerwas's work are authoritative and competent because they have tested Christian beliefs in their lives and found that these beliefs make sense. Ricoeur's reflections on testimony helped us to understand the complex relation between witness as verbal testimony and witness as *testimonium vitae*. Yet, it also revealed some shortcomings. Most importantly Hauerwas implicitly inverts the relation between verbal witness and witnessing in life and because of that he obscures the typical characteristics of witnessing as a particular speech act. Finally, we found that Agamben's analysis of the testimony of the survivor challenges Christians and Christian theologians such as Hauerwas.

Chapter 4 was an examination of *Scripture*. Some crucial Bible texts on witnessing in Isaiah, Acts, Revelation and John were analyzed. We found that these Bible books affirm Hauerwas's idea that God calls people as his witnesses and that through the assistance of the Holy Spirit, Christians serve God by witnessing in the ongoing battle between truth and lies. The strongest support is offered by Revelation. Both in Hauerwas's work and in Revelation, the ministry of witness is to remain faithful in a world without certainty. However, in book of Acts and the gospel of John, we find no support for Hauerwas's idea that Christians are called to bear witnesses through their lives. In Acts and John the ministry of the disciples consists of the proclamation that Jesus is the Christ.

Finally, in this chapter, three rules of discourse for the theological reflection on witness were formulated with the help of Scripture. We have examined whether and to what extent Hauerwas complies with these three rules. The conclusion of this systematic theological analysis is clear. Despite some inadequacies and omissions in his account of Christian witness, Hauerwas basically conforms to the three rules of discourse. In Section 4, however, we found that in one respect Hauerwas's account of witness is one-sided. Next, I'll briefly reiterate the conclusions of this chapter.

1. In his reflections on the character of Christian witness Hauerwas takes into account that the human act of witnessing to God is preceded by God's act of calling people as his witnesses and that God calls these witnesses to make himself known to the world.

It's not immediately obvious that Hauerwas complies with this first rule of discourse. His considerations on the necessity of witness by the church are prone to being misunderstood. Hauerwas could be understood if he suggested that witnessing simply begins as a practice in which God and men are working together in a synergic relationship. But, as we have indicated, this reading is superficial and fails to take into account that in the work of Hauerwas, God and man are not portrayed as *natural* partners. The story of God and man is far more dynamic and exciting. As it does in Isaiah and Acts, this story begins with a powerful but gracious God calling an incompetent and unknowing people. This vocation should be understood as a redemptive act. God saves his people from its blindness and deafness and invests it with the ministry of witness. On the one hand, this calling is a constitutive summons. Through God's calling the church becomes a witness to the triune God. But it is also a command. Through this calling the church learns what it must do. It has been called to bear witness to the Father, the Son, and the Holy Spirit.

2. In his reflections on the character of Christian witness Hauerwas takes into account that man can only answer God's call to be his faithful and truthful witnesses with the help of the Holy Spirit.

It's not difficult to argue that Hauerwas also complies with this second rule of discourse. Christians must respond to the call "you are my witnesses" and, the same as Israel in Isaiah 43 and 44, and the disciples in Acts 1, they can only respond properly through the work of the Holy Spirit. The Spirit does not create these communities of witnesses in one single act, but through a gradual process of training. Witnessing truthfully and faithfully is a communal skill which can only be learned step by step, through moral and intellectual exercise. Moreover, we've suggested that all Hauerwas's ethics and theology could and should be understood as an exploration of how the Holy Spirit helps the church to answer its vocation as a witness. One of the crucial aspects of this answer is peacefulness. By being a peaceful community the church bears witness that God's peace is an alternative to a politics of violence and death. Indeed, through the guidance of the Spirit, the church is trained to participate in the self-revelation of the triune God and become more like Jesus Christ who lived and died as a true and faithful witness.

3. In his reflections on the character of Christian witness, Hauerwas takes into account how, in a world of mendacity and treacherousness, witnesses make known the one true God, and vouch for the truth of their testimony—without the false pretension that they have control over the One of whom they bear testimony.

The witness's claim to the truth is a significant but complex issue and that's why most of this chapter is dedicated to the third rule of discourse and why it was necessary to give three more detailed formulations of this rule. First, we have argued that the witnesses Hauerwas speaks of communicate in a rather specific way: they bear witness through their lives. By living in a particular way they show what it means to be human, what the world is like, and who God is. But though this is a special way of making things known, Hauerwas does not mean to say that Christian witnessing is in itself a unique form of communication. What can be found in Acts is also indicated in Hauerwas's work: what is being communicated is the thing that's unique, not the mode of communication. Secondly, we've seen that these people are involved in a conflict between truth and lies. And with regard to this issue we reached a similar conclusion. On one side, Hauerwas stresses that to remain truthful and faithful to their vocation Christians cannot keep themselves aloof but must take part in this conflict. But he does not mean to say that Christians are able to solve the conflict between truth and lies. Like the faithful disciples in Revelation, the Christians in Hauerwas's work are no more than witnesses present at a trial to testify as best as they can that what they've found is true. Thirdly, we've indicated that the witnesses Hauerwas speaks of are people who vouch authoritatively for the truth of their testimony. In "cultural linguistic" terms one could say that these witnesses have acquired authority through testing Christian faith in their lives. They've found that Christian convictions offer a way to live truthfully in world without certainty. In "revelational-theological" terms we could say that, like Israel in Isaiah and the disciples in John, Acts, and Revelation, these people have been taken into the service of God's self-revelation. But while Hauerwas speaks of Christian witnesses as people having the authority to claim that their testimonies are true, he does not mean to say that they control or possess the truth. Indeed, Hauerwas suggests that the *testimonium vitae* of the church, this practice which is neither self-referential nor self-justifying, indicates that the triune God, to whom these practices refer, is true. Finally, we remarked that the circularity in Hauerwas's reasoning is quite similar to circularity we found in the gospel John. And it's not that of a closed circle but of a spiral which moves men from the position of an audience to that of a people being addressed by the redemptive vocation of the one true God.

4. In his reflections on the character of Christian witness, Hauerwas does not take into account that witnessing is not just showing through life but also referring by words and by gestures.

Finally we discussed three issues which required more examination: vocation and violence; training and crisis; and showing and referring. As for the first issue, our conclusion supported Hauerwas's account of witness: vocation does not necessarily presuppose violence. For the second issue, we concluded that though Hauerwas does not reflect on the notion of testimonial crisis, he's not unreceptive to it. It's indeed possible within his pneumatological account of training and exercise to take this notion seriously and respond to the challenge of the testimony by the survivors. But our third conclusion is the most far-reaching. In one respect, Hauerwas's account of witness is one-sided. He does not see what the New Testament suggests, namely that there's another way of witnessing: not witnessing as showing but witnessing as *referring*. In a full theological account of Christian witness, both showing *and* referring must be conceived as obedient answers to Christ's calling.

In the introduction I mentioned a tension in this study between *words* and *life*. Hauerwas uses the *word* "witness" to understand what's going on in the Christian *life*. This word and how Hauerwas uses it in his theological reflections have been subjected to our tests and evaluations. But what the word refers to—the "testimonial life," so to say—cannot be subjected to examination. When we reflected on these lives, we could not but say "so to say." This tension could not be solved, but it must be endured and this is what I have tried to do in the five chapters of this book. It became especially visible in the structure of the current chapter where I interrupted my argument to tell stories about witnessing. In some ways these stories are a crucial part of my argument. They prove that Hauerwas's account of witness helps us to understand what's going on in Christian life. But in another way these stories refer to what's beyond argument, to how the lives of Fedde Schurer, the Monks of Tibhirine, and Bono bear witnesses to the one true God.

THE TESTIMONY OF STANLEY

Perhaps the best way to end this book is by quoting from the epilogue of *Hannah's Child*.

> I would like to think that this book might fall into the category of "testimony," but I am not confident that what I have done deserves that description. When I was a

child I often heard testimonies in church. They usually came during services on Sunday night. A member of the congregation would suddenly "feel moved" to declare to those assembled what God had done in her life. Such heartfelt testimonies made by unsophisticated people in straightforward language impressed me then and impress me now. I trusted their testimonies.

I am a theologian. I have been trained too well to be able to trust claims that I might make about what God may or may not have done to make my life possible. I believe, however, that God has made my life possible. Yet how do you write a testimony, a witness, to testify to God's presence in your life that does not make more of you than your life has been? How do you testify to God's presence in a manner that does not tempt you to say more about God than you know? (286)

For Hauerwas *Hannah's Child* is a testimony, a witness to what God has done in his life. I hope this study has made clear that his work is devoted to witness in almost every way. And maybe it has also shown how he gives a heartfelt testimony through his writing. But what about us, his readers? In many ways we are his congregation. His testimony is given to us. It is up to us to judge if it can be trusted. And it is we who must consider whether Stanley Hauerwas says no more about God than he really knows.

Bibliography

Agamben, Giorgio. *Remnants of Auschwitz: The Witness and the Archive.* Translated by Daniel Heller-Roazen. New York: Zone, 1999.

Aland, Barbara, et al. *Novum Testamentum Graece.* 27th ed. Stuttgart: Deutsche Bibelgesellschaft, 1993.

Assel, Heinrich. "Zeugnis. Begriff—Dogmatisch—Ethisch." In *Religion in Geschichte und Gegenwart*, edited by Hans Dieter Betz et al., 8:1852–54. 4th ed. Tübingen: Mohr Siebeck, 2005.

Assayas, Michka. *Bono on Bono: Conversations with Michka Assayas.* London: Hodder & Stoughton, 2005.

Ballentine, James A. "Testis unus testis nullus." In *A Law Dictionary of Words, Terms, Abbreviations, and Phrases which are Peculiar to the Law and of Those which Have a Peculiar Meaning in the Law*, 495. Indianapolis: Bobbs-Merrill, 1916.

Baltzer, Klaus. *Deutero-Jesaja* 2. Kommentar zum Alten Testament. Gütersloh: Gütersloher Verlagshaus, 1999.

Barrett, C. K. *A Critical and Exegetical Commentary on the Acts of the Apostles.* 2 vols. International Critical Commentary. Edinburgh: T. & T. Clark, 1994.

Barth, Karl. *Anselm: Fides Quaerens Intellectum. Translated* by Ian W. Robertson. Cleveland: World Publishing, 1962.

———. *Church Dogmatics* I/2. Translated by G. T. Thomson and Harold Knight. Edinburgh: T. & T. Clark, 1956.

———. *Church Dogmatics* II/1. Translated by T. H. L. Parker et al. Edinburgh: T. & T. Clark, 1957.

———. *Church Dogmatic*, IV/3. Translated by G. W. Bromiley. Edinburgh: T. & T. Clark, 1961.

———. *The Christian Life: Church Dogmatics* IV/4. Translated by G. W. Bromiley. Grand Rapids: Eerdmans, 1981.

———. *Der Christ als Zeuge.* Munich: Kaiser, 1934.

———. *Witness to the Word: A Commentary on John* 1. Translated by Walther Fürst. Grand Rapids: Eerdmans, 1986.

Beale, G. K. *The Book of Revelation: A Commentary on the Greek Text.* New International Greek Testament Commentary. Grand Rapids: Eerdmans,1999.

Beauvois, Xavier. *Of Gods and Men.* Sony Pictures, 2010. Orignial French release title: *Des hommes et des dieux.* Why Not Productions, 2010.

Bellotto, Nicoletta, and Simonetta Ponchia, eds. *Witnessing in the Ancient Near East.* Padova: Sargon, 2009.

Bender, Harold S. "Testimony." In *Global Anabaptist Mennonite Encyclopedia Online* (1959). http://www.gameo.org/encyclopedia/contents/T4994.html.

Berges, Ulrich. *Jesaja 40–48*. Herders theologischer Kommentar zum Alten Testament. Freiburg: Herder, 2008.

Beuken, Willem A. M. *Jesaja IIIa*. De prediking van het Oude Testament. Nijkerk: Callenbach, 1989.

Blenkinsopp, Joseph. *Isaiah 40–55*. Anchor Bible 19A. New York: Doubleday, 2002.

Bluhme, Hermann. *Etymologisches Wörterbuch des deutschen Grundwortschatzes*. Munich: Lincom Europa, 2005.

Bolt, Peter. "Mission and Witness." In *Witness to the Gospel: The Theology of Acts*, edited by I. Howard Marshall and David Petersen, 191–214. Grand Rapids: Eerdmans, 1998.

Browne, Harry. *The Frontman: Bono (In the Name of Power)*. London: Verso, 2013.

Brueggemann, Walter. *Theology of the Old Testament: Testimony, Dispute, Advocacy*. Minneapolis: Fortress, 1997.

Bunnin, Nicholas, and Yu Jiyuan. "Fideism." In *The Blackwell Dictionary of Western Philosophy*, 255–56. Malden, MA: Blackwell, 2004.

Buskes, J. J. *Vier vrienden*. Apeldoorn: Semper Agendo, 1971.

Cavanaugh, William T. "Stan the Man: A Thoroughly Biased Account of a Completely Unobjective Person." In *The Hauerwas Reader*, edited by John Berkman and Michael Cartwright, 17–32. Durham: Duke University Press, 2001.

Chergé, Christian de. "Testament of Dom Christian de Chergé." Order of Cistercians of the Strict Observance. http://www.ocso.org/index.php?option=com_docman&task=cat_view&gid=100&Itemid=149&lang=en.

"The Child Witness to Violence Project." childwitnesstoviolence.org.

Childs, Brevard S. *Isaiah*. Old Testament Library. Louisville: Westminster John Knox, 2001.

Coady, C. A. J. *Testimony: A Philosophical Study*. Oxford: Clarendon, 1992.

Coenen, L. "Witness, Testimony." In *The New International Dictionary of New Testament Theology*, edited by Colin Brown, 3:1038–47. Grand Rapids: Zondervan, 1986.

DeCurtis, Anthony. "Bono: The Beliefnet Interview." *Beliefnet*, February 2001. http://www.beliefnet.com/Entertainment/Music/2001/02/Bono-The-Beliefnet-Interview.aspx.

DeHart, Paul J. *The Trial of the Witnesses: The Rise and Decline of Postliberal Theology*. Malden, MA: Blackwell, 2006.

Derrida, Jacques. "Poetics and the Politics of Witnessing." In *Sovereignties in Question: The Poetics of Paul Celan*, 65-96. New York: Fordham University Press, 2005.

———. *The Instant of My Death/Demeure: Fiction and Testimony*. With Maurice Blanchot. Stanford: Stanford University Press, 2000.

Durantaye, Leland, de la. *Giorgio Agamben: A Critical Introduction*. Stanford: Stanford University Press, 2009.

Elshtain, Jean Bethke. "Theologian: Christian Contrarian." *Time*, September 17, 2001, 76–77.

Epictetus, *Discourses*. Translated by Thomas Wentworth Higginson. Edinburgh: Thomas Nelson, 1890. http://www.archive.org/stream/epictetusdiscour01epicuoft#page/2/mode/2up, book 1.9, 1102.

Erler, Adalbert, et al. "Eid." In *Handwörterbuch zur deutschen Rechtsgeschichte*, edited by Adalbert Erler and Ekkehard Kaufmann, 1:861-70. Berlin: Schmidt, 1971.

———. "Hörensagen." In *Handwörterbuch zur deutschen Rechtsgeschichte*, edited by Adalbert Erler and Ekkehard Kaufmann, 2:238-41. Berlin: Schmidt, 1978.

Ernst, Josef. *Das Evangelium nach Lukas*. Regensburger Neues Testament. Regensburg: Pustet, 1993.

Felman, Shoshana, and Dori Laub. *Testimony: Crises of Witnessing in Literature, Psychoanalysis and History*. London: Routledge, 1991.

Fischer, Matthias Gerhard. "Zeugen." In *Handwörterbuch zur deutschen Rechtsgeschichte*, edited by Adalbert Erler and Ekkehard Kaufmann, 5:1684–93. Berlin: Schmidt, 1998.

———. "Zeugnis." In *Handwörterbuch zur deutschen Rechtsgeschichte*, edited by Adalbert Erler and Ekkehard Kaufmann, 5:1684–97. Berlin: Schmidt, 1998.

Fodor, James. "Postliberal Theology." In *The Modern Theologians: An Introduction to Christian Theology since 1918*, edited by F. David and R. Muers, 229–48. 3rd ed. Oxford: Blackwell, 2005.

The Fortunoff Video Archive for Holocaust Testimonies. library.yale.edu/testimonies.

Fox, George, et al. *A declaration from the harmless and innocent people of God, called quakers, against all sedition, plotters, and fighters in the world*. The Religious Society of Friends. http://www.quaker.org/minnfm/peace/A%20Declaration%20to%20Charles%20201660.htm.

Frei, Hans W. *Types of Christian Theology*. Edited by George Hunsinger and William C. Placher. New Haven: Yale University Press, 1992.

Fricker, Elizabeth "Varieties of Anti-reductionism about Testimony—a Reply to Goldberg and Henderson." *Philosophy and Phenomenological Research* 72 (2006) 618–28.

Friedman, Saul S., ed. *Holocaust Literature: A Handbook of Critical, Historical, and Literary Writings*. Westport, CT: Greenwood, 1993.

Gerlitz, Peter, et al. "Martyrium." In *Theologische Realenzyklopädie*, edited by Gerhard Krause and Gerhard Müller, 22:196–220. Berlin: de Gruyter, 1992.

Giesen, Heinz. *Die Offenbarung des Johannes*. Regensburger Neues Testament. Regensburg: Pustet, 1997.

Gilissen, John. *Historische inleiding tot het recht*. Antwerp: Kluwer, 1989.

Glare, Peter, et al. "Auctor." In *Oxford Latin Dictionary* I, edited by P. G. W. Glare. 2nd ed. Oxford: Oxford University Press, 2012.

———. "Auctoritas." In *Oxford Latin Dictionary* I, edited by P. G. W. Glare. 2nd ed. Oxford: Oxford University Press, 2012.

Green, Garrett. *Scriptural Authority and Narrative Interpretation*. Philadelphia: Fortress, 1987.

Griffiths, Paul J. "Witness and Conviction in *With the Grain of the Universe*." *Modern Theology* 19 (2003) 67–75.

Gustafson, James M. "The Sectarian Temptation." In *Moral Discernment in the Christian Life: Essays in Theological Ethics*, edited by Theo A. Boer and Paul E. Capetz, 142–45. Louisville: Westminster John Knox, 2007.

Hamm, Thomas D. *Quakers in America*. New York: Columbia University Press, 2003.

Hauerwas, Stanley. *Against the Nations: War and Survival in a Liberal Society*. Minneapolis: Winston, 1985.

———. "Aristotle and Thomas Aquinas on the Ethics of Character." In *Character and the Christian Life: A Study in Theological Ethics*, 34–56. San Antonio: Trinity University Press, 1975.

———. "Character, Narrative, and Growth in the Christian Life." In *A Community of Character: Toward a Constructive Christian Social Ethic*, 129–54. Notre Dame: University of Notre Dame, 1981.

————. *Christian Existence Today: Essays on Church, World, and Living in Between.* Durham, NC: Labyrinth, 1988.

————. "Christian Practices and the Practice of Law in a World without Foundations." *Mercer Law Review* 44 (1993) 743–51.

————. *Christianity, Democracy, and the Radical Ordinary: Conversations between a Radical Democrat and a Christian.* With Romand Coles. Eugene, OR: Cascade, 2008.

————. "Christianity: It's Not a Religion; It's an Adventure." *U.S. Catholic* 56 (June 1991) 6–13.

————. *Christians Among the Virtues: Theological Conversations with Ancient and Modern Ethics.* With Charles Pinches. Notre Dame: University of Notre Dame, 1997.

————. "The Church as God's New Language." In *Christian Existence Today: Essays on Church, World, and Living in Between*, 47–65. Durham, NC: Labyrinth, 1988.

————. *A Community of Character: Toward a Constructive Christian Social Ethic.* Notre Dame: University of Notre Dame, 1981.

————. "Connections Created and Contingent: Aquinas, Preller, Wittgenstein, and Hopkins." In *Performing the Faith: Bonhoeffer and the Practice of Nonviolence*, 111-34. Ada, MI: Baker, 2004. Originally published in *Grammar and Grace: Reformulations of Aquinas and Wittgenstein*, edited by Jeffrey Stout and Robert MacSwain. London: SCM, 2004.

————. "Courage Exemplified." In *Christians Among the Virtues: Theological Conversations with Ancient and Modern Ethics*, 149–65. With Charles Pinches. Notre Dame: University of Notre Dame, 1997.

————. "Disciplined Seeing: Forms of Christianity and Forms of Life." With Brian Goldstone. In *Working With Words: On Learning to Speak Christian*, 33–60. Eugene, OR: Cascade, 2011.

————. *Dispatches from the Front: Theological Engagements with the Secular.* Durham, NC: Duke University Press, 1996.

————. *Een robuuste kerk: De christelijke gemeente in een postchristelijke samenleving.* Translated by Herman Paul et al. Zoetermeer: Boekencentrum, 2010.

————. *Hannah's Child: A Theologian's Memoir.* Grand Rapids: Eerdmans, 2010.

————. *The Hauerwas Reader.* Edited by John Berkman and Michael Cartwright. Durham, NC: Duke University Press, 2001.

————. "Hooks: Random Thoughts by Way of a Response to Griffiths and Ochs." *Modern Theology* 19 (2003) 89–101.

————. *Living Gently in a Violent World: The Prophetic Witness of Weakness.* With Jean Vanier. Resources for Reconciliation. Downers Grove, IL: InterVarsity, 2008.

————. *Matthew.* Brazos Theological Commentary on the Bible. Grand Rapids: Brazos, 2006.

————. "Moral Character as a Problem for Theological Ethics." PhD dissertation, Yale University, 1968. Subsequently published as *Character and the Christian Life: A Study in Theological Ethics.* San Antonio, TX: Trinity University Press, 1975.

————. *The Peaceable Kingdom: A Primer in Christian Ethics.* Notre Dame: University of Notre Dame, 1983.

————. "Remembering as a Moral Task: The Challenge of the Holocaust." In *Against the Nations: War and Survival in a Liberal Society*, 61–90. Minneapolis: Winston, 1985.

——. *Resident Aliens: A Provocative Christian Assessment of Culture and Ministry for People Who Know that Something Is Wrong.* With William H. Willimon. Nashville: Abingdon, 1989.

——. *Sanctify Them in the Truth: Holiness Exemplified.* Edinburgh: T. & T. Clark, 1998.

——. "Self-Deception and Autobiography: Reflections on Speer's *Inside the Third Reich.*" With David Burrell. In Stanley Hauerwas et al., *Truthfulness and Tragedy: Further Investigations into Christian Ethics,* 82–98. Notre Dame: University of Notre Dame, 1977.

——. *The State of the University: Academic Knowledges and the Knowledge of God.* Malden, MA: Blackwell, 2007.

——. "The Testament of Friends." *The Christian Century,* February 28, 1990, 213–16.

——. *Unleashing the Scripture: Freeing the Bible from Captivity to America.* Nashville: Abingdon, 1993.

——. *Vision and Virtue: Essays in Christian Ethical Reflection.* Notre Dame: Fides, 1974.

——. "Why 'The Way Words Run' Matters: Reflections on Becoming a 'Major Biblical Scholar.'" In *Working with Words: On Learning to Speak Christian,* 94–112. Eugene, OR: Cascade, 2011.

——. *Wilderness Wanderings: Probing Twentieth-Century Theology and Philosophy.* Boulder, CO: Westview, 1997.

——. *With the Grain of the Universe: The Church's Witness and Natural Theology; Being the Gifford Lectures Delivered at the University of St. Andrews in 2001.* Grand Rapids: Brazos, 2001.

——. "Witness." With Charles Pinches. In *Faithful Reading: New Essays in Theology in Honour of Fergus Kerr,* edited by Simon Oliver and Karen Kilby, 134–54. London: T. & T. Clark, 2012.

——. *Working with Words: On Learning to Speak Christian.* Eugene, OR: Cascade, 2011.

Healy, Nicholas M. *Church, World, and the Christian Life: Practical-Prophetic Ecclesiology.* Cambridge, UK: Cambridge University Press, 2000.

——. *Hauerwas: A (Very) Critical Introduction.* Interventions. Grand Rapids: Eerdmans, 2014.

——. "Karl Barth's Ecclesiology Reconsidered." *Scottish Journal of Theology* 57 (2004) 287–99.

——. "The Logic of Karl Barth's Ecclesiology: Analysis, Assessment and Proposed Modifications." *Modern Theology* 10 (1994) 137–57.

——. "Practices and the New Ecclesiology: Misplaced Concreteness?" *International Journal of Systematic Theology* 5 (2003) 287–308.

Holzhauer, H. "Meineid." In *Handwörterbuch zur deutschen Rechtsgeschichte,* edited by Adalbert Erler and Ekkehard Kaufmann, 1:447-58. Berlin: Schmidt, 1983.

Hovey, Craig. *Bearing True Witness: Truthfulness in Christian Practice.* Grand Rapids: Eerdmans, 2011.

Hunsinger, George. *How to Read Karl Barth: The Shape of His Theology.* New York: Oxford University Press, 1991.

Hütter, Reinhard. *Evangelische Ethik als kirchliches Zeugnis: Interpretationen zu Schlüsselfragen theologischer Ethik in der Gegenwart.* Neukirchen-Vluyn: Neukirchener, 1993.

————. "Karl Barth's 'Dialectical Catholicity': Sic et Non." *Modern Theology* 16 (2000) 137–57.

Jaki, Stanley L. *Lord Gifford and His Lectures: A Centenary Retrospect.* Macon, GA: Mercer University Press, 1986.

James, William. *The Varieties of Religious Experience.* New York: Mentor, 1958.

Jansen, Mechteld M. *Talen naar God: wegwijzers bij Paul Ricoeur.* Gorinchem: Narratio, 2002.

Johnson, William Stacy. *The Mystery of God: Karl Barth and the Postmodern Foundations of Theology.* Louisville: Westminster John Knox, 1997.

Jones, L. Gregory, et al. *God, Truth, and Witness: Engaging Stanley Hauerwas.* Grand Rapids: Brazos, 2005.

Kadri, Sadakat. *The Trial: A History, from Socrates to O. J. Simpson.* New York: Random House, 2005.

Kallenberg, Brad J. *Ethics as Grammar: Changing the Postmodern Subject.* Notre Dame: University of Notre Dame Press, 2001.

————. "The Strange New World in the Church: A Review Essay of *With the Grain of the Universe* by Stanley Hauerwas." *Journal of Religious Ethics* 32 (2004) 197–218.

Kierkegaard, Søren. *Kierkegaard's Journals and Notebooks.* Vol. 4, *Journals NB–NB 5.* Edited by N. J. Cappelørn et al. Princeton: Princeton University Press, 2011.

————. *The Moment and Late Writings.* Edited by Howard V. Hong et al. Kierkegaard's Writings 23. Princeton: Princeton University Press, 1998.

————. *Søren Kierkegaard's Journals and Papers.* Vol. 4, *S–Z.* Edited and translated by Howard V. Hong and Edna H. Hong, assisted by Gregor Malantschuk. Bloomington: Indiana University Press, 1975.

Kiser, John. *The Monks of Tibhirine: Faith, Love, and Terror in Algeria.* New York: St. Martin's Griffin, 2003.

Klein, Ernest. "Wit, Witness, n." In *A Comprehensive Etymological Dictionary of the English Language* ii. Amsterdam: Elsevier, 1966.

Levi, Primo. *The Black Hole of Auschwitz.* Edited by Marco Belpoliti. Translated by Sharon Wood. Cambridge: Polity, 2006.

————. *The Drowned and the Saved.* Translated by Raymond Rosenthal. New York: Random, 1989.

————. *If This Is a Man/The Truce.* Translated by Stuart Woolf. London: Abacus, 1987.

Levinas, Emmanuel. "Truth of Disclosure and Truth of Testimony." In *Basic Philosophical Writings,* 97–108. Bloomington: Indiana University Press, 1996.

Liemburg, J. *Fedde Schurer, 1898–1968. Biografie van een Friese koerier.* Leeuwarden: Friese Pers Boekerij, 2010.

Lietaert Peerbolte, L. J. *Paul the Missionary.* Leuven: Peeters, 2003.

Limpitlaw, Amy. "The Gifford Lectures: Over 100 Years of Renowned Lectures on Natural Theology." *Theological Librarianship* 3.1 (2010) 6. https://journal.atla.com/ojs/index.php/theolib.

Lindbeck, George. *The Nature of Doctrine: Religion and Theology in a Postliberal Age.* Philadelphia: Westminster, 1984.

Lipton, Peter. "The Epistemology of Testimony." *Studies in History and Philosophy of Sciences* 29 (1998) 1–31.

Lüpke, Johannes von. "Zeuge, Zeugnis ii: Theologie." In *Historisches Wörterbuch der Philosophie,* edited by Joachim Ritter et al., 12:1324–29. Darmstadt: Wissenschaftliche Buchgesellschaft, 2004.

Mangina, Joseph L. "Bearing the Marks of Jesus: The Church in the Economy of Salvation in Barth and Hauerwas." *Scottish Journal of Theology* 52 (1999) 269–305.

Marquardt, Friedrich-Wilhelm. *Theological Audacities: Selected Essays.* Edited by Andreas Pangritz and Paul S. Chung. Eugene, OR: Pickwick, 2010.

Marshall, Bruce D. *Trinity and Truth.* Cambridge: Cambridge University Press, 2000.

Mather, Willam. *A brief charactor of the antient Christian Quakers.* London: Printed for S. Clarke in George-Yard in Lombard-Street, 1695. http://openlibrary.org/works/OL10489021W/A_brief_charactor_of_the_antient_Christian_Quakers.

McClendon, James W. *Systematic Theology 1: Ethics.* Nashville: Abingdon, 1985.

———. *Systematic Theology 2: Doctrine.* Nashville: Abingdon, 1994.

———. *Systematic Theology 3: Witness.* With Nancey Murphy. Nashville: Abingdon, 2000.

Miscamble, Wilson D. "Sectarian Passivism." *Theology Today* 44 (1987) 69–94.

Molendijk, Arie L. *Getuigen in missionair en oecumenisch verband: een studie over het begrip 'getuigen' in documenten van de Wereldraad van Kerken, de Rooms-Katholieke Kerk en de Evangelicalen in de periode 1948-1985.* Leiden: Interuniversitair Instituut voor Missiologie en Oecumenica, 1986.

Nation, Mark Thiessen. "Stanley Hauerwas: Where Would We Be Without Him." In *Faithfulness and Fortitude: In Conversation with the Theological Ethics of Stanley Hauerwas*, edited by Mark Thiessen Nation and Samuel Wells, 19–39. Edinburgh: T. & T. Clark, 2000.

Neusner, Jacob, trans. *Pesiqta deRab Kahana: An Analytical Translation.* Vol. 1, *Pisqaot 1-14.* Atlanta: Scholars, 1987.

Neyrey, Jerome H. *The Gospel of John.* New Cambridge Bible Commentary. Cambridge: Cambridge University Press, 2007.

Novak, David. "Defending Niebuhr from Hauerwas." *Journal of Religious Ethics* 40 (2012) 281–95.

Ochs, Peter. "On Hauerwas' *With the Grain of the Universe.*" *Modern Theology* 19 (2003) 77–88.

Paul IV, Pope. *Evangelii Nuntiandi.* Rome, December 8, 1975, section 43. The Vatican Archive Online. http://www.vatican.va/holy_father/paul_vi/apost_exhortations/documents/hf_p-vi_exh_19751208_evangelii-nuntiandi_en.html.

Penn, William. "An Epistle from Friends of Pennsylvania and Jersey to Friends in Britain" (1683). Reprinted in *The Yorkshireman: A Religious and Literary Journal, by a Friend* 1-1, second edition (1835) 194. Google eBook. http://books.google.nl/books?id=TRAEAAAAQAAJ&dq=%22An+Epistle+from+Friends+of+Pennsylvania+and+Jersey+to+Friends+in+Britain%E2%80%9D&hl=nl&source=gbs_navlinks_s.

Pervo, Richard I. *Acts: A Commentary.* Hermeneia. Minneapolis: Fortress, 2009.

Peters, John Durham. "Witnessing." *Media, Culture, & Society* 23 (2001) 707–23.

Plaisance, Patrick Lee. "The Journalist as Moral Witness." *Journalism* 3 (2002) 205–22.

"Practice," and "Tribalism," Rundell, Michael, and Fox, Gwyneth, *Macmillan English Dictionary*, 2nd ed. (Macmillan Education, 2007), Macmillan Online, accessed June 24, 2013, http://www.macmillandictionary.com/dictionary/british/practice. / http://www.macmillandictionary.com/dictionary/american/tribalism.

Radscheit, Matthias. "Witnessing and Testifying." In *Encyclopaedia of the Qur'ān*, edited by Jane Dammen McAuliffe, 6:442–505. Leiden: Brill, 2006.

Rasmusson, Arne. *Church as Polis: From Political Theology to Theological Politics as Exemplified by Jürgen Moltmann and Stanley Hauerwas.* Lund: Lund University Press, 1994.

Rayner, John D. *Jewish Religious Law: A Progressive Perspective.* New York: Berghahn, 1998.

Reeling Brouwer, Rinse. *Grondvormen van theologische systematiek*. Vucht: Skandalon, 2009.

Ricoeur, Paul. "The Hermeneutics of Testimony." In *Essays on Biblical Interpretation*, translated by David Stewart and Charles E. Reagan, 119–54. Philadelphia: Fortress, 1980.

———. "L'hermeneutique du temoignage." *Archivio di Filosofia* (La Testimonianza) 42 (1972) 35–61.

Rippin, Andrew. "Witness to Faith." In *Encyclopaedia of the Qur'ān*, edited by Jane Dammen McAuliffe, 6:488–91. Leiden: Brill, 2006.

———. *Oneself as Another*. Chicago: University of Chicago Press, 1992.

Rowe, C. Kavin. *World Upside Down: Reading Acts in the Graeco-Roman Age*. New York: Oxford University Press, 2009.

Rundell, Michael, and Fox, Gwyneth. "Practice," and "Tribalism." In *Macmillan English Dictionary*, 2nd ed. Macmillan Education, 2007. Macmillan Online, accessed June 24, 2013, http://www.macmillandictionary.com/dictionary/ american /practice. / http://www.macmillandictionary.com/dictionary/american/tribalism.

Satake, Akira. *Die Offenbarung des Johannes*. Kritisch-exegetischer Kommentar über das Neue Testament 16. Göttingen: Vandenhoeck & Ruprecht, 2008.

Sellert, W. "Zeugnispflicht." In *Handwörterbuch zur deutschen Rechtsgeschichte*, edited by Adalbert Erler and Ekkehard Kaufmann, 5:1694. Berlin: Schmidt, 1998.

Scheuer, Manfred, and Peter Fonk. "Zeuge, Zeugnis, Zeugenschaft." In *Lexikon für Theologie und Kirche*, edited by Walter Kaspar et al., 10:1442–43. 3rd ed. Freiburg: Herder, 2001.

Scheyhing, R. "Eideshelfer." In *Handwörterbuch zur deutschen Rechtsgeschichte*, edited by Adalbert Erler and Ekkehard Kaufmann, 1:870-72. Berlin: Schmidt, 1971.

Schneider, Gerhard. *Die Apostelgeschichte* i. Herders theologischer Kommentar zum Neuen Testament 5. Freiburg: Herder, 1980.

Scholz, O. R. "Zeuge, Zeugnis I." In *Historisches Wörterbuch der Philosophie*, edited by Joachim Ritter et al., 12:1317–23. Darmstadt: Wissenschaftliche Buchgesellschaft, 2004.

Schurer, Fedde. *De gitaer by it boek*. Baarn: Bosch & Keuning, 1966.

Schwemer, Anna Maria. "Prophet, Zeuge und Märtyrer: Zur Entstehung des Märtyrerbegriffs im frühesten Christentum." *Zeitschrift für Theologie und Kirche* 96 (1999) 320–50.

Schwöbel, Christoph. "Systematic Theology." In *Religion Past & Present: Encyclopedia of Theology and Religion*, edited by Hans Dieter Betz et al., 12:233–34. Leiden: Brill, 2012.

Second Vatican Council. *Lumen Gentium*. Rome, 1964, section 31. The Vatican Archive Online. http://www.vatican.va/archive/hist_councils/ii_vatican_council/ documents/vat-ii_const_19641121_lumen-gentium_en.html.

Simian-Yofre, H. S. "עוד'wd." In *Theologisches Wörterbuch zum Alten Testament*, edited by G. J. Botterweck et al., 5:1107–28. Stuttgart: Kohlhammer, 1986.

Stambaugh, John E., and David L. Balch. *The New Testament in Its Social Environment*. Philadelphia: Westminster, 1986.

Stiver, Dan R. *Theology After Ricoeur: New Directions in Hermeneutical Theology*. Louisville: Westminster John Knox, 2001.

Stockman, Steve. *Walk On: The Spiritual Journey of U2*. Winter Park, FL: Relevant Books, 2005.

"Stories of the Cambodian Holocaust: From Sideshow to Genocide." http://www. edwebproject.org/sideshow/index.html.

Tanner, Kathryn. *God and Creation in Christian Theology: Tyranny or Empowerment?* Minneapolis: Fortress, 2005.

Tertulian. "Apology." In *Ante-Nicene Fathers* iii. *Latin Christianity: Its Founder, Tertullian.* Edited by Allen Menzies. Grand Rapids: Eerdmans, 1885.

Theobald, Michael. *Das Evangelium nach Johannes* 1. Regensburger Neues Testament. Regensburg: Pustet, 2009.

Thomas, Günther. "Witness as a Cultural Form of Communication." In *Media Witnessing Testimony in the Age of Mass Communication*, edited by Paul Frosh and Amit Pinchevski, 89–101. New York: Palgrave Macmillan, 2009.

Thyen, Hartwig. *Das Johannesevangelium.* Handbuch zum Neuen Testament 6. Tübingen: Mohr Siebeck, 2005.

Trites, Allison. *The New Testament Concept of Witness.* New York: Cambridge University Press, 1977.

U2. "Acrobat." *Achtung Baby.* Compact Disc, Island Records, 1991.

———. "Gloria." *October.* Compact Disc, Island Records, 1981.

———. "Grace." *How to Dismantle an Atomic Bomb.* Compact Disc, Island Records, 2004.

———. "I Still Haven't Found What I'm Looking For." *The Joshua Tree.* Compact Disc, Island Records, 1987.

———. "Moment of Surrender." *No Line on the Horizon.* Compact Disc, Island Records, 2009.

Vaan, Michiel de. *Etymological Dictionary of Latin and the Other Italic Languages.* Leiden: Brill, 2008.

VerSteeg, Russ. *Law in the Ancient World.* Durham, NC: Carolina Academic, 2002.

Webb, Stephen H. "The Very American Stanley Hauerwas." *First Things*, June/July 2002, 14–17.

Wells, Samuel. *Transforming Fate into Destiny: The Theological Ethics of Stanley Hauerwas.* Carlisle: Paternoster, 1999.

Wengst, Klaus. *Das Johannesevangelium.* 2 vols. Theologischer Kommentar zum Neuen Testament 4. Stuttgart: Kohlhammer, 2001.

Wiesel, Eli. "The Holocaust as a Literary Inspiration." In *Dimensions of the Holocaust*, 9. Evanston, IL: Northwestern University Press, 1977.

Witherington, Ben. *Revelation.* New Cambridge Bible Commentary. Cambridge: Cambridge University Press, 2003.

Wittgenstein, Ludwig. *On Certainty.* Translated by Denis Paul and G. E. M. Anscombe. New York: Harper, 1969.

———. *Philosophical Investigations.* Translated by G. E. M. Anscombe et al. Malden, MA: Wiley-Blackwell, 2009.

———. *Tractatus Logico-Philosophicus.* Translated by C. K. Ogden and Paul Kegan. London: Routledge 1960.

World Council of Churches. *Christian Witness in a Multi-Religious World.* http://www.oikoumene.org resources/documents/wcc–programmes/interreligious–dialogue–and–cooperation.

Yoder, John Howard. "Armaments and Eschatology." *Studies in Christian Ethics* 1 (1988) 43–61.

———. *The Christian Witness to the State.* Newton, KS: Faith and Life, 1963.

Zmijewski, Josef. *Die Apostelgeschichte.* Regensburger Neues Testament. Regensburg: Pustet, 1994.

Index

Scripture References

For an account of witnessing and testimony in the Old Testament, see 68–71; for the New Testament, see 71–75.

Printed in Great Britain
by Amazon